# C. C. MARTINDALE

*A Biography*

Also by Philip Caraman

John Gerard
*The Autobiography of an Elizabethan*

William Weston
*The Autobiography of an Elizabethan*

Henry Morse
*Priest of the Plague*

The Other Face
*Catholic Life under Elizabeth I*

The Years of Siege
*Catholic Life from James I to Cromwell*

Saint Angela
*The Life of Angela Merici, Foundress of the Ursulines*

Henry Garnet
*1555–1606 and the Gunpowder Plot*

# C. C. Martindale

*A Biography by*
## Philip Caraman

*Longmans*

LONGMANS GREEN AND CO LTD
48 Grosvenor Street, London W1
*Associated companies, branches and representatives*
*throughout the world*

© *Philip Caraman* 1967
*First published* 1967

*Printed in Great Britain by Western Printing Services Limited, Bristol*

Evelyn Waugh
*Master and Friend
and to his wife*
Laura

# Contents

# Illustrations

# *Preface*

Towards the end of his life Fr. C. C. Martindale reconciled himself
to the certainty that his biography would be written. On his retirement from Farm Street Church in 1953 he gave me many personal
papers. Later, he told me that it was his wish that I should write the
'Life'. By that time he knew the kind of book he might expect from me.

My concern has been more with the man than with his work. For
this reason I have given much space to his early years, both before
and after he entered the Society of Jesus in 1897. It was the method
he pursued in his own biographies, particularly in his book on the
young Renaissance saint, Aloysius Gonzaga. He would go into details
of pedigree, upbringing and environment in order to set the scene
for the portrayal of manhood life. He believed that only in this way
could character or sanctity be made comprehensible. In so far as I
have done this, I have met his wishes which, happily, coincided with
my own principal interest.

This method was made possible for me thanks to the help I received from his family, and particularly from his half-sister, Miss
Helen Martindale. I have drawn also on a massive journal which he
wrote in Denmark during the second world war. This contained
many long autobiographical passages. There were, in addition, some
fragmentary pieces of autobiography which he gave to me.

I have not discussed at length the many enterprises with which he
was connected. They belong more properly to the history of the
Catholic Church in England in the first half of this century than to
this biography. However, when I came to return the mass of letters
and papers lent to me, I realised how selective I had perforce been in
my use of detail. I have aimed at presenting the priest in a way which
might interest a wider public than he himself was able to reach, in
spite of his prodigious activity.

After his family, my main debt is to John Willem Gran, Bishop of

Oslo, who ungrudgingly allowed me to write this book in time that belonged to him. Below is a list of persons who helped me with letters or recollections. If any names are omitted it is through oversight. They are given in alphabetical order without attempt to discriminate the measure of assistance I owe to them.

Mr. Robin Anderson, Mgr. John Barton, Rev. E. Basset, S.J., Mr. Neville Braybrooke, Most Rev. Matthew Beovich, Archbishop of Adelaide, Mr. R. K. Browne, Rev. Sebastian Bullough, O.P., Miss M. Butler, Mr. Francis Bywater, Mr. Carey J. Carrington, J.P., Rev. R. Clarke, S.J., Miss M. Coates, Mrs. P. F. Collins, Rev. Richard Copeland, S.J., Rev. Joseph Corbishley, S.J., Rev. Francis Courtney, S.J., Rev. Joseph Christie, S.J., the late Earl of Craven, Rev. M. C. D'Arcy, S.J., Squadron Leader S. H. R. L. D'Arcy, Miss Brenda de Butts, Mgr. Valentine Elwes, Rev. Francis Fenn, S.J., Mrs. Gerard Fiennes, Rev. M. J. Fitzsimons, S.J., Miss G. Frith, Mr. Arthur Gannon, Mr. Graham Greene, Hon. Mrs. Anthony Grigg, Fru Grundy, Mgr. P. V. Hackett, Dom Michael Hanbury, Rev. F. Hannon, S.J., Mr. and Mrs. Hudleston, Sister Anne Hughes, Rev. Martyn Hughes, Brigadier W. Hynes, Père R. Isaac, S.J., Lady Kelly, Rev. J. E. Keegan, S.J., Mr. Peter Laversuch, Rev. F. C. Lennon, S.J., Rev. Peter Levi, S.J., Mrs. Lowndes Marques, Rt. Rev. Hans Martensen, Bishop of Copenhagen, the late Dr. G. McElligot, Mr. A. R. McElwain, Mr. Jim McKay, Most Rev. P. T. B. McKeefry, Archbishop of Wellington, Rev. D. O'Connor, S.J., Rev. Michael O'Halloran, S.J., Professor Hugh O'Neill, Miss M. Pearson, Mr. Harold Pitman, Rev. Patrick Plunkett, S.J., Mr. John F. Power, Rev. Francis Rea, S.J., Lady Reay, Rev. F. Roberts, S.J., Mr. E. Osborne Ryan, Rev. Ignatius Scoles, S.J., Mr. Robert Speaight, Mrs. V. Spencer-Bull, Miss Phyllis M. Stone, Mother Superior, Horseferry Road Convent, Miss Stella Sweetman, Mr. R. J. Taylor, Mrs. M. Thain, Mr. Stephen Trappes-Lomax, Mr. Charles Vivian, Mr. R. P. S. Walker, Rev. O. Waring, the late Mr. Evelyn Waugh, the Earl of Wicklow, Mgr. Humphrey Wilson, Rev. E. Yarnold, S.J., and Mrs. M. Yates.

P.C.

*Akersveien 5, Oslo*
*1 May 1966*

*Ancestry of*
*C. C. Martindale*

John Martindale of Breeks Hall, Ormside, nr Appleby*

John Martindale

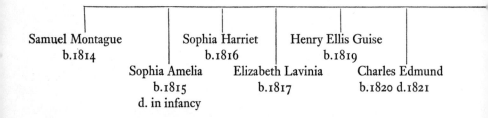

Samuel Montague
b.1814

Sophia Amelia
b.1815
d. in infancy

Sophia Harriet
b.1816

Elizabeth Lavinia
b.1817

Henry Ellis Guise
b.1819

Charles Edmund
b.1820 d.1821

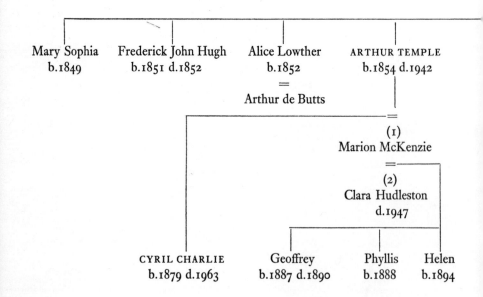

Mary Sophia
b.1849

Frederick John Hugh
b.1851 d.1852

Alice Lowther
b.1852
=
Arthur de Butts

ARTHUR TEMPLE
b.1854 d.1942

=
(1)
Marion McKenzie

=
(2)
Clara Hudleston
d.1947

CYRIL CHARLIE
b.1879 d.1963

Geoffrey
b.1887 d.1890

Phyllis
b.1888

Helen
b.1894

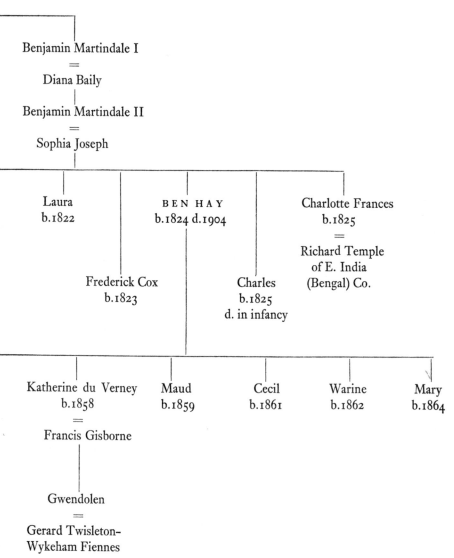

Benjamin Martindale I
=
Diana Baily
|
Benjamin Martindale II
=
Sophia Joseph

Laura
b.1822

BEN HAY
b.1824 d.1904

Charlotte Frances
b.1825
=
Richard Temple
of E. India
(Bengal) Co.

Frederick Cox
b.1823

Charles
b.1825
d. in infancy

Katherine du Verney
b.1858
=
Francis Gisborne

Maud
b.1859

Cecil
b.1861

Warine
b.1862

Mary
b.1864

Gwendolen
=
Gerard Twisleton-
Wykeham Fiennes

* Mr. Mather, vicar of Ormside, wrote to Sir Arthur Martindale: 'Benjamin (I) was obviously the son of John Martindale of Breeks Hall', but he gave no reason. There was a John Martindale at Breeks Hall, with sons called John and Benjamin, about the appropriate date, but nothing more can be stated with certainty.

# I

# Background

Cyril Charlie Martindale, the only child of Arthur and Marion Martindale, was born at his grandfather's house in Kensington Gardens Square on 25 May 1879.

The early records of the family were destroyed in the eighteenth century by Cyril's ancestor, Miles Martindale, a puritanical but mad gentleman who considered such things worldly. There remain a few charming family miniatures, miscellaneous fragmentary sources and a number of entries in the pages of two family Bibles preserved by his half-sisters.

The family originated in Martindale, now a partly cleared forest at the south-west of Ullswater; the Martindale arms are found there —argent, two bars gules, over all, a bend azure. Cyril, who at an early age interested himself in heraldry, traced their modifications as the family passed over to Avondale and eventually into Wales; in the country churches he visited as a boy he noted their quarterings with the Musgraves, Dacres and other northern families. Owing to gaps in the pedigree it was impossible for his father to establish technically his right to use the arms; Cyril urged him, when he received his knighthood, not to take out a new version for himself.

'My remoter family must have been incredibly dull; the nearer ones pretty fair scallywags,' Cyril wrote in one of his attempts at autobiography.[1] His interest in his own heredity could never be wholly satisfied. His mother died before he knew her. To her family, which played little part in his early life, he ascribed everything which he could not explain through his paternal ancestry—his poetic inclinations and particularly his early intoxication with colour and

---

[1] Cyril began one autobiographical essay in the third person, calling himself Robert. This has not survived.

I

form, the curves of leaves, fountains, and, above all, the quality of mystery he found everywhere. It was this last characteristic that isolated him in childhood both from adults, to whom he could not explain it, and also from other children, who did not share it. He experienced it most intensely in Latin countries and in warm climates.

On 22 December 1881 Colonel Ben Hay Martindale, R.E., C.B., Cyril's grandfather, compiled for the benefit of his son, Arthur, some notes entitled 'My Ancestors and Their Life'. He had been born on 1 October 1824 in Marylebone and was able to recollect his own grandfather, Benjamin Martindale I, 'a small, highly polished man who would never sit down till every lady in the room was seated'. Benjamin I had married Miss Diana Baily whose family owned the famous coffee house named after it, in Leicester Fields. He was a man of great wealth, was a member, with his brother John, of the disreputable entourage of the Prince Regent with whom they were on intimate terms. The well-known painting by Romney, now in Kenwood House, of a young girl in white dress and bonnet, seated in a landscape, with her hands crossed on her lap and with a lamb to her right, is of John Martindale's daughter.[1] John and his wife, either separately or together, were also painted by Romney, but the portraits have not been traced or identified. The two brothers were connected in a managerial capacity with White's and jointly owned Crockfords, the celebrated gaming house.

At Crockfords the brothers played chuck-farthing with sovereigns and there also they lost most of their inherited fortune. The financial ruin of the family was completed by the negligence or rascality of lawyers.

Benjamin Martindale's son, also called Benjamin, married Sophia Joseph, 'than whom a better or more unselfish woman never lived'. She belonged to an opulent Jewish family settled in Liverpool. At the time of her marriage her parents had retired from the banking business and were living in Bedford Square. It was said that Sophia, until she met Benjamin Martindale II, had never put the sole of her foot to the ground out of doors but always went in a carriage as was

[1] The sittings were on 21 and 23 June 1781; and on 3 and 7 February 1782.

2

the custom with ladies of her wealth. The Joseph fortune was eventually invested in land on which Birkenhead and its docks were later built.

Sophia Joseph became a Christian on marriage and was consequently cut off from her share of the family inheritance. When her young husband was about to start a career in the army, he was informed by his father that the family was ruined and that he would have to make his own way for himself.

With his wife he went to live at Dunkerque, but he could never adjust his style of living to his comparative impoverishment. He always lacked money; nevertheless, with the help of relatives he was able to give his children a good education. Ben Hay was the tenth child and the youngest surviving boy. Cyril, who when writing of his contemporaries betrayed an astringency that was wholly lacking in his dealings with them, wrote of his grandfather in terms that scarcely did justice to his remarkable character. To Cyril he was always the absolute autocrat, a mixture of Abraham and Jupiter, puritanical and self-contradictory. Yet in some ways Cyril resembled him; in both there was the same restlessness, the endless application and drive.

From Dunkerque, Ben Hay had been sent to Rugby under Doctor Arnold and from there had passed into Woolwich. By sheer application he had won as a cadet the Sword of the Academy and the Survey Prize: before his entry his education had been classical and only with the help of a crammer had he been able to reach the required standard in mathematics, science and German. From his first posting, Gibraltar, he had gone to Corfu. There at the Palace on 12 September 1848 he married Mary Elizabeth Knocker, a member of a Kentish family and the grand-daughter of Sir John Holland of Upper Deal. In 1852 he was back in England and put to work on the defences of Dover during the 'French panic'. Later he was stationed at the War Office as second 'guinea-pig' (he received a guinea a day in lieu of all allowances and in addition to his pay) until 1857, when with his eldest three children he sailed to New South Wales to organise on behalf of the Colonial Office the public works department there. On his arrival he was installed as Commissioner for Railways; then, in addition, for Roads and Telegraphs. When soon afterwards the department of Lands and Works was divided, he became secretary also for Works. Eventually his various responsibilities merged into a single Commission for Internal Communications. 'It really was a gigantic task,' he wrote, 'and the photos taken of me at that time are of a man as old as I am now only with black curly hair. A good deal of natural jealousy arose (I now think) at the enormous power invested in one man, and the position became unenviable.'

Ben does not go into the details of his resignation; the New South Wales papers did. His critics found his manner unconciliatory; he himself was impatient of red tape. In his accumulation of posts many small officials felt themselves pushed aside. His policy was challenged in Parliament; his integrity, however, was never doubted nor his soundness of judgement. The final battle was fought on the question of railway tolls. The colonists complained that they were too high. When Martindale refused to alter them, they were cut down by a ministerial Act, which proved him right when at the end of the year the deficit was increased by £3,000. Every minute action of his was scrutinised by the Assembly with the aim of making political capital out of it.

Before Captain Martindale offered his resignation to Sir William Denison, the Governor-General, he had completed the construction of the railway over the Blue Mountains. On the eve of sailing he received a public address signed by persons in the government, some leading citizens of Sydney and the acting Chief Justice. After acknowledging his 'uniform courtesy' and his readiness always to supply information about the progress of public works, the address continued: 'On your arrival in the colony railway communication was in a crude and unformed state: [now] it has assumed a defined and firmly established character. Electrical telegrams, then scarcely known, have been extended throughout the length and breadth of the land, affording facilities of intercourse and conducing to the public prosperity in a degree that future ages only can realise.' For this if for no other reason Captain Martindale's period of office would 'ever stand forth prominently in the annals of the progress of this land'.

All the travellers in the interior of the colony [one paper wrote] 'from the gentry who travelled on the main roads in their own vehicles, down to the teemsters, whose dray wheels were constantly embedded in the soft clay, young and old, rich and poor—all the travellers through the interior—for want of knowing any other culprit, united in casting the blame on Captain Martindale'.[1] Many journalists came out in his defence. In one of the Sydney museums there exists still a collection of his exquisitely careful paintings.

Ben, who as a young lieutenant at Corfu had 'begun to know the Lord', was unperturbed. He sailed home with Denison and was well received at the War Office where, from 1862 to 1868, he was Superintendent of the Barracks Department. When the Control Movement took place in the spring of 1868 he was selected to inaugurate it. This he did successfully from Aldershot until he was ordered to Canada a year later to inaugurate Control there. During his Canadian service he witnessed the Fenian Outbreak, the Red River Affair and the withdrawal of English troops from Canada: in fact, except for General Hamilton, he was the last officer to leave the country.

In Canada he had again overworked. He was never able to refuse any job offered him and in addition to his Control duties he had shared in the Admiralty administration. On his return to England he had completed thirty years' service in the Engineers. He retired when no attractive military task was suggested to him, and through the good offices of a friend he was given the post of Controller of St. Katherine Docks. With his pension from the Army and his substantial salary he was now well off. He was offered the K.C.B. but refused it as idly increasing his expenses. His large family and his constant charity to his cousins forced him still to live economically.

2

Arthur Temple Martindale, Ben's eldest surviving son, had been born at Dover on 13 March 1854. At his christening on 27 March his godparents were Ben's sister, Elizabeth Lavinia, and Sir Richard Temple of the East India (Bengal) Civil Service, who was married to Charlotte Frances, the youngest of Ben's sisters.

On his father's return from Australia Arthur was sent, at the age

[1] *Sydney Morning Herald*, 15 January 1861.

of seven, to a preparatory school at Blackheath. Ben, writing to a friend in Australia on 26 October 1861, reported: 'Arthur is doing well at Blackheath and is growing into a manly, truthful boy. He is a favourite at school with his great brown eyes and open face which you remember.'

He was also Ben's favourite. From Blackheath he passed into Cheltenham and then, like two uncles before him, he entered the Indian Civil Service. He was only twenty-three, a sociable, serious, slightly romantic person, an upright almost military figure, when he married Isabelle Marion McKenzie at St. Thomas' Cathedral, Bombay, on 17 November 1877.

Marion McKenzie was the daughter of Captain C. F. McKenzie. Her family were distant cousins of the Evans, Derbyshire gentry, from Allestree, four miles from Derby. It was there that Marion McKenzie (Cyril referred to her always as May), orphaned in early childhood, was brought up by Sir Walter Evans, member of Parliament for Derbyshire for thirty-six years. The other three McKenzie children, Alastair, Colin and Claire, were allocated to Darley Abbey, a smaller house in the neighbouring village, belonging to Mr. William Evans, Sir Walter's brother, who had married Susan Gisborne, a sister of Sir Walter's wife, Mary Gisborne; and to Holme Hall, the Gisborne home.[1]

Marion McKenzie was a delicate and intelligent girl, volatile, carefree, fascinating but not strictly beautiful. Arthur Martindale had visited Allestree during his first home leave from India and had instantly fallen in love with her. At the time he was a Junior Attaché at the Foreign Office, Calcutta. Marion, only eighteen, had already considered several suitors. Owing to his small salary Arthur was not prepared to propose marriage there and then, but some months after his return to India he made the offer in a letter addressed to Mr. William Evans. His sister, Alice, noted in her journal on 3 March 1877:

> About a month ago Papa [Ben Hay] received a letter from Arthur: he proposed engaging himself to May McKenzie and en-

[1] For the Gisborne connections see Appendix I, p. 239.

closed Papa a letter for her for Mr. Evans. In spite of all the attention she has received in Derbyshire, she and Arthur have kept faithful during sixteen months of absence. He did not propose to marry till May '78 as then his income would be larger, etc. Papa sent on his letters to Allestree—May was staying with Katie[1] at Holme Hall: they telegraphed to return home immediately. She said, yes, at once to Ard's letter and all her people fully approved.

In July Arthur applied for home leave, but on account of the Indian famine he was refused. Eventually it was decided that Marion should go out to India for the wedding. On 11 September Aunt Alice wrote again:

Arthur sends terrible accounts of the famine and distress in Madras and his district: many thousands of poor natives all starving and only five Europeans there to superintend them: many die every night. We are so thankful he keeps well. Soon we trust all will be arranged for his wedding and May at length will go to him, as he *can't* come to her! She is much stronger now. Many of their household possessions have been already sent out to Coimbatore.

Mr. Evans escorted Marion to India. When the girl saw the country where Arthur's career lay she hesitated, but she was told firmly that there was now no going back on the engagement. The marriage took place from the Bombay residence of Sir Richard Temple who also lent the couple a country house for their honeymoon.

Arthur worshipped his wife more than she did him but they were ill-matched partners. Cyril himself wrote later: 'I doubt whether the marriage would have worked well.' Marion Martindale was already a consumptive before leaving for India. There her condition quickly deteriorated. In May, the year after her marriage, she was sent back to England; Arthur, himself on sick leave, followed her in June. Reaching Southampton on 14 July he had to be nursed for some time before he could rejoin his wife at Allestree for convalescence.

[1] Katherine, Arthur's sister, married to Francis Gisborne.

Meanwhile Marion's own health had not improved. Before Christmas she had a second haemorrhage of the lungs. She was now pregnant, and in this condition she was considered too frail to return to India with Arthur at the end of February. 'The parting was *terrible* to both her and Arthur, but she was quiet with us and I did all I could,' wrote Aunt Alice.

This was the last meeting between Arthur and his young sickly wife. On 25 May her child was born in Ben Hay's house in Kensington Gardens Square. Alice noted: 'He was so delicate that they had a hard matter to save him, but Dr. Paul's great skill mercifully succeeded. He was forced immediately to have a nurse and Elizabeth Nevett was chosen.' 'It was very difficult to make me be born,' Cyril wrote of the event. 'I was rather black and after (they said) two hours of slapping, and of hot and cold water, etc., I signalised my entry into the world by a lament. I cried. I didn't like the world; nor do I.' When he was well enough he was brought down to the drawing-room and exhibited on a cushion. About a month later, on 25 June, he was christened Cyril Charlie by the Reverend Daniel Moore at the Church of the Holy Trinity, Bishops Road, Paddington. His godparents were Mr. Evans, who had accompanied Marion to Bombay, Mr. Evans' daughter, Mary, and Charlie Lucas of Warnham Court, Hersham. It was after Charlie Lucas that the boy received his second name. Cyril never knew him but received from him a silver gilt-lined christening mug and silver knife and fork which he was permitted to use on his birthdays.[1]

Marion Martindale never rallied after her son's birth. She spent five weeks with her sister-in-law, Alice, then moved to Allestree. Her decline was rapid and she died there on 27 October. Later Cyril was told how at the very end she had asked to see him, had sat up in bed, stretched out her arms, had a violent haemorrhage and died. 'I was told,' wrote Cyril, 'that at that moment I looked exactly like her.' He was five months old.

The funeral was delayed until 1 November to allow Arthur time

---

[1] The mug was later given to Archbishop Downey to sell for his Liverpool cathedral project, but was put in a glass case with other elegant objects. The knife and fork were presented to Campion Hall.

to return from India. On reaching Allestree, Arthur went to his own set of rooms and spoke to no one. His wife was buried in Allestree churchyard about half-past three the following afternoon. Shortly afterwards Arthur returned to India. Cyril, when he became conscious that he had lost his mother, was never allowed to mention her: 'It would cause pain.' He wrote:

> I picture her in association with Allestree. She used to go dancing about the park among the clover (I can never forget its smell), buttercups, daisies and meadow-sweet. I cannot believe that I have constructed this picture from what I have been told: anyhow, I *see* her as playing around, in her white frock, in the Allestree park.

### 3

The earliest description of Cyril is given by his aunt Alice, who had been appointed the child's guardian. Six days after Marion Martindale's funeral, Alice wrote:

> Little Cyril came to stay with us on 7 November 1879—delicate but healthy. He was five and a half months old—very fair, rosy, blue eyes, light hair—fat and with a first tooth just through. He soon made friends with us all and proved very sweet-tempered and winning. He has been the pleasure and comfort of our lives ever since and has got on very well.

Then writing on a later date which she does not record:

> Now he can say a few words, is cutting his double teeth and has just learnt to walk. He is a universal favourite.

Arthur, back in India by December, had lost his Foreign Office post in Madras. He was sent to Tanjore, then to the Godaveri district which his sister Alice believed 'savage and remote'. He was in constant touch with her by letter. 'He has just killed his first tiger!' she noted in her diary.

Alice was heavily oppressed by her responsibilities. Recollecting his earliest childhood, Cyril wrote: 'She moralised everything; and if I did anything at all awkward, even like upsetting my milk, she made me feel that it would make God angry and my father grieved, about *ex aequo*.' Nevertheless she was devoted to her charge. 'It seems a wonderful two and a half years since he came to us,' she wrote on Cyril's third birthday. 'He is a dear little child, very gentle and good and loving to us; looking fat and rosy but always needing great care. He picks up a few French words prettily. He is very fair, but not quite so pretty as he used to be.' On his third birthday he had 'a buttercup wreath, and sponge cakes for tea'. His photograph should have been taken that day and sent to his father, but the rain prevented it. Two days later he was taken to Ryde and enjoyed a long visit to the pier. The weather was warm; Alice and her sister Maud bathed; Cyril was photographed.

Cyril had a vivid memory of his grandfather's high and narrow house in Kensington Gardens Square. It was full of massive mahogany furniture of the period, bronze ornaments, pastel portraits and enchanting cabinets crammed with odd pieces—Venetian glass, phials of amber and overseas curios. On the top floor was Cyril's nursery. 'My first recollection is isolated,' he wrote, unable to give even an approximate date, 'and one of unmitigated malice. How old is one when one wears a lace veil and rides in a pram? Well, I had been told that I mustn't suck my veil. When my nurse was tipping my pram down a kerb, I thought: "Now for a quick nibble!" I took my chance, like St. Augustine and the pears. I knew I would have no time to enjoy it (and my veil, like my cot-curtains, had a special taste). I nibbled out of pure wickedness, entirely because I had been told not to, *diabolo suadente*.'

Shortly before his fourth birthday he attended on 13 April 1883 the wedding of his mother's sister, Claire McKenzie, to Captain Duncan Johnson, R.E. at St. Margaret's, Westminster. 'Cyril was sweet in pure white and blue sash.' A few days later, on his fourth birthday, Aunt Alice noted: 'Little Cyril had toys, and some children to tea, and was supremely happy. He was very well and bright.'

Often when Alice travelled north, visiting sometimes her friends the Hudlestons at Hutton John, near Penrith, Cyril was sent to live with her younger married sister, Katherine. Cyril liked her by far the best all of his aunts; unlike Alice, she was worldly, and, as Cyril always remembered, she gave him his first glass of Sauterne which he enjoyed greatly. Katherine's husband, Francis Gisborne, had inherited Holme Hall, Bakewell, which his father, who had married a Russian lady, had purchased on his retirement from the consular service in Russia and Corfu. Francis died young and there was only one child, Gwendolen, about Cyril's age, whom he very early vowed to marry.[1] Cyril was four and Gwendolen five at the time of this childish romance. They were good playmates and early in 1884 it was decided that the two children should be taken to Sorrento to meet Arthur, then returning from India on his first home leave since the loss of his wife.

On 15 January 1884 Cyril sailed, in the care of Alice, from Gravesend in the *John Elder*, carrying emigrants to Australia. He was sick several times during a rough crossing of the Bay of Biscay 'but what I remember acutely was tying my tin bucket to a string and trying to fish up some sea water. Naturally the bucket was swept away and is now somewhere in the bottom of the Mediterranean. Even then I hatched the germ of an idea—you cannot pull up the sea in a bucket. This grew and grew and provided some intelligent basis for my period of adolescent agnosticism many years later.'

While they awaited Arthur's arrival, Cyril and Gwen were taken for walks by the sea. Gwen recalls also how they used to go out together in panniers strapped to a mule: stones were put in Cyril's so that his weight should balance hers. There were picnic lunches of chocolate and bread. In the hotel annexe where they had their supper the two children played a game of giving the residents names suggested by their appearance, like *L'ambassadeur* and *Le Joli Moustache*. Churches were visited; there were fireworks and a procession in honour of some saint; the children were enthralled as they watched his image heave through the streets on swaying shoulders. Vesuvius was moderately active; at night red-hot lava dribbled from the crater. Cyril was awed by it and very angered when his grandfather, in his innocent geniality, referred to the volcano as 'old Vessie'. One

---

[1] Gwendolen actually married Gerard Twisleton-Wykeham-Fiennes. For much of the information in the following pages I am indebted to her.

incident might have been taken as an omen. Outside the hotel gates was a seated statue of St. Peter. One day, coming home from a walk, Cyril fell and cut his knee on it.

The highlight of the visit to Sorrento was Arthur's arrival. The family was frightened that Cyril might be shy, hang back or talk little. So the child was rehearsed. He must run up to him, stretch out his arms and hug him. All this he did because he had been told (truthfully) what a good and loving man his father was. Nevertheless, because he was made to act, there was set up at their first conscious meeting a screen of unreality between father and child. Apart from riding about sometimes on his shoulders, Cyril remembered nothing more of his father at Sorrento.

It took Arthur some time to get used to his son's precociousness. In Rome, on their way back to England, Cyril astonished his father by his absorption in the dome of St. Peter's which he kept on drawing from the Pincio hill. Only five years old, he took back with him impressions of a dazzling sky and buildings of pale tawny stone with an ethereal horizon. But it was the fountains that held him—the white, moving, noisy sheafs of water. Trevi was a disappointment. Later, when he found his way back to it without asking, he understood the reason: the water was too subordinate to the statues, rockeries and great façades behind it. He preferred the humble, little, single-jet fountains under ilex trees. Of the rest of his journey home he remembered little except, again, a fountain in an hotel garden by one of the great lakes. He imagined the jet played high when he was good; when he was bad, it would hardly rise at all. Already he was engaged in a childish form of mental play-acting.

As he grew up, the screen between him and his father became denser, particularly when Cyril realised that he could never become the kind of man or lead the kind of life Arthur saw for him. On their return to London the difference between the two was revealed in a trivial incident. Arthur wanted the nursery at Kensington Gardens Square to be re-papered with hunting scenes; Cyril insisted on fairies among wild flowers. In the end two walls had Arthur's paper, two Cyril's.

From the days he could first remember, colour was one of the enchantments of his childhood, particularly when it was united to form. An all-year fascination was his kaleidoscope with its endless combination of shades and shapes. He loved especially the more intense and pure colours made by the prisms. In the Queen's Road there was an artists' shop and in the window a palette, with large daubs of paint, which induced such excitement that he insisted always on stopping to gaze until his nurse wrenched him away. Every year there was a sort of miracle in store for him with the appearance of the first snowdrops, greenish white with drooping heads. Crocuses he liked till they became overblown. Already he had discovered how to see things framed within and across other objects. When he lit his toy theatre from behind its wings and turned out every other light, it became a magical cavern. In the same way when he looked at a laburnum or almond tree from some distance between the rows of regular dull houses, it was transformed into a thing of magic, like a patch of heaven. In a different way a door, if shut or ajar, was a challenge to exploration. The very first essay he published, apart from juvenilia, was about Janus and the mystery of doors.

In his nursery in London, Cyril was permitted to speak only French with his governess, Emma, until dinner time, and even after dinner would often continue in French; he preferred the sound of French words. His walks in Kensington Gardens were sometimes marred by sights that caused him real terror. He was never to forget the impression made on him during these walks by two men he often passed in the street on his way to the Gardens. They played a barrel-organ and wore white coats. Both of them had lost an arm. Above the organ was a double picture: the lower half showed one of the men, as a small boy in blue, having his arm broken by a dray that ran over him. Above, the second man's arm was being sawn off by a piece of machinery; blood spouted from it; other men were running towards him, also in white coats. The first time he saw it Cyril screamed and had to be taken home by his nurse. After that, even the glimpse of a white coat in the distance made him hysterical. In the end that particular street where the organ-grinders played was avoided.

A more subtle and inexplicable horror was created for him by certain types of London houses, usually flat-fronted, without ledges or cornices, blank and passive like the two men in white coats. When he passed them, unaccountably he felt a sense that something very alive and wicked was lurking in them, ready to pounce: the windows became real eyes. The differentiation between these houses and others was always sharp. Sitting up in his cot at night he worked over these impressions. He imagined all kinds of things that might be going on inside them and made up stories, which he told Gwendolen, of horrible tortures. In these stories he was always the prince and Gwendolen the princess.

More difficult to place exactly is Cyril's first recollected visit to a Catholic church. It was on his way back from Kensington Gardens after his afternoon walk. As it was beginning to rain, Emma, in search of shelter, took him into the Carmelites[1] in Church Street. All Cyril recalled were the small red windows of the clerestory. The Brompton Oratory not unnaturally produced a more enduring impression. He was vaguely frightened, especially by the Calvary Chapel. In a different way he felt the impact of the Sacred Heart statue, now on the left of the entrance. It produced on him an indefinable effect of being alive and looking at him. The tabernacle passed unnoticed but then, as always later, in a manner he could not analyse, a Catholic church, no matter how full of ugly objects, always felt different from any other church. Later he explained it by saying it gave him a sense of being lived in.

4

During his leave in the summer of 1884 Arthur Martindale visited Hutton John, about five miles south-west of Penrith, Cumberland, where his sister Katherine Gisborne was a frequent visitor. There he proposed to Clara Hudleston, six years younger than himself.

About the same time Cyril's aunt, Alice, became engaged to Arthur, son of General de Butts, an old friend of Ben Hay. Their marriage took place at Bickley on 11 May 1885.

[1] Bombed during the war and now entirely rebuilt on the same site.

This appearance of Arthur in his son's life was brief, yet sufficient to give a slender substance to a legendary figure. That his father loved him, Cyril had to take on the word of his aunts: he had been taught always 'to put others before himself' and presumed that his father also did. While his father was at no time in the forefront of the child's mind, his aunts, in their loyalty, never allowed him to recede into its background. Ben Hay, the grandfather, was the colossus of his home: he pressed heavily on the boy, who was not sympathetic to him. On his side, Cyril was aware that while his grandfather loved him, it was chiefly for his absent father's sake. Moreover, Ben was subject to occasional outbursts of rage which frightened Cyril; his wife, however, was a fountain of affection and gave the child the amount of softness he needed; possibly she expended her motherly love on him rather than on her husband who believed that he ruled her completely.

When Alice married,[1] her sisters Maud and Mary (known as Daisy or Day) took a larger part in Cyril's life. Maud was reputedly clever, wore pince-nez and was crotchety; Day was very mannered until in later life she took up work, first in Japan among the lepers, then in London for the Church Army. She became a favourite of London barmaids whose affection made her able to dispense with affection. At Temple Grove, his preparatory school, Cyril developed a cult of her; although spasmodically she later wanted to follow her nephew into the Church, a hundred slender strings bound her to Anglo-Catholicism, like Gulliver in Lilliput.

Yet it was a devoted household into which Cyril, without a mother and with an absent father, fitted coherently. The religion of his grandparents and aunts was stolidly conventional; ethics played a more emphatic part in it than dogma. The creed, rather than the conviction, that things could not be other than they were, made the next generation more likely to detach itself from all creeds when things did turn out differently. It was a religion very proper to the period and mixed with much sentimentality, yet it never wholly convinced their young charge; he had impressed deeply on him the

[1] Her daughter, Merriel (Mrs. Thain), has given me much help with this chapter and allowed me to see Cyril's letters to her.

difference between right and wrong behaviour, but could not make his elders understand his awareness of evil, nakedly opposed to good and solidified in the wicked houses he passed on his walks. He was, of course, officially taught religion by his aunts but perhaps in a too personal manner: God was angry, or at least grieved, when he was naughty. He believed that, but inferred from it that his elders, primarily his grandfather, perhaps also his father, who had the advantage of being 'invisible', were much more closely associated wth God than he could ever be. Indifferently he was told that 'God' and his 'Father' would be hurt if he did certain things he wanted to do, but he quickly appreciated that God knew, while his father had to be told. This did not help him to like either. He was never told to love God. Sometimes, when God was presented in this manner, he would shut himself up in the lavatory and call God all the bad names he knew—ugly, naughty, nasty, unkind. Such behaviour may have been a sort of revenge on God's unfair advantage of omniscience or the defiance of an inferiority complex that was consistently inoculated into him when God was mentioned. Certainly it was not a reaction to a Calvinistic upbringing: the taint of the English version of this was very slight in the family. He was taught that the human heart was exceedingly wicked, but this was not the predominant emphasis in the family's religion.

Every day before breakfast Ben Hay read morning prayers, with the servants kneeling apart at the far end of the room. These prayers, and the readings from Scripture that followed them, meant nothing to Cyril who found the 'special holy voice' used by his grandfather unreal and distasteful. The family knelt at leather chairs buttoned into puffs, and Cyril would spend the time pushing the puffs in and watching them slowly recovering their rotundity; or he would press his fingers on his eyeballs and produce a kind of granulated electric-green circle which expanded and contracted. In Ben Hay's absence his wife would read in a *sotto* voice. Once Cyril joined in with 'tuppety, tuppety, tup', which was what he sincerely believed she had said, and was rebuked without explanation.

In the evening Cyril recited his own prayers to Alice, then later to Maud or Day: first for blessings on his family, then for virtues in a hierarchy of Victorian emphasis: 'Make me good and obedient and true and gentle and loving and patient.' His aunt would ask, 'Do you remember doing anything today to tell God you are sorry for?' If he had done anything wrong, he resented telling his aunt something the all-seeing God had already observed; if not, he was ordered to think again. He was never allowed to ask his aunt directly for anything: if it was good for him, she would give it to him. He composed his first spontaneous prayer: 'Pray God, if it be good for me, may I be taken to see the coloured fountains.' But he had to be careful not to pray like this too often: he could express his wishes to his aunt only via God.

Churchgoing distressed him. He followed nothing of the service and hated the musty smell of the pews, hassocks, and the entire buildings that had been unused all week. His prayer-book had half-a-dozen ribbons in it, intended as markers; the different colours entertained him sufficiently during the service. Whenever he asked a question on a religious subject, he was usually told he would learn when he was older. Once he asked what 'Incarnation' meant and was put off in this way; it sounded similar to 'fornication' which recurred when his grandfather read the Apocalypse with such gusto. He was left with a dim suspicion that 'Incarnation' was something wicked also.

Although the formal exercises of religious worship made no appeal to his imagination, some excellent Anglican picture-books did. In his cot he had to look at these books before he turned to others. They consisted mostly of Old and New Testament stories. It was, in fact, in the story of the Good Samaritan in a book called *The Parables* that he first discovered he could read a word or two. He was never taught the Life of Our Lord as such. Christmas, of course, brought its decorations, presents and hymns; Easter its coloured eggs and usually a stay in the country; but there was no instruction in the dogma enshrined in these feasts. Aunt Alice found the story of the Crucifixion too sad to mention; later she did not tell it to her own children. The imaginary stories he made up about the Apostles before going to sleep soon merged into romances about himself and Gwen.

But for the greater part the religion he was taught was more theism than Christianity. The Sunday papers, which supplemented his picture books, illustrated the Broad and Narrow Ways and presented similar devices. There were also missionary magazines, which inspired him with a loathing for palms, cowrie shells, black babies and, in particular, for St. Paul. Sundays, until tea-time, were especially distasteful. There was church, then holy reading. Cyril was made to learn the current collects by heart. When he could read well enough, he was made to join the 'Young Scripture Readers' Union'. This meant that he had to read five to ten verses a day, then think, select the verse he liked best and recite it later by heart. This practice had its use but it did not assist his imagination.

Meanwhile a minor religious ferment was taking place in his mind. The stimulus came from a book entitled *The Angel of the Iceberg*. An angel saw a ship crushed between two bergs and resolved to melt one of them. First the angel lit a fire; this did nothing. Then it swaddled the berg with rags; this also was useless. Finally the berg on its own account floated into the Gulf Stream, i.e. the Love of God, and melted.

The story was the first revelation of the love of God to his childish mind and did him more good than weighty moral exhortations. Both the *Angel* and the tale of *Timothy Tuttle and the Little Imps*[1] fostered in him a germ of real religious growth independently of all that was forced on him by his grandfather and aunts. The unreality of their teaching was impressed on him one day after he had prayed to God via Aunt Maud for a small model shop. Infallibly he got it. When he brought it down to the drawing-room to exhibit, a visitor asked, 'Who gave you that?' His answer was, 'God'. The lady replied with evident mockery in her voice, 'Did an angel fly in with it through a window?' Cyril knew perfectly well that it had come in a brown-paper parcel. He was offended and turned his back.

Nevertheless, the narrow London house in Bayswater was always

[1] Timothy Tuttle was an opulent merchant who had settled down for his after-dinner nap and found himself in a desecrated cathedral (his soul), full of black imps (his thoughts). There were two choked-up fountains (baptism and repentance) and an old lady (conscience). Gradually the place was cleared up; the imps were dipped and cleaned, and finally Timothy Tuttle woke up innocent.

full of affection and often real love. Perhaps in greater measure than most children Cyril suffered from extreme boredom, and a feeling that 'this will never finish'. At the same time he was tormented by the idea of growing up and becoming like the people who were held up to him as models. In the grave interpretation they put on their task, his aunts impressed on him that somehow, in a way he could not comprehend, the entire future (whatever that might mean) depended on him. This responsibility, and his shyness, increased his isolation from other children (except his cousin Gwen) and from his elders. Already he was independent of their opinions about him, as later of most other persons'—or perhaps, more accurately, was unaware of them. But with this went an instant alertness to what was passing in other people's minds. Later this sense developed into an uncommon power of sympathy that made it possible for him, almost inerrantly, to answer other people's thoughts rather than their words.

There was much that combined to drive him inwards on himself. As a child he felt incapable of communicating his feelings; and later also, when the matter was in any degree spiritual. Yet in other ways it was a typical Victorian childhood, filled with wonder, light, colour and excitement. Frequently he was in bed with bronchitis; seldom did he feel completely well. He was certainly not heading for a robust and conventional boyhood.

# 2
## *Childhood*

When Cyril was seven, he was told that his father was marrying again. Arthur's marriage to Clara Hudleston of Hutton John was fixed for 4 August 1886 at Greystoke Church. Some weeks before the event the entire family moved up to Keswick. It was Cyril's first visit to the country from which the Martindales stemmed. Emma took him for excursions in the district. The Barrow falls disappointed him; although the water descended in a single stream, its bulk was small. Lodore was different. Cyril climbed to the top hoping to see a dramatic edge over which the water fell sharply; instead, it came over divided between rocks, not in one sheet. Everywhere he asked Emma to find him a girl with really golden hair and really blue eyes, such as he had known in his fairy tales, but again he was disappointed: the hair was always yellow or bright brown and the eyes a feeble china blue or tinted with green or grey. He began to be conscious of shortcomings in natural scenery, physical beauty, even also in himself. 'There was certainly here,' he wrote afterwards, 'the roots of pessimism going as far as despair, from which God has constantly had to rescue me.'

On the morning of the wedding all went by train from Keswick to Penruddock. The elders continued to Hutton John; Gwen and Cyril were deposited in Greystoke churchyard to eat their lunch. Afterwards Cyril was taken to the vicarage where he changed into a white sailor suit with blue cuffs and collar. In the wedding picture the bridesmaids appear in the hideous straw hats that the Royal Family then affected. The reception at Hutton John was on a grand scale. Between the road and the house two large triumphal arches were erected; the servants were apparelled in the Hudleston colours (gules and argent), the maids in white frocks with red trimmings.

Through the great hall, restored by Clara's grandfather, with all the Hudleston quarterings on panels in the ceiling—Fenwicks, Huttons, Chaucers, Stapletons, Inghams—the guests passed on to the terrace with its perfect row of high ancient yews. All Cyril remembered of the journey home was that, when the train approached London, he was shown Harrow with its spire black against an angry red sunset. 'That,' he was told, 'is where you will go to school some day.' His heart sank miserably.

Clara Hudleston was a remote figure in Cyril's life. From the beginning he could not be persuaded to call her 'mother', so eventually his father settled for Cara, a compromise of Cyril's choice, which satisfied all. After the marriage Marion Mackenzie's brothers and sister, who had never been conspicuous in his childhood, faded almost completely from his nursery horizon. Only Claire, an alleged beauty, given to stale epigrams, had impressed herself at all on his recollection.

Because of his delicate health it was judged prudent for Cyril to be moved from London to the country. A series of temporary homes was found, while Ben Hay searched for a permanent place at a convenient distance from London. The family first moved to Chisel-hurst, then to Bickley. Their stay in both places was brief.

At Chislehurst the old Princess Eugénie was the Martindales' neighbour. Cyril was taken to see her. He recalled the dignified Queen Anne house which had been made to look so French inside and also the chapel where the Prince Imperial was then buried, but he was not allowed to visit it too frequently for fear of being caught by the glamour of Rome. He attended a kindergarten in the district and 'fell in love' with its dancing mistress.

The house at Bickley, now a built-up area, was large, vulgar and opulent. When the family was at dinner, Cyril used to get up from bed, adorn himself in any fancy clothes he could lay his hands on, and patrol the passages. Once, when Aunt Mary came up to say her last good night, she felt the boy's cold hands and knew that he had been out of bed. Cyril denied this, but the servants had reported him. To be detected in a lie was an act of consummate wickedness. The next day he had to take his meals alone. He was permitted to speak to no one and had to write and confess his iniquity to his father, whose answer from India began: 'Your letter gave me a great deal of sorrow and a great deal of joy.' More than ever Cyril believed that grown-ups never understood anything. His father must have known that he would never have written like that unless he had been found out and ordered to write, and as for mendacity, he could not see that it mattered so much. There were plenty of lies he would never have dreamed of telling.

From Bickley, Ben Hay moved to Bromley. The house there, Oldfield, was to remain Cyril's home until he was halfway through Harrow. Behind and in front of it were fields; the drive up to it was edged by evergreen shrubs. In the inner hall, between the book-shelves, were hung tiger skins, horns and other imperial relics; the walls of the dining-room were covered with ancestral portraits and pastels; all the objects, so familiar to Cyril, that had adorned the Bayswater house, were exhumed from storage in London and given a place in the drawing-room. At the back a French window opened on to a terrace and a grassy slope below it led on to a second terrace. Below that was a tennis-court with a small transverse copse behind it; and, beyond the copse, a kitchen garden ending in a row of elms. When the family was settled, Emma gave place to a German governess who taught Cyril German songs which he yelled at the top of his voice. The Fraulein had a difficult task. Cyril called her *du alte Hexe!*; she retorted with, *Teufelskind!*

It was during one of these moves, probably when the family had settled at Bromley, that Cyril was sent as a boarder to his first preparatory school, Amesbury House. He was then about seven. The headmaster was a Mr. Moore, a correct, bearded gentleman with a baritone voice, and was assisted by a Mr. Statham who appeared to Cyril a mysterious and mephistophelean character with a scar on his neck that greatly intrigued the boys. The layout of the grounds, particularly a 'cliff' that fell down to a hard tennis-court, left more impression on him than the dismal interior of the house.

On the first day at the first class newcomers were asked their names. When asked his, Cyril gave his Christian name and was instantly covered with derision. Moore's was such an adult establishment that it was unthinkable for any boy to possess either a Christian name or a female relative.

At first Cyril was popular, then, when it was discovered that he could not play games, the reverse. However, when the boys were taken to Penge swimming baths, he regained some of his lost esteem. He was by a long way the best swimmer in the school.

Naturally he made a few friends: two brothers called Swan, whose father had amassed a fortune by inventing an electric lamp, a half-French boy, de la Condamine, who attained later fame by writings on higher paganism, and lastly, an important character called Alderman, who set himself up as the guardian of school morality. When he caught Cyril reading *The Mystery of a Hansom Cab*, he snatched it away for fear he would learn swear-words: unaccountably Alderman knew them all already.

A simple incident occurred that made Cyril indelibly conscious of his isolation. In the garden beyond the tennis-court was a hazelwood copse in which the boys played hide-and-seek. One day a boy called Elder could find nobody, lost his way out and began shouting, 'Where are you?' Cyril wrote later: 'I became conscious of myself too, completely isolated in my own self-hood, so that I have never been able to think of people in the mass, even when I was speaking to thousands at a time or broadcasting. I have always had to think of each separate personality as of something with which I could never get into complete contact; while, in proportion as one *was* approaching the middle of a soul, the experience was almost terrifying.'

His friend, Robert de la Condamine, had all the affectations, though not the accent, of a stage Frenchman: in fact he was a good actor in the conventional manner of the day and was well informed about the theatre. In school theatricals he was cast as Portia and Cyril as Nerissa in the trial scene from *The Merchant of Venice*. In another play Cyril, who always disliked women's parts and performed them with little success, was the heroine and de la Condamine the maidservant. But it was in a much more curious manner that the French boy entered Cyril's private life. He was, at least technically, a Catholic, though he had not continuously been brought up in his faith. One day, either at school or at his home, which Cyril occasionally visited, he announced that he was going to make a private chapel, which would contain a piece of the Host. 'What is the Host?' Cyril asked. 'A sort of biscuit,' he was told. Cyril, who required only a stimulus of this kind to set him off on his own trail, resolved to make his own shrine. He painted a picture of an angel flying up through a ray of light with murk around it. At the time he believed that when any good person died, he or she became an angel. In front of the picture was a fairy-light, a small bronze Roman lamp, and flowers when he could find them. The shrine was dedicated to his mother. Although he knew nothing about prayers for the dead, he felt that this was the way to honour her. What, in retrospect, seemed so strange to him was his readiness, first under the influence of de la Condamine and then of others, to accept so readily this kind of quasi-Catholic behaviour, when something rather like it, not the practice itself, was suggested to him.

Once only in adult life did Cyril hit the trail of de la Condamine. He was at Blenheim and happened to pick up one of his books, *The Upper Garden*.[1] He mentioned that he had known the author and the Duke of Marlborough said, 'My wife always likes these sexual oddities.' De la Condamine achieved no great notoriety even in his own circles; he appears to have become a kind of Aubrey Beardsley, with a spark of genius and considerable command of imagination and language.

Whatever education was given at Amesbury House, Cyril remembered little of it. He could not see that the problems of Euclid were problems; it seemed to him that they became difficult only when one was asked to prove them. He wept conspicuously over sums. In history he always fastened on what made persons human, like Prince Charles Edward's cold, but could not see the importance of dates. 'You always remember what does not matter,' his irritated master told him. But books were beginning to play their part. Harrison Ainsworth's *The Tower of London* and *The Lancashire Witches* satisfied to the full his craving for the mysterious and macabre—sliding panels, passages within walls, ghosts and decapitations. The politics of the novels had no interest for him, but the colours of the costumes, par-

[1] Methuen (1911).

ticularly 'black cloth of gold', and horrific details, did. He would draw pictures of decaying corpses dangling from gibbets over putrid marshes in the sunset. He preferred Grimms to Hans Andersen, perhaps because of the macabre element in them.

Although he did not mind what he drew himself, he became almost hysterical at the representation of horrors by others. At home his grandfather, who, like many retired Victorian colonels, was interested in the Apocalypse, produced a brochure in which the author identified with anti-Christ Prince Jerome Napoleon, whose name, he said, added up to 666.[1] On the back was a scene showing a crowd in the Tuileries, all with 666 printed on their foreheads; in the background a guillotine, with a severed head lying in a small pool of blood. The picture made him almost delirious. He knew where the brochure had been placed in the bookcase and could see its slim back from the corridor. He did all he could to prevent himself from passing it, and, if he did, from seeing it. The occasional sight he got of it made him feel sick for an hour or longer.

Cyril was beginning to dislike his grandfather and at the same time beginning to think that he would never be able to like his father when he returned again on leave. His grandmother remained the dearest person in his home.

It was while he was a weekly boarder at Amesbury House that he had a curious experience he recorded in later life. It occurred one night in the dormitory which was occupied by five or six boys. That morning in school a sixpence had been missing. Either for a tease or for some other reason Cyril was accused of taking it. He was miserable. As always later, when in a state of misery or pain, he felt his grief would never end. In the dormitory that evening, while it was still light, he saw the outline of a woman pass quickly across the room. When it was exactly opposite his bed, in front of the fireplace, it turned and looked at him, passed on and vanished. He believed undeniably that he had had this impression, followed by a total revulsion of feeling. He saw no features but was aware of motion, shape and turning. For a cause he could never afterwards explain, he

[1] Fr. Martindale's best work in Scripture are his commentaries on the *Apocalypse*: for instance, his chapter on this book in the *Catholic Scripture* Commentary, and his *St. John*.

concluded that it was his mother. Such full-length photographs of her as he had seen showed her in swathing dresses like a princess. On this figure only a few simple folds were indicated; there was not exactly any colour, but here and there an intensification of the atmosphere, producing the effect of a yellowish green.

About this Cyril wrote later: 'I never elaborated the experience. I could have drawn it then as I would now. I did not connect it with anything religious, like my prayers. I have not even the beginnings of an explanation or definition of it.'

The conclusion was a childlike incident. The boys had saved up for a nocturnal feast the same night. It consisted of dates, cream chocolate bars and coconut. Cyril had finished his share, except for one specially large date which he had heroically resolved to keep until the next morning. But when he came to eat it in the daylight, he found that it was grey with mould. This he did not hesitate to ascribe to his guardian angel's intervention.

There were other childhood experiences that isolated him for reasons he could not communicate. He was always frightened by the 'charity' processions of benevolent societies that commonly paraded the streets on Sundays with bands playing. Usually their banners represented a widow and two orphans at a paternal tomb, over which presided an angel in pink. Their utterly expressionless faces somehow corresponded to the blank-fronted houses in Bayswater, behind which he had imagined some force, more fearful than an evil person, lurking in readiness to pounce. Obscurely he felt that not only in the banners but in the whole procession of these blank-faced, black-coated and often top-hatted men, there was some real and evil force. A show of respectability was always associated with it and, in an unexplained manner, the revulsion involved the lower middle-class Protestantism of his childhood days, half-genuine as it was and half-hypocritical. Even at a spiritual level he had an unconscious abhorrence of it.

*The Angel of the Iceberg* still acted as a counterpoise to this terror; and also other books, including George Macdonald's *The Princess and the Goblins*, in which the religious message was not over-emphasised, but could be taken or left. By these indirect means he began to understand that he could use familiar, even humorous, terms about divine things. In this he was not to change, particularly in his conversation. Moralisation, most of all when it came from his grandfather, always blighted for him everything to which it was attached. It dragged the mysterious down to the level of goodness, which, for him, meant proper Victorian behaviour.

There were two churches the family patronised for Sunday worship, St. Matthew's at Bickley and St. Luke's at Bromley. Neither the buildings nor the localities attracted him. At St. Luke's the vicar, a Mr. Woodhouse, put out some timid tentacles towards a high-Anglican form of worship.

During this time St. Luke's was visited by Archbishop Benson. Cyril remembered vividly how he went in procession round the church, superior but bland, his hair curling over the back of his collar, because (as he discovered when he came to write the life of his son, Robert) he thought that an Archbishop's hair should curl in that manner. The concerts of sacred music appealed to Cyril. Parry's Cantata, *The Holy City*, he found enthralling, especially the vision-like prelude, and some of Wesley's more mystical hymns, like 'Love divine, all loves excelling'. He was not particularly religious, but he had a craving always for something he did not comprehend. He took part also in charitable tableaux.

But it was still colour and form that gave him his most intense experience of pleasure. He tried to paint the vivid yellow autumnal colours, then other impressions, like the shimmer of gold and silver, framing his pictures in heavy crimson curtains. He developed also an acute sense of smell. Throughout his life he was aware of all sorts of scents; some flowers practically suffocated him, especially syringa, tuberoses, freesia, lime trees in full bloom. And there were smells also in a different range: the series, for instance, connected with cricket—flannels, cricket-bat oil, cropped grass and the pavilion woodwork. Like the angels, each scent was *sui generis*. A hyacinth smelt like a hyacinth and nothing else; bonfires in autumn had their special fragrance. His last summer term at Amesbury House came back to him wholly in terms of the massed roses in the school garden with their unique but mildly intoxicating odour. Later he discovered that he shared with St. Aloysius an inability to endure any stale scent.

Every year at Amesbury House his isolation was enhanced. There was a boy around whom there formed a gang from which Cyril felt excluded. He knew nothing of indecency at the time, but one afternoon when he was doing sums at one end of the long school-room and the gang was huddled at the other, he felt anxious to share in what was being said and done. He never said anything about this but his family must have guessed that something was agitating him. Ben Hay put to him what seemed totally meaningless questions. Again Cyril felt he lived in a different world, and that it would be useless to attempt an explanation. He did not speak to Mr. Moore or to any boy. But one day the headmaster gave a long talk to the school. All attended except Cyril. The same evening he was taken away.

He was also ill. He was sent to Hutton John for a rest. In the night train he tried to wake up early in order to see the dawn. He expected it would be sudden and was disappointed when it was slow and cold. For the second time, but in a less childish way, he took pleasure in the north country—in the old house with no hint of suburbs around it, in the clipped yew-trees, the becks and fells. He was completely satisfied.

Although his departure from Amesbury House was unexpected, he was unlikely to have continued there much longer. Already he had developed an habitual sense of tiredness; at home, but never at school, he showed an inexhaustible capacity for tears. Even his grandmother could not discover the cause. All Cyril could say was, 'I am so tired of everything', meaning that he had a distaste for all that made up his life at school. Possibly at the age of eight and a half he was beginning to experience the troubles of adolescence. He had an intense desire for what he vaguely understood to be peace. The idea haunted him; the hymn, 'Peace, perfect peace', educed floods of tears. Probably he was anxious for nothing more than to be left alone.

2

Temple Grove, Cyril's second preparatory school, was at East Sheen,[1] in an open countryside through which the boys walked to Richmond Park. The school had closer links with Eton and Winchester than with Harrow, but it was chosen in preference to Elstree, probably for its connection with the Temples. The old Georgian part of the house had been built by Sir William Temple. It had a simple dignity but had been extended at each end; later a long wing had been pushed out to form an L; later still, this was prolonged first by a cloister, and then, in Cyril's time, by a chapel.

Mr. Edgar, the headmaster, was a low-Church clergyman true to type. He was devoid of humour and a devout believer in the schoolboy code of honour, and was never prepared to admit that his charges could be guilty of any serious moral misdemeanour. He chewed constantly a greying moustache and desired to be thought more alarming than he was. His wife, known among the boys as 'Blackie-Bluejah', was a large, kind-hearted lady, who in her full dresses progressed through the school like a galleon. There were two daughters, Mabel, the elder one, wizened, nervous and pious; the second, Edie, was more worldly. Both petted Cyril mildly when he was ill. The sub-master, Mr. Allen, lived in a house of his own, and because he was a connection of the Hudlestons, insisted on addressing Cyril as 'cousin'. The matron was a Mrs. Bostocke, known as 'Dame Boss'. Cyril was frequently in her care. If Mrs. Edgar was a galleon, Dame Boss was a man-of-war.

From his first term, under the care of Mr. Packe, who later left to become a clergyman, Cyril progressed effortlessly through the school. He was never beaten and, until his last year, was intensely happy. If he did not come out first in his class, he was seldom below second. There is a letter of his that has survived from this period. It is addressed to 'Darling dearest Aunt Daisy':

> I *hope* you are perfectly well. I am so glad the party went off well. Did they eat all the eclairs? I am really getting on pretty well

[1] It was later removed to Eastbourne and then to Lord Rankeillour's house, Heron's Ghyll, at Uckfield.

with my work, I think, and I also think I am still top. I have copied out the Apostles' gems. They are on the next page. [Then follows the list, headed by 'Andrew: the sapphire, emblem of his heavenly faith', and so on through to Mathias.] The colours you can find in your book.

I have learnt the collect for today. It is very beautiful. I have read day and night out of my testament, and I have put your photo where I can see it day and night. I always kiss it before I go to sleep.

The matron is very nice, but tremendously fat. On the next page I shall make a sketch of her. She is strict and threatens a great deal, but I shouldn't think they come off [*sic*].

[At the top of the fourth sheet is a pen drawing of Dame Boss.][1]

Now, darling Aunt Day, Goodbye. Ever yr *very* loving nephew Cyril.

The letter is endorsed 'Privateish'.

During his frequent visits to the sick bay at Temple Grove he read voraciously whatever books came his way. Dickens' *Tale of Two Cities* stirred new fancies. The first half he found grim and second-rate. The French part made him feel that his proper home was France, and, in spite of the wicked Marquis, aristocratic France. A visit to Paris during one of his vacations was the beginning of his life attachment to that country. He believed that he had some French blood, but his grandfather's insistence that all inquiry into his forebears was a worldly pursuit made it impossible for him to settle the point.

Another book that influenced him enduringly was Lytton's *Last Days of Pompeii*. Although he was incapable of detecting its psychological absurdities, it opened for him the classical world into which he would perhaps never otherwise have found his way. Since his father intended him for the diplomatic service, he had been placed on the modern side of the school; he already knew French fluently and could speak a little German. While he was good at mathematics, except arithmetic, by preparatory school standards, his interests did

[1] See illustration, p. 84.

not lie there. In his very first term the new boys, by way of a test, were made to sit round a table in the library, translate some English sentences into Latin and then take them through to Mr. Edgar's study for correction. Cyril finished his at once. Mr. Edgar scowled, gnawed his moustache and asked, 'What's the matter?' The sentences were done correctly; the headmaster was annoyed. Cyril continued with Latin, though he remained on the modern side. Mr. Ellis, the Latin master, said that he thought in Latin. Already he was entranced by the Georgics and wanted to set them to music. Like French, Latin came to him naturally. He began Greek only in his second year at Harrow.

Rider Haggard's *King Solomon's Mines* woke his interest in Africa. Cyril envied the superb Zulus and would have liked to have exchanged his nervous frame for theirs. On bath nights he and a boy called Innes used to prance about attired in a *moocha*, or a long towel hanging down in front. *Cleopatra* formed a link with what he had read in *The Last Days of Pompeii* about the cult of Isis, and he became interested in the Egyptian atmosphere and in hieroglyphics. At the age of ten he demanded Renouf's *Egyptian Grammar* as a Christmas present and began to haunt the British Museum during his holidays, sometimes in company with a school-friend called Codrington.[1] He filled a large note-book with Egyptian drawings and was soon able to read inscriptions on obelisks with fair ease. He had no guidance. The interest, however, did not survive his education at Harrow. There seems to have been little orderliness in anything he learnt outside the schoolroom.

During a second sojourn in the sick bay Cyril came across *The Ingoldsby Legends* which stimulated his taste for the macabre and bloodthirsty. After the visit to Hutton John for his father's wedding he had become interested in heraldry. The *Legends* fostered this. Unconsciously he was responding to the Rabelaisianism in many of

---

[1] Humphrey William Codrington (1879–1942), son of Rear-Admiral William Codrington, C.B. From Temple Grove he went to Winchester, which he left in order to become a Catholic. In 1903 he joined the Ceylon Civil Service. He wrote *Ceylon Coins and Currency*, *A Short History of Ceylon*, and contributed to learned periodicals including the *Eastern Churches Quarterly*. The January 1943 issue of this review contains an obituary of Codrington written by Dom R. H. Connolly.

the poems. The medieval and Catholic elements stirred up afresh an unexplained craving that had been dormant for some time. Poetry meant principally Longfellow, particularly *The Golden Legend*, *Hiawatha* and *Evangeline*. At Harrow, when he needed it most, the prayer to the Sacred Heart came back to his memory in an almost preternatural way, along with the recollection of the statue in the Brompton Oratory. At home he resolved to produce the *Golden Legend* on his miniature stage. The sonerousness of the lines, rather than the Catholic ideas, captivated him. He used the *Legend* for his prayers. Later Tennyson began to count equally with Longfellow, principally his poems like the *Idylls* that had some religious colouring. *Maud* interested him only moderately; he could not see the point of it.

Cyril appears to have been popular at Temple Grove. His proficiency at swimming prevented his lack of interest in other sports altogether outclassing him. At the same time, he seems to have made fewer friends than at Amesbury House. Other boys began mildly to bore him, but a strange affinity, and also an antagonism, declared itself very early between him and a short, sturdy, round-faced, bespectacled boy called Edghill, who had been christened Albert Edward after his godfather, the Prince of Wales. Edghill's father had been Chaplain-General to the Forces, and his son had already determined to become a clergyman. He was exactly suited to the establishment as it then was, and indeed, after leaving Eton, he entered the Church and satisfied family tradition by writing a learned treatise on Amos.[1]

Edghill was somehow different from the ordinary run of boys. He was Cyril's regular companion during his holidays. Together in the grounds at school they created a world of fiction, making secret paths and hiding places in the shrubberies from which they watched other boys pass unaware of their presence. However, they made it a point of honour never to eavesdrop on their conversation. Edghill was solid, while Cyril was flimsy. Now, as so often later, Cyril was attracted by those most unlike himself physically: athletes, dockers,

---

[1] In the Oxford Commentaries Series. His last book was published in 1911. He died in this or the previous year as the result of an accident at a boys' camp he was conducting.

stokers and prize-fighters. There were also Codrington, Cyril's companion at the British Museum, Percival Innes, who later became a member of Parliament, and a youth of almost excessive refinement, A. E. A. Napier. When in adult life they crossed his path and wished to renew acquaintance, Cyril never responded; possibly he felt they would be out of sympathy with his calling.

Through Edghill's influence Cyril developed an interest in ritualism. When he stayed at Edghill's home, or Edghill at his, they went round churches, seeing whether the incumbent had placed two candles on the Communion Table or wore coloured stoles. On Cyril's side there was only a small religious element in this. It was more a search for something mystical or belonging to the other world for which he continuously craved.

At school, under Edghill's influence, Cyril found himself carrying out a strange rite of his own, surreptitious and unrevealed even to his friend; he always had to translate the practices of others into a version of his own.

In the dormitories each boy had a china mug for brushing his teeth and also a hard biscuit to eat before coming down to first schools. When he believed that all were asleep, Cyril would get out of bed, fetch the mug and biscuit, return to his bed, kneel down on it and (as he would have said later) 'put himself in the presence of God'. At the time he intended to do no more than isolate himself from everything past and future. He would then solemnly eat a portion of the biscuit and drink a little water. Long afterwards he could recall the peculiar taste of the biscuit and of the water, just a little dusty, drunk out of a china mug. During the ceremony he would think of himself as a prophet filled somehow with the Holy Ghost, though he could not say exactly what he meant by either. His idea of Holy Communion was vague. He knew that grown-ups sometimes stayed behind in church for a second service, but he had not been told what happened at it—that would come later. And in any case, both for his own Low Church family and for Mr. Edgar, Communion would have been something done 'in memory of the Lord'. There was no question of anything changed, even for a few moments, into something else. 'To all intents and purpose,' Cyril wrote later, 'my *rite* was my own invention, *and*, I should suppose, a gift, and a great gift, from God.'

This was a kind of apex in his religious life. None of the chapel services stirred him but certain religious hymns kept their appeal. He was placed in the choir because he was considered devout, not for his voice. The overture to *The Holy City* fitted exactly into his absorption with the Apocalypse. His preference was for celestial hymns and a few sincere moralising ones, like

> *Father, let me dedicate*
> *All this year to you.*

His love of hymns remained with him all his life and often as a priest he would recite those he had learned at Temple Grove. Through them he first gained a sense of words, or perhaps phrases, and of the shape of sentences.

At this time he wrote little outside school exercises, except some verses which began

> *The mother was sad for her son and got*
> *A place in the Burmese fighting hot . . .*

And so through a large number of lugubrious stanzas in each of which one of her children met a morbid end.

At Temple Grove there was a boy called Maltby with whom he formed an unenduring friendship. In a spell of infantile hooliganism induced by this companion, Cyril scratched his name on a church pew (it was before the chapel was built) and also worked out an elaborate system of cribbing by which notes were passed from locker to locker along a secret wire. Maltby also imparted to him much inaccurate information about sex, a subject that was treated very seriously by the boys. Henceforth Cyril could claim to be 'in the know' and was not excluded from any secrets passed round the school. Sometimes the boys discussed how often it was healthy to do certain solitary acts. Public opinion settled roughly for once a week. No notorious love affairs came to his knowledge, but it was assumed (perhaps wrongly) that one existed between an older boy and a certain master. Code commanded that it was nobody's business to pry.

The notion of sin did not enter into such relationships, though, if a culprit was discovered, the matter at once became grave. Sex was taboo both to masters and parents and cloaked by a *laissez-faire* morality, even by a certain fatalism. Psychologically this was a mistake. Cyril always wanted to pry into mysteries, even if it was only to see what lay behind a stage curtain or a closed door.

As at Amesbury House, women were scarcely mentioned. Boys were still of the age when it was inadmissible to acknowledge that they had sisters, though aunts were accepted as a regrettable necessity.

### 3

Twice during his time at Temple Grove Cyril went for Christmas to Allestree, which had now been inherited by William Gisborne. His Aunt Sophy, William Evans' sister, was there on both occasions, and also Gwen. Sophy had become a Catholic, but this made less impression on Cyril than her elegant black draperies and auburn wig. Despite *The Ingoldsby Legends* Cyril did not know that Catholics in fact existed. Still less did he believe that there could be one in his family.

Cyril performed in the Christmas plays. He danced well and won applause at the Servants' Ball by flirting violently with the chief parlour-maid. Then, and still more on his summer visits, Allestree cut deep into his memory. Of Christmas he recalled mainly the bitterly cold train journeys to Derby, his meeting the footman at the station, the ride to the Hall in a brougham smelling deliciously of leather. But in its summer beauty Allestree was a place of endless enchantment. In several early books he described the house, the park and, always, the knoll:

> The Knoll is really a very considerable hummock of ground, and you can see right away round a big arc of country, to where the hills shut in the valley five or six miles away. The home woods come round the bottom of the Knoll and you only see the roof of the house and its annexes peering up among them more than ever

like a village, with their stable belfry and the dove-cote and their irregular pitch. You can't see the gardens, for the woods hide them, but then the park slopes away down to the Pool, as it's called, and then rises again a little to its further limit, which is Crawford-in-the-Dale, the lower village. The Pool is a little lake, in two levels: the water trickles over the old wall that crosses it and holds up the higher part of the Pool, and this trickle keeps the stonework always one mist of maidenhair; snapdragon grows on it too, and on the middle of the wall is an island, which we call Goat's Island, after Niagara. Water fowl nested there.[1]

Allestree brought out the gaiety that he had deep in himself; home and Temple Grove suppressed it partially, Harrow totally. It revived again briefly on his becoming a Catholic and during the French period of his noviceship.

There were occasional visits also to Hutton John. Cyril was old enough now to be impressed by its history. Below the upper terrace it was possible to see, most sharply in the evening sunlight, the form of the old Saxon house with its line of mounds and ditches, built on the site of an ancient Roman fortress. The first record of the Hutton home went back to 1240. In 1346, the year of Crécy, it had been burnt to the ground by David Bruce, the son of Spider Bruce, in a raid in which nineteen hamlets were destroyed. Four years later, a hundred and fifty yards higher up the hill, a tower was constructed with encircling walls, and onto this, in the next two centuries, the new castle was built. In 1450 Thomas Hutton added the Hall on the wall facing east, and just ninety years later Cuthbert Hutton, an official of Henry VIII's court, who knew Hampton Court well, added the south wing. He also constructed the terrace and planted the yew trees.[2] The house passed into the hands of the Hudlestons in the sixteenth century, when Marie Hutton, the heiress of Hutton John, married Andrew Hudleston, whose family remained Catholic until the Restoration.

---

[1] *The Waters of Twilight* (1914), 18–19: see also pp. 197 sq. and *In God's Nursery* (1913) and *The Castle and the Ring* (1955).
[2] Cf. F. Hudleston, *A Short Description of Hutton John* (Cumberland and Westmorland Antiquarian and Archaeological Society Transactions: Kendal, 1924).

What most intrigued Cyril were the heart-shaped windows in the lower wall of the Elizabethan wing. They had been inserted shortly after the Restoration by the Cavalier, Andrew Hudleston, the brother of the Benedictine monk, Fr. Hudleston, who received Charles II into the Church on his death-bed. Andrew had been in France and influenced, perhaps, by the emergent devotion to the Sacred Heart. The library had been his chapel, and there was a vague tradition of a ghost which Cyril was never allowed to mention.

Cara, Arthur's wife, who disliked India as much as Cyril's mother had done, was frequently at Hutton John during Cyril's visits. She had lost her eldest child Geoffrey who had been born in Quetta in May 1887 and had died at Hutton John at the age of three; he was the only son she was to bear Arthur. But it was her mother whom Cyril remembered distinctly. On the very first day of this visit, old Mrs. Hudleston told Cyril he might play in the beck, then suddenly remembered that he had complained of a severe headache the previous day and called him back at once: 'I knew you were your father's son,' she said to him, 'and that whatever you did, you would do immediately.'

From Hutton John, Cyril made expeditions to the local games. Their principal feature was always Lord Lonsdale with his primrose yellow carriages and postilions; then later, his automobiles in the same colours. From the fell above the house it was possible to see Dacre Castle at the far end of the estate and, some distance beyond it, Lowther; and to the left of it, the tower of Greystoke Castle. Lady Mabel Howard was then at Greystoke. Cyril had met her at a concert near Ullswater, where he had rapturously applauded her songs. Not long afterwards, when Cyril sat one afternoon playing the piano in the drawing-room at Hutton John, Aubrey Herbert and his sister Victoria were shown in with their governess. 'I'm afraid everyone's out,' Cyril said. 'Would you like me to show you the house?' Lady Victoria appeared dazzling in her blue dress, and instantly Cyril fell in love with her. As they were climbing the spiral stairway in the wall of the tower, Cyril asked whether he might carry her cloak and wished it were heavier that he might endure more for his beloved. They would meet also in Greystoke Church, full of

Howard and Hudleston hatchments, in horse-box pews on opposite sides of the aisle.[1]

The north country always brought out Cyril's romanticism. He loved the stone walls, fells and becks, the dry texture and colour of the heather, the yellow ragwort and wild geraniums. He felt this was his home. The same feeling, more strangely, came to him in France and also, but less intensely, in Italy even before he could read the Latin classics or speak Italian. The faded photos of his visit to Sorrento always made him sick with longing for that country. At the end of his life Portugal became the third country of his adoption.

Once during Cyril's time at Temple Grove his father, with two of his brothers, took some shooting in Kircudbrightshire, in south-west Scotland, renting a house called Drumstinchel. Cyril went with them, but he found his gun too heavy and had no desire to kill anything. During these days he always wanted to be alone, away from the crowd and from his father's party. It was not a happy holiday. He felt shy, he was looking for affection and he cried much. His time was passed mostly near the house in a wood which he made his own. To reach it he had to cross a stream. As he did so, he would hang over the bridge and consider drowning himself. He knew he did not really mean this, that the stream was too shallow and that, in any case, he could swim. But with despairing conviction he now understood that he could never be like his father, still less his uncles, that he could never fish, shoot, and drink 'pegs' as they did, or even wear the clothes that suited them. All he wanted was to be ordinary and unnoticed. He was not conceited, but he was made to think himself inferior.

### 4

With the large measure of freedom allowed the boys at Temple Grove in preparation for Eton, Cyril had been happy until his last term. The change was caused by a boy called Owen Berkely-Hill, who possessed a fiendish power of provoking and maintaining enmities. His ability to spellbind other children was something Cyril

[1] Cyril never met Lady Victoria Herbert again, though she was once pointed out to him in London when she was leaving Herman Norman's house as he was entering it; nor did he ever meet Aubrey's wife, Mary Herbert, who became a Catholic in 1923.

never met in later life. Using his arts, he put Cyril at enmity with Codrington. The happy atmosphere of Temple Grove was shattered irreparably. Moreover, Cyril was very ill. He spent many of his last weeks there in the sick-room and found life excessively harsh.

During these years he had become aware of sex and religion. His appetite for the macabre had also developed, but at this stage of his life there was nothing morbid about it. His religion was of a rollicking brand, and the macabre was scarcely alarming, certainly not horrific. Sex was a dimly understood hint of what time would bring. But in so far as it went, the medieval Catholic content in his religion, which seemed natural to him, provided a door through which he could later step and breathe a more congenial air. The lines from *The Ingoldsby Legends* kept recurring in his memory:

> *O, taper shall burn and bell shall toll,*
> *And Mass shall be said for my stepson's soul.*

He did not know what the lines meant and had no idea that the *res Catholica* could ever matter to him.

Finally he was sent up to Harrow to sit the mathematics scholarship. At the time he was in quarantine for mumps and did his papers in Mr. Bowen's rooms. There were seventy entrants and only two scholarships available. Cyril did the modern-side Latin paper so effortlessly that he asked also for the classical papers. After his return home (he was too sick to continue at school) a telegram was sent to Ben Hay: 'Grandson gets scholarships for classics and mathematics combined.' In fact, a special scholarship was created for him. This achievement should have indicated to his grandfather that Cyril would do better if transferred immediately to the classics, yet for a time still at Harrow he continued with mathematics.

Later Cyril never considered his education (until he went up to Oxford) at all satisfactory. He was taught to do things right, not well —to read Virgil, not to appreciate him. He was never asked what his interests were, never directed to read anything worth while. After *A Tale of Two Cities*, he was prepared to read more Dickens, but no one suggested it. For the rest of his life he remained poorly read in the English classics. He could have assimilated much more than he was given at Temple Grove. In art he was self-taught, also in music and Egyptian which no one urged him to continue. It should have been seen that his French classes were a waste of time; he knew the language well enough to read Racine and Molière. Throughout these years he was never made to struggle. He was able always to do easily what was set. There was no liberal education. At the end of his life he considered that the only subjects he had really studied were his Oxford books, allied University subjects, particularly Greek and Roman religion, some Scripture and the life of St. Aloysius. Yet in fairness it must be said that the Temple Grove education was directed, not to Harrow, but to Eton. Had he gone there, he would have enjoyed more intervals of real happiness.

# 3
## Harrow and After

Cyril arrived at Harrow in the summer of 1893 and went to Mr. E. W. Howson's small house for two terms. It lay on the way up to the chapel and looked out towards London.

Mr. Howson, the son of a distinguished clergyman, Dean Howson, was an idealist with no notion of how to manage boys for good or ill. His wife, a tall, good-looking lady with red hair and white skin, was kind but inexperienced. There were about twelve boys in the house. Its head was Cameron of Lochiel, a weakling who later developed into a sturdy laird and married Lady Hermione Graham. Cyril's room companion was Gilbert Hamilton, son of Lord Claud Hamilton. All arrived briefed in the ways and formulas of Harrow of which Cyril was ignorant.

He was placed in the Upper Remove, on the modern side, under Mr. H. Davidson, an old-fashioned and icy schoolmaster whose manner frightened him. Immediately he came out on top, though in the course of the term he yielded his place once or twice to an inky little mathematician called Smithe. He did little work, was despised as a swot, and because he was too shy to talk at table, was considered 'pi'. Days at Harrow were then spent in the minimum of necessary work and the maximum of congenial games. In the evenings, when work was over and the topic of games exhausted, conversation tended sometimes to indecency. The feminine influences of Cyril's home had not prepared him either for the smut or for the hearty Rabelaisianism from which the boys seldom shrank. He knew himself an alien and feared he would be more of an alien when he went up to the Large House.

It was at the suggestion of his grandfather, who was anxious that he should learn perspective, that he was put into the drawing class. In

fact, perspective came naturally to him. Although he liked copying
the nude statues in art books, he preferred to sketch the Sistine and
other Madonnas; and for this reason his art master, Mr. Hines, looked
on him as a sort of angel. Hines was an accomplished artist himself in
a finnicky style, but had no notion how to teach his subject. As usual,
Cyril went his own way. He would sketch the school buildings and
grounds, the red brick and the elms. But he liked best to experiment
with skies. There were still extensive views, unspoilt by villas, from
the Terrace to London and from the churchyard to Windsor, and,
had he known it, to the Beaumont beeches.

Cyril also took music, but the teaching was poor. He would have
heard few Harrow songs in his first term. Later he appreciated their
splendid tunes, but with some exceptions, such as the traditional
'Forty Years On', 'Queen Elizabeth' and a few others, he found the
words fatuous or excessively sentimental. His grandfather and his
aunt Mary came for his first speech day, which he remembered
mainly for the white waistcoat he was made to wear. On the occasion
of his first Harrow and Eton match he wanted to go home, but Mr.
Howson told him he would lose caste if he did not attend Lords for
at least one of the days. His top hat gave him a headache; his button-
hole of tuberoses made him sick.

His first summer holidays were spent in Jersey with his aunt
Claire. He returned to find himself in the Third Fifth, the lowest
form in the Upper House. This involved wearing tails which he had
difficulty always in keeping tidy. But the term proved important, for
Hamilton went on to another house and Cyril, thrown back on himself, began to develop more individually. As at Temple Grove, the
services in the Harrow chapel meant nothing to him. Sundays were
idle and consequently brought more noise, breakages and bawdiness
than other days. None of the preachers held his attention, except, for
his oddities, the headmaster, Mr. Welldon, who believed (and indeed
wrote) that what boys required was sentiment, not doctrine—a view
that fitted neatly the wishes of most parents, afraid as they were of
dogma, both high and low. At times Welldon moved the boys to
mockery. He would exclaim in chapel: 'I do not believe there is any
bad language in this great school; I do not believe there is any im-

morality. Should there come to be any, it must be put down. It *shall* be put down!'—or such phrases that were more provocative than deterrent. Outside chapel he would appear often in a ridiculous light. Both a snob and a bully, he was unaware how absurd he looked to the boys as he rode down the High Street, beaming and scowling at the town as if he owned it, or preening himself when royalties or duchesses visited the school. Winston Churchill, Cyril's elder contemporary at Harrow, was however more favourably impressed by Welldon, who took a personal interest in him and his struggle to learn the classics.

In his subsequent appointments, first as Bishop of Calcutta, then as Dean of Manchester and finally of Durham, Welldon had hardly greater success. Possibly he was a man of extreme simplicity, doing what he conceived his duty. Certainly he was naïve, as his novel *Gerald Eversley's Friendship* showed. It was inconceivable to Cyril that in June 1937 when Welldon lay dying at Sevenoaks, he asked him to visit him. Cyril, then a priest, arrived only after his death.

Under Welldon the boys learnt little Christianity unless, as it rarely happened, a house-master made good the official lack of it. An exception was Mr. Done Bushell, unashamedly a high churchman, who presented a gilded altar to the chapel, decorated with paintings of innocuous Old Testament youths such as the boy Samuel; these were held up as models to the school. There was no ritual at all, and the stained-glass windows were crude though there was one that Cyril liked. It contained the *Te Deum* figures—prophets, apostles, angels and martyrs—at which he would gaze during the services. Night prayers were composed and well read by Mr. Howson.

Only a handful of Harrow figures impressed themselves on Cyril. There was Mr. Searle, the secondary Master in Welldon's house, a man with a crippled hand, a fine golden mane and beard, no clerical mannerisms, but a number of extreme eccentricities. He taught higher mathematics. If the boys crowded round his desk, he would send them back to their places with a cry, 'To your tents, O Israel!' Once when Cyril was stooping to see what he was writing, Searle exclaimed, 'Kneel! boy! kneel!', and then added in a whisper, 'No better position in the world!' Only Searle regularly, and Canon (later

Bishop) Gore, on the occasion of a visit, left in Cyril's mind a vague and ill-understood impression of holiness. Gore was preaching on the Feast of the Ascension. Cyril forgot his sermon but remembered the effect. When next they met, Bishop Gore appeared to Cyril a much tormented man. It was in the House of Lords after Gore, twitching the entire time, had made a speech. Later they met on several occasions at Oxford during the first world war. Gore was not prepared to allow that there was any spiritual movement at all in France, which was represented for him exclusively by Blondel, Laberthonière and rationalist thinkers. He was unwilling to admit the existence of anything he was unprepared to acknowledge.

Apart from Searle and some lesser figures, E. E. Bowen was the only other personality to make an impression on Cyril. He wrote the best school songs, some of them too fantastic even for sophisticated taste, preached athletics and a Spartan life for all, and taught history in a way that made the boys aware of countries other than England and also of foreign personages, like American presidents and even Popes. It was remarkable how most delinquents naturally went to him; he was not a parson nor even a believing Christian.

It was after his return for his second, the autumn term, that Cyril invented for himself his new religion, similar in points to the one he had devised at Temple Grove. At night in his room he used to spread a cloth on his table in the manner of altar linen. Over it he placed a pale antimacassar and on this set two candles and a box, covered with a white silk handkerchief, not unlike a tabernacle. Above he put a drawing he himself had made of Thorwalden's *Christ*, but with the curious addition of a red heart. He then bought an inkpot with handles; this he converted into a censer in which he burnt brown paper. Finally he made a disc of cardboard like a host. Then he prayed. He lifted the disc as high as he could reach, burnt it, mixed the ashes with water and swallowed them.

What he imagined he was doing he did not know; only once had he attended, with Edghill, an Anglican Mass. This was a rite of his own. Holy Communion had little meaning for him at the time and the prospect of it played no part in his life. The boys went to Communion only after Confirmation, which was still a remote event. Here was something of his own contriving which he could not explain even to himself.

But this rite was altogether different from another of his religious practices. In some romantic novel he had read the second half of the *Hail Mary* and immediately felt an urge to recite it. Instinctively he resisted. At home he had been taught that it was idolatry to pray to the Virgin. The temptation grew more imperative. At last, one night, as he stood on his window-sill, the top frame pulled down and his elbows resting on it, his head in his hands, he almost cried with the effort to hold back the prayer. 'At last I yielded,' he wrote. 'It was like being wrapped up in a great dark warm velvet cloak. I never had any inclination to stop saying it, let alone to repent: in fact, I made ten little discs of cardboard and threaded them on a string and said the *Hail Mary* on each. I am morally certain I had never seen or even heard of a rosary, let alone how it should be said. The full essence of this *attack* on me to make me say what I could of the *Hail Mary* (I don't know when I picked up the first part) was *not* from any sub-conscious memory, etc: it came from outside, and I have never doubted it; and the *Hail Mary* is part of my spiritual life, and I can't help it.'

These practices were secret, a refuge from a world he found increasingly harsh. Far from regarding himself as at all good, he lived in baffled isolation, always more alert to his difference from other boys. Already he was aware in himself of something that never ceased to fascinate him when he discovered it in others: he called it the 'co-existence of contraries in the same person'. It was a theme he sometimes pursued to extremes, as in his much-criticised Memoir of Fr. Roy Steuart. He realised it acutely about this time when he drew a picture that he considered obscene and beside it made a sketch of the Sacred Heart. He then asked himself which way of life he would choose. He struggled with intermittent courage to act rightly, but was haunted by a line of Longfellow that constantly recurred to him, about the abyss:

> *From which nor plummet nor rope*
> *Ever drew up the silver sand of hope.*

In his third term at Harrow, Cyril went up with Mr. Howson to his large house, Druries, which had been evacuated by Mr. Griffiths. It was in a bad state, both materially and morally. The W.C.s were outside in a yard, where a kind of stump cricket was played. Cyril, who was pathologically shy, waited until medicine forced him to rush, at night, to the only indoor W.C. which was used by forty or fifty boys. There was always one House that had the supposed reputation of being the most immoral: Druries had now acquired this glory. However Cyril met no boys from other Houses and few from his own. He wrote later:

> I was puzzled even then at the small effect immorality seemed to have on boys. A very few kept aloof on principle; others out of fastidiousness, disguising their dislike by saying, 'I don't want to spoil my football' etc. Most took to it by fits and starts, especially when House matches were over and there was no incentive to 'keep fit'. I could never have taken immorality in that easy-going way. I could not see that 'purity' mattered very much, but in order to make it do so, I would have had to transfer it into an enthralling mystery, which indeed *real* purity is. I was neither admired nor bullied for not being 'in' with that gang, but rather sneered at. I was inferior, therefore, to the average whose exploits up-to-date would not have suited me.

Cyril formed no romantic friendships. Mr. Howson, on taking over Druries, sacked a large number of older boys and by this action ruined the House athletically without improving it morally. The residual middle group of boys merely copied their elders. Moreover, Howson wrote a circular letter on Uplift and manly behaviour that did no more than rile the boys.

The division lay between 'Bloods' and 'Non-Bloods', the former being exempt from the 'swagger rules' which created the sense of tradition and hierarchy that governed behaviour more than the masters, unless of course a master exercised a special influence through his personality. Until a boy was above these rules, he was precluded from certain privileges, such as wearing a coloured waistcoat or using a rolled-up umbrella. Cyril had a year of fagging which meant little to him, but at last he was transferred to the classical side. He found himself in a form where boys were reading Aeschylus when he hardly knew the Greek alphabet. He never showed the same instinct for Greek that he already had for Latin.

2

During his second Lent term, Cyril developed a desire for penance. His friend Cameron, the Catholic laird, had given him two small oval pictures of the Crucifixion and of Our Lady by the Cross. He hung them in his room and brought derision on himself. Perhaps after being hurt by others, he wanted to hurt himself. He maltreated himself. He denied himself sugar and sweets. He put pieces of wood in his bed, and got up whenever he woke at night, however cold it might be, to say some prayers. As a consequence he became ill enough to be sent home. From home he went to his aunt Alice at Folkestone, where he spent Easter. The parish church there was 'high' in a medieval manner, and very fashionable. The white-haired, mild and mystical-looking Rector impressed him. On a later visit Cyril tracked him down to Sandgate and demanded to go to confession. Unluckily this time the Rector was wearing embroidered velvet slippers which took the edge off his asceticism; he had no idea what to say after confession, and Cyril decided to give up the search for help.

Twice, on this visit to Folkestone, Cyril entered the Catholic Church there. The first time, when he was sitting in a back bench, a priest came up to him and asked whether he was a Catholic. Cyril answered, no. The priest mumbled something and passed on. On the second occasion he came in during the evening service and was shocked by the way the priest rushed through the Rosary. Afterwards at Harrow he visited the old tin church, then later the new building that replaced it in 1894. The priest appeared to him rough and unctuous. Cyril asked to see inside the tabernacle but was refused.

Still later, when his father was staying at Winchester, he entered the Catholic Church there; by accident he had passed under the old

47

arch leading to it. Taking up a hymn-book he hit on *Daily, daily, sing to Mary*. The next moment acolytes entered the sanctuary and lit candles; a priest followed; then precisely that hymn was struck up. Cyril felt justified in pocketing the hymn-book.

In none of these encounters with the Catholic Church did any priest help him towards it, though he believed that some clergymen possibly helped him out of Anglicanism.

Until the end of his first year at Harrow, Cyril retained many of the pleasures and pursuits he had brought with him from Temple Grove. Egyptology was forgotten, but he kept an old interest in butterflies. The Warren at Folkestone gave him an interest in fossils. His grandmother had presented him with a fine birds' egg cabinet, but he could never bring himself to take risks in climbing trees. Once or twice he dissected dead birds from sheer determination to overcome his horror of the operation. Probably it was his envy of those physically unlike himself that brought on a phase during which he drew massive athletes with thick necks and square shoulders. Again he was pitying himself for what he could never be.

At the end of his fourth term, his second summer term, Cyril was sent to Le Havre to re-learn French: at Harrow it was considered insufferably conceited and effeminate to speak any foreign language with a correct accent. His grandfather had found a French family which was not only good, but Protestant. Cyril went, unaccompanied.

While he was waiting for the boat at Southampton he wandered round the town looking for the Catholic Church. Too shy to ask for it, he was about to give up his search when he crossed a street, saw a photographer's shop, then suddenly the church. In the porch he asked a smug sacristan whether there was Mass going on. 'Ow naw . . . only Mass in the mornings.' He had been showing off and felt snubbed. But he had his compensations. At the entrance to the sanctuary were statues of the Sacred Heart and Our Lady. They were neither beautiful nor unusual but, as at the Oratory, Cyril was thunderstruck. He did not pray. He almost reeled out of the church to find himself confronted by two pictures in the porch, a copy of Millet's 'Angelus' and another with the title, 'The Sacred Heart'.

From the church he went straight to the boat but could not eat or sleep during the crossing. He passed the night on deck, repeating at times the prayer in *Evangeline*: 'Sacred Heart of the Saviour, O inexhaustible fountain, fill our hearts this day with love and forgiveness and patience', which he alternated with the *Hail Mary*. Although he did not know the Angelus, he linked this prayer with Millet's picture. He did not attach any theological meaning to the Sacred Heart nor did he, in fact, seek definition. He rested content in his unique experience.

From the quayside at Le Havre, where he was met by two boys (one of them formerly at Amesbury House), he was driven towards the cliff on which the upper town is built. On the way he noticed instantly a church with an elongated dome under which were the letters *D O M*, which he took to mean what it would have meant in German, namely Cathedral.

Madame de Conick, the lady of his grandfather's appointment, in whose house he stayed, was a rabid Calvinist and quickly seized the chance of telling him that, while Roman Catholics were inevitably damned, the Church of England was worse, in so far as it tried to effect a compromise: the Lord would vomit them both out of his mouth and she, Madame de Conick, convinced of her election, would exult in the ensuing conflagration. Cyril immediately asked her how to reach the 'Dom'. 'Nous n'avons pas içi de Dôme,' she replied chillily. But not all the disagreeableness of the de Conick family, who must have disliked Cyril as much as he did them, could alter his feelings of being at home in France. On his first day he recognised the smell of French bread, butter and coffee and liked the de Conicks' large, rambling house and its typically ill-kept garden.

On the afternoon after his arrival, Cyril went out alone in search of the 'Dom', which turned out to be the Church of St. Michael, backed against a cliff in a narrow street of poor houses. Behind the high altar was an apse containing a statue (as he learnt later) of Our Lady of Lourdes. Outside this apse, to the left and right, were two more images, St. Michael, and a well-groomed, almost hermaphroditic St. John in mauve. Towards the entrance on the left, at the bottom of the church, hung a great crucifix; on the other side there was the chapel of the Sacred Heart. Immediately on going out he found a confectioner, bought some fondants and returned to eat them in the church. Again he did not pray. There was no repetition of his experience in Southampton. Once or twice on later visits he chanced on Benediction with the ciborium. He also attended a High Mass. The details distracted him. It seemed fidgety and scrappy; the Ministers appeared to walk, sit and act with no continuity. When the celebrant made the ritual signs of the cross over the chalice, Cyril truly thought he was driving away the flies.

It was St. Michael's he mainly haunted. On occasion he would climb to the small shrine high up on the cliff looking out towards the Channel. He described it in *The Goddess of Ghosts*:

> All manner of votive offerings tapestried the walls, many of them models of ships, little nets, little bits of wreckage, a compass, a telescope. Others were toys and nursery appliances: a pathetic rattle and several dolls. There were wreaths in plenty, and everywhere, everywhere, tiny hearts. In Elinor's ears the offerings spoke, the hearts beat: from all over the world, throughout history, hope and gratitude set, like a great tide, towards Mary.[1]

Nearby Cyril bought a small *objet de piété*, like a monstrance. The friendly woman who sold it to him instructed him to place a *cierge* behind it.

At Le Havre he did much painting, often in the public gardens, where he drew the fountains exactly and the surrounding trees with moderate realism. He swam a great deal. In company with a Winchester boy, who was also staying with Madame de Conick, he went on escapades which he would never have initiated himself. At night they climbed down the creeper outside his window and visited the cabarets of the town—the more sophisticated ones and the small sleezy dives patronised by the lowest type of sailors and by prostitutes. Several times alone, and occasionally with the Winchester boy, he went to the annual Le Havre fair. He remembered the gingerbread stalls and peep-shows, exhibiting bloody tragedies or feeble indecencies and also the marionettes. One performance of 'The Temptation of St. Anthony' particularly impressed him. A lady in

[1] *The Goddess of Ghosts* (1915), p. 196. There is a description of St. Michael's in one of the stories he wrote for *The Pylon*.

scarlet satin was engaged in enticing the saint with a gold champagne beaker; the devils assaulted him, yelling, 'Démolissons, démolissons son ermitage!' Finally Anthony was received into glory.[1]

There was also a lady who kept an alleged menagerie, which was really an *affaire d'alcove*. The fatuity of her remarks and the squalor of the place offended Cyril more than her immorality. Still he pretended to debate whether he would or would not sell his soul to the devil. He was aware, of course, that he could not do such a thing; but then his character was such that, while he could not keep away from Catholic churches at one extreme, at the other he was drawn to opposing attractions. He felt himself constantly swinging between the two. Strangely the Church of Rome was an entity distinct from the church buildings he entered. There was still something wicked about them. There were even features in the services that displeased him: the way, for instance, that priests gabbled and were careless of dirt. What provided immoveable features were the tabernacle, the Sacred Heart and Our Lady.

Back at Harrow after his second summer vacation, his life was not particularly eventful. He persisted in some of his surreptitious religious practices. In France he had purchased a rosary, which was soon discovered and impounded by the matron during a period of sickness in the infirmary. From the shape of his forehead the matron pronounced that he had no real intelligence; in any case, nobody who used Roman Catholic objects could have. Once on a visit to London he escaped before breakfast to attend Mass at the Oratory. At Laslett's, a Catholic repository across the road, he ordered an ivory-coloured statue of the Sacred Heart. When it reached Harrow in a package addressed in a commercial hand, Mr. Howson, suspecting that it might be some indecency, demanded that Cyril should unpack it in his presence.

Throughout Cyril's years at Harrow, Longfellow remained in favour. He translated the whole of the fifty-third chapter of Isaiah into Evangeline-like hexameters. Mr. Owen, his English master, introduced him to Browning. Certain lines from 'Rabbi Ben Ezra', 'Abt

[1] One of Fr. Martindale's first essays in hagiography was on St. Anthony of Egypt in *On God's Holy Hills* (Burns, Oates, 1919).

Vogler', the 'Fano Guardian Angel', and not least 'Pictor Ignotus' (especially the conclusion) produced an enduring effect on him. They seemed to contain a hint that a kind of total abnegation was required of him. The words also fascinated him. It was only the spell cast by words that made him attend to anything taught in language classes. Virgil continued to suit his moods, especially his lines on the night: he repeated them often—*Dum intempesta silet nox*, in particular. Before going to bed he would stand at his window-sill and try to imagine that night existed outside time and so lead himself to the illusion that he need never start another day. But relentlessly the school clock chimed the quarters and he knew that everything would happen as before. He hated life. At home, and on his way back to Harrow in the train, he still cried. At school, life was beyond tears. The *Aeneid* gave him some consolation and in a remote manner held for him a hint of a Rome, eternal and universal. What was good enough for his grandfather more than ever seemed empty for himself.

But he was far from being unhappy in mind all the time. His progress through the school was effortless. As the number of books on his shelves increased, he developed a self-assertiveness. He began to write poetry. One splendidly macabre piece included a Virgilian notion:

> *Gaze where yon black waters sleep.*
> *Pale images shall pass your eyes.*
> *Lift a stone from yonder heap,*
> *Ah! with a soft child's voice it cries . . .*
> *Enter that entangled grove,*
> *Tear apart the straining shoots,*
> *Blood distils, and heart-strings move*
> *Palpitating at the roots.*

This poem was somehow associated with a lady called Diomed:

> *Her accents linger*
> *Tremulous across the air*
> *While the moonlight's fiery finger*
> *Traces glories in her hair.*

Cyril enjoyed these exercises and the opportunities they gave for alliteration. His principal effort, which he never completed, was called 'A Nightmare of Religions'.

He rejected the religion of China, about which he knew nothing:

> *Dreadful dragons dimly dart*
> *Angry-grinning down my days.*

and that of Egypt:

> *And all the while Osiris sang*
> *Sad songs of the declining day*
> *And all the while the bull-frogs rang*
> *Their chants and changes where they lay*
> *Along Amenti's mystic marsh*
> *Their voices now repressed, now harsh*
> *Shattering the consecrated hush.*

There was also a Canto about Pompeii:

> *All the golden afternoon*
> *On Pompeii's banks of thyme*
> *I lay and listened to a tune*
> *The campanile's slender chime . . .*
> *Look, new lights begin to glimmer*
> *Tinted fires begin to burn;*
> *Leaping waters shine and shimmer*
> *In a fairy fence of fern.*
> *Where the tinkling footsteps go,*
> *Fifes and flutes fly shrill and sharp*
> *Lightly spraying to and fro*
> *Cool arpeggio from a harp.*

Finally the religion of England. A church set among the trees rang its bells for evensong:

> *Beating bells, withhold your clamour,*
> *Chime your changes to the tomb!*
> *Conscience, hearing, learns to stammer*
> *Words that better had been dumb.*

To rhyme 'noon' with 'tune' was perhaps at that date impermissible, but to transfer the adjective 'slender' from the campanile to its chime shows sensitivity, perhaps even an instinct for poetry. There was in 'The Nightmare' a kind of guilty agnosticism. Cyril was pretending that all religions were failures, but in his heart he knew he could not cut himself off from what he later described as the *res Catholica*. Here also were the beginnings of his interest in the comparative study of religions, a subject in which he was a pioneer among English Catholics.

### 3

Towards the end of Cyril's time at Harrow his grandfather decided that the family should visit a young, remote kinsman who had married a Swiss and was living in a chalet almost overlooking the lake of Brienz. With Ben Hay went aunts Maud and Mary. Cyril detested the chalet. The mountain air made him tired. He became obstinate. He refused to paint the scenery, even a splendid waterfall. To his grandfather's annoyance he insisted on taking as his subjects certain lugubrious saints with whom he had become acquainted at Harrow. He resisted excursions that were proposed, and spent most of his time on a chaise-longue reading light novels. When the party went on to Mürren, he refused to admit that he was impressed by the mountains: in fact, he was stunned by their grandeur: the Jungfrau, the Eiger, the Black and White Monks, and the Lauterbrünnen valley. However, he consented to make the unexacting ascent of the Schilhorn. On his way down he had an accident that was almost fatal. Chasing a butterfly he slipped on some dry turf and just saved himself from slipping over the lip of a deep precipice.

The climb proved that he was not altogether malingering. He could not breathe properly at high altitudes, and for a long time afterwards he had nightmares in which he dreamt that he was painfully climbing unending hills.

At Beatenberg, at the hotel where the family stayed, there was a young American lady with a peach-bloom complexion and misty golden hair. As at Greystoke with Lady Victoria Herbert, Cyril fell moodily in love with her. His aunts derided him, but he succeeded in getting an introduction to the girl. When she spoke, her saw-like voice quickly ended all romance. In Berne and Basle on the journey home he sulked more than ever. One of his aunts begged him to be rather less moody. The disease of adolescence was on him.

This was the time the family moved to Albury, about five miles from Guildford. On his first holidays there he learnt that his grandfather had become an Irvingite. The old man now lent Cyril a book on Irving which left him uninterested, and once took him to an Irvingite High Mass. The minister 'spoke in a tongue' and was followed by a member of the church who interpreted him. Cyril asked his grandfather what it was all about but the old gentleman appeared not to know.

Guildford had some really 'high' churches, but they left Cyril unaffected. He recognised something authentic in the friary at Chilworth, but at the same time was put off by what he considered the un-Franciscan ways of some of the friars he met there. The pilgrims' path to Canterbury inspired him, but he was for the most part restless and bored in his new home surroundings. More than ever he was displaying what he himself would have called 'self-contradictory characteristics'.

He was duly confirmed at Harrow. There is no record of names of confirmation candidates in the Registers; but it was probably in the autumn term 1896. 'On Saturday, November 28,' the *Harrovian* notes, 'the Archbishop Elect of Canterbury,[1] late Bishop of London, confirmed about a hundred boys; the service lasted about an hour and a half, the Archbishop addressing the candidates for about half an hour.' Cyril took the sacrament seriously. Merely to fuss the headmaster, he told him that he was hesitant about going to Communion because he did not know whether Anglican orders were valid; but before he was due for Communion Leo XIII had issued his Bull.[2] Perversely Cyril conformed, since he could say that he 'knew' he was not 'receiving'. At the same time he was shocked by boys who referred to the service as 'early breakfast' or attempted to drink enough of the chalice to force the celebrant to prepare another.

Cyril appears not to have known where he stood, or even where he

[1] Frederick Temple.    [2] *Apostolicae Curae*, dated 13 September 1896.

wanted to stand. He entered briefly a period of agnosticism. A book by Mrs. Besant was given to him. For a time he tried to persuade himself that Christianity was only one form of essential religion. With other boys he took the pose of regretfully abandoning it as a lovely myth. He pushed his crucifix into the back of a drawer, but did not destroy it. Certainly he wanted to believe Christianity was untrue or, at least, unproven. Years later, making an appeal for the temporal support of 'convert' clergymen, he referred briefly in public to his state of mind in his last year at Harrow: 'I can hardly remember a time when I liked the Anglican Church; but I well remember seeing with devastating clarity that the Roman Church was a lie. I can remember my feeling of downright seasickness when I began to perceive that the lie was truth.'[1]

It was the fashion of his House to be unrefined. Cyril followed it, but he continued to hate blasphemies. He wanted to be a sinner in an eclectic and individual manner, remaining superficially decent. He was given Littledale's *Plain Reasons*[2] which distressed him. He liked to think that an interior decay was at work. He asserted himself more. There were more violent oscillations now between the explicitly obscene *inédits* of Aubrey Beardsley and his own ceaseless drawings of Our Lady of Lourdes. In *The Illustrated London News* he had read an article on Lourdes and from this he went on to Emile Zola's book which by chance had been sent to him.[3] Its anti-clericalism did not affect him, for he was already anti-clerical, but he was overwhelmed by Lourdes itself and the tale of Bernadette. He wrote to his Catholic aunt, Sophy Gisborne, for more literature on the subject.

In this last year at Harrow he sat for the Balliol scholarship. It was only a preliminary canter. At Oxford he stayed with the Lambs, relatives of his stepmother, and one afternoon went into St. Aloysius' Church where he heard Fr. Joseph Rickaby, the Jesuit, give a conference on *Romans*. He was uninterested. Invited to dinner by Edward Caird, he and Raymond Asquith sat on either side of the

[1] Annual Report of the Converts Aid Society, 1929.
[2] R. E. Littledale, *Plain Reasons against joining the Church of Rome* (Christian Knowledge Society, 1880).
[3] *Lourdes*, the first volume of a trilogy entitled *Les Trois Villes* (1894).

Master. Cyril showed off somehow, for one of the Dons wrote of him: 'There is too much fluff about Martindale.' Raymond Asquith was awarded the scholarship.

It has been said that Cyril was compelled to leave Harrow on announcing his decision to become a Catholic. This is incorrect. The incident that led to his leaving was this.

As a member of the Sixth Form he had fags and was also responsible for a landing on the top floor of his House. In one room was a small boy, a dirty, ugly, unpopular youth who was a nuisance to all. It was Cyril's duty, as well as right, to visit him and see whether he was doing his 'prep'. If the boy was not working Cyril usually helped him, but in a cruel way; he made him writhe under his mockery, knowing well what he was doing.

On his return from Balliol Cyril was too tired to take further responsibility or even to be unkind. Instead he said to the boy, 'We will bury the hatchet'; then dramatically he buried a knife in the ashes of his fire. The boy answered, 'It's too late.' That night Cyril heard him shuffling along the corridor. He thought, 'Can't the little beast even walk decently', but he determined to let him alone. It did not occur to him to ask the boy where he was going at that time of night.

The boy ran home. The next day Cyril was summoned to the headmaster. How Welldon had heard of his unkindness, Cyril never discovered; certainly his housemaster, Howson, knew nothing of it. Welldon, however, appeared much more concerned with the reaction of the boy's father, who was a member of Parliament, than with the maltreatment the boy had received at Cyril's hands. As often later, when he was questioned about his actions, Cyril made no attempt either to defend or explain himself; and in any case, all that Welldon said by way of accusation was, 'And you are the boy who came to me with your religious difficulties.' Cyril acknowledged that his difficulties had not been real, nor yet part of a game, but rather preoccupations. On his return to his House he saw Howson, who told him that he had grown sarcastic and cynical, and was no help to him. He let Cyril understand that if Welldon proposed to send him away, he would raise no objection. Either he or Welldon telegraphed to Cyril's

grandfather informing him that there was trouble. The old gentleman arrived and was mystified. Meanwhile Cyril's loathing of school
life had come to a stormy head. He was fatalistic. Somehow he knew
that the end of his school career was bound to be like this and had
determined to return home with his grandfather. He was not expelled, but merely went to Welldon to announce his own decision.
In the end-of-term printed lists he was put down as 'absent sick'.
Absent he undoubtedly was.

<h2 style="text-align:center">4</h2>

Cyril arrived home with a sense of liberation, but altogether unconscious of the shock the news would give his father. He was also
uncontrite. Only later did he feel a sense of guilt over the harm he
believed he had done during his emancipated spell.

After a few days Harrow vanished from his immediate consciousness. A nightmare was over. Later he learnt that he had left no ill-will
behind. He was spoken of as brilliant. The *Harrow Register* was sent
to him regularly, and after his triumphs at Oxford, his name at
school was covered with a kind of posthumous glory. He was asked
to organise an appeal for money in order to hang Cardinal Manning's
arms in the Speech Room. Only twice, however, did he return to the
school: the first time with some Jesuit students who had asked to see
Harrow, the second time in 1951, when he drove out from Mount
Street with Mr. R. W. Moore in order to address the Catholic boys.
But always, whenever he looked at the buildings as he passed in the
train, he would ask, 'Was that really I ?' He considered that he should
have been removed after two years, given a private tutor and made
to travel. But this was beyond his grandfather's conception, and his
father was too remote to appreciate his unhappiness.

His family assumed that he would still be going up to Oxford, and
accordingly after a few happy weeks at home he was sent to the
Reverend Yorke Faussett at Clifton to be tutored. At the same time
he was turning more definitely in the direction of the Catholic
Church. He wrote to his father and complained unjustly that his
career at Harrow would not have ended in this way had he been

58

allowed to become a Catholic. He also asked his father's permission to enter a monastery. It was not that he knew a great deal of the monastic life or its many forms, but he wanted to be different from others.

Faussett was the correct, thin-lipped, cultured type of parson, and Cyril took an instant dislike to him. Possibly he was chosen by his grandfather less for his own sake than that of his wife, a good-looking, vivacious but rabid North of Ireland Protestant. Had a good inoculation against Anglicanism been needed, Faussett was the man to provide it. Cyril was grateful to him for opening his musical ear to Chopin and Grieg.

His life continued to be spiced with religionism. He inflicted harsh penances on himself but at the same time became increasingly sour. He began another long poem, but it came to nothing. Its subject was unpromising—a long gas-lit avenue in a well-to-do suburb: there were blank villa-garden walls on either side and a church in the distance. Behind a wall lay a murdered man, presumably the adulterous lover of the lady of the house; the street was hard and empty, like humanity, and at the end of it in the tabernacle the Blessed Sacrament was locked up.

At intervals he would enter the Catholic pro-Cathedral at Clifton and bring azaleas for the statue of Our Lady of Lourdes; then he bought a gold heart that he tied round the neck. He would return and read Cicero and John Stuart Mill with the scholarly Mr. Faussett. He felt that his life was a swamp.

Eventually his grandfather wrote to say that Arthur had given his consent to his joining a monastic novitiate for a period, but he was not to become a Catholic. Presumably he believed that Cyril would soon sicken of the rigorous life. Perhaps also he feared that if he became a Catholic, priests would soon have him in their clutches. Kind but impractical as the plan was, it gave Cyril an opportunity of making his first continuous contact with the Catholic Church.

Possibly at Arthur's suggestion a house of Anglican Benedictines was approached on Cyril's behalf, but Cyril made it clear that he wanted a Catholic monastery. From Clifton he wrote to his aunt Sophy, who invited him to come to Bournemouth where she was then living. He had a conscientious scruple, which he explained to her: during an earlier period of flirtation with the Church he had promised his father not to become a Catholic until he had reached the age of twenty-one. He considered himself still bound by this undertaking, and proposed that during his years of waiting he should live anonymously in some Catholic hospital and do menial work there. He told his aunt: 'I want to make a clean cut and do the exact opposite of everything I have done so far.' Sophy Gisborne was horrified at the effect this proposal would have on the family. Pressed by Cyril, she was forced to admit that there was a good Catholic hospital in Bournemouth, St. Joseph's, which was run by nuns. Immediately Cyril hustled her into a cab and drove there. The Superior, Sister Clare Liddin, was aghast. Cyril attempted to put her at ease: 'My aunt will guarantee my fees,' he told her, 'and that I will not steal your spoons.' He was told that if he came he must not eat with the male servants and would have to sleep in a small dressing-room that was vacant.

Aunt Sophy, one of the *grandes dames* of the Jesuit parish at Bournemouth, sought the counsel of the Superior there, Father Cooney. Utterly bewildered but eager to snatch at a convert, Fr. Cooney endorsed Cyril's proposal. At once Cyril wrote to his grandfather to explain his intention. The old gentleman replied that he agreed that he should not sleep in a male ward and, in a letter to the Reverend Mother, added that he must not spoil his hands by blacking boots; nor must he have a holiday from intellectual work. It was hoped that he would soon tire of his chosen life and sit a second time for the Balliol scholarship.

On his return to Clifton, Cyril purchased a Catholic Truth Society pamphlet on St. Aloysius, which he sent home, fully realising how absurd, pharisaic and even downright immoral it would appear to his grandfather and aunts. He would have been hard put to it to answer had they written back, 'You are too like St. Aloysius yourself. You are running away from your duty as he did, and taking the easier path, however penitential it may seem to you.' On the other hand he was aware of what he called a certain personal pressure that the saint was exercising on him. At the time he knew nothing of the

Renaissance, or of the saint's family and background, and barely understood his personality, but the influence was there in spite of the pamphlet and pictorial presentations, which were more a deterrent than an aid to devotion. The influence continued to the end of his life.

On 17 March 1897 Cyril left Clifton for Bournemouth. On his way from the station to St. Joseph's he clearly understood that this was his chance for a new life and sincerely prayed that it might prove so. His liberation from Harrow had been merely negative: he saw himself now approaching what he had falteringly sought for so long. While he was resolved to bury himself and his past in obscurity, he foresaw inevitably a certain amount of Catholic petting and even flattery. The latter was never to his taste, for he was always as aware of his shortcomings as anyone else, but praise was different: it might be justified, and, therefore, healthy.

In this mental, perhaps spiritual, condition it is not surprising that he suffered a reaction against his home and upbringing. His letter to his father was an instance of it. When he thought of his relatives, he was disdainful. Although his childhood religion contained plenty of good, he could not see it now. Mentally he tried to cut himself off from his past and all persons connected with it. He did not feel that he had reached home; he realised now that he had always been there. It was a sense that always remained with him and indeed gave him a balance in all the fluctuations of his early career in the Society of Jesus.

He had not been long at St. Joseph's when he began to lose weight. Sentimentally he entertained the idea that he would die young as Aloysius had done. He could not imagine the future. He knew he could not go on nursing the sick for ever. At St. Joseph's he made beds, swept the wards, ran errands for the sick but did not have as hard a life as he had planned for himself. Perfunctorily he read some Greek and Latin. In the afternoon he would go to the Jesuit presbytery to receive instruction from Fr. Cooney; sometimes with another priest, Fr. Bearne, he would go the rounds of the parish sick. What he saw of the Jesuits did not draw him to them. Fr. Cooney was too hearty; Fr. Bearne appeared externally so melancholic that a Wesleyan patient in St. Joseph's Home declared that he was living proof that the Catholic religion was false. A third priest there, Fr. Redmond, play-acted (so Cyril thought) in the pulpit. There was also Fr. McAleer, who said little but struck him as a truly devout, simple gentleman.

He was not in the frame of mind to follow with interest Fr. Cooney's instructions. The arguments the priest used did not impress; more accurately, they did not back up what he already knew. It was as though Fr. Cooney were trying to prove the existence of the air which Cyril was already breathing. He was given to read the works of a late Victorian Jesuit, Fr. Sylvester Hunter, but he preferred dogmatic exposition to apologetics. From a purely literary point of view he found Catholic books mostly inferior to what he had read. Only the works of Bishop Hedley gave him satisfaction. Anglicanism, entwined with home and Harrow, was nevertheless a bygone thing.

Meanwhile he fussed around the sacristy at St. Joseph's. He dusted, beat carpets, bought flowers for the altar, arranged them. He made detailed sketches of various events in the lives of the patron saints of the Sisters; these, until they faded, hung in their cells until recently. He found some fine Venetian glass cruets, which would not pour, then substituted for them a more practical pair with silver bands. He also purchased a coarse, highly coloured statue of St. Aloysius which was erected in the chapel and, before he left, he hung his silver crucifix round its neck. He showed off a good deal, read the Little Office of Our Lady in the street, and tried to flog himself with his rosary. Somewhere he bought a hairshirt and found it useless. In Holy Week he intended to spend an entire night before the altar of repose in the Church of the Sacred Heart, but gave up the attempt at three in the morning and slept the remainder of the night on a sofa in the presbytery parlour.

Yet he had made life sufficiently hard for himself to find the noviceship comparatively easy. When he called in shabby clothes to see his aunt Sophy at the Norfolk Hotel, he came suddenly to realise that he was too much of a gentleman-servant. He had abdicated only by half, and wanted to go the whole distance. He protested to Fr. Cooney that he needed the sacraments and was being spiritually starved. With consummate folly Fr. Cooney replied, 'We must see whether we can receive you secretly.' Cyril rejected this course and pointed out that the age of twenty-one was merely a legal fiction. He would be no wiser the day after his birthday nor more ignorant the day before it. He added that he would write in this sense to his grandfather and retract his promise. If Fr. Cooney would not receive him, he would find a priest who would.

After an interval, Ben Hay replied that Cyril's father had really given permission for his son to become a Catholic, but it had been withheld, not unreasonably, in the belief that he was going through a phase of religiosity.

The date of his reception into the Catholic Church was fixed for 8 May 1897.

# 4
## Roehampton and Aix

It was with mixed joy and fatalism that Cyril awaited the day of his reception into the Church. When free to choose, he disliked committing himself even to what he wanted. He believed because he could not help believing; sincerely as he desired to be a Catholic, he was loth to take the step. He saw a vision of the truth, and walked blindly towards it.

He had anticipated that the ceremony on 8 May at the Sacred Heart Church would be quiet and private. He had invited only his aunt Sophy and a few Catholic friends he had made in Bournemouth, the Scott-Murrays and the Colthursts. Fr. Cooney had different ideas. For reasons best known to himself, he had asked a large number of parishioners. The church has half full. Cyril was cruelly embarrassed when, in the middle of the ceremony, he was taken aside for confession and emerged from the box scarlet and shame-faced. Afterwards he was the victim of much chaff. In the sacristy Fr. Cooney said: 'Well, you're a bloody Papist at last.' The few sincere and spiritual words addressed to him by Fr. McAleer touched him more. Three days later, on 11 May, he made his first Communion.

He continued to live at St. Joseph's. His future had to be settled. He felt certain he was drawn to the Society of Jesus. He knew nothing of the Redemptorists and did not consider the Dominicans or Franciscans. Fr. Bede Camm suggested the Benedictines on the ground that they and the Oratorians were all 'gentlemen', but this was enough to make Cyril decide definitely against them. Eventually Fr. Cooney suggested to him the Society, though it was clear to Cyril how carefully he had hitherto refrained from mentioning it.

It was arranged that he should go to the noviceship, Manresa

House at Roehampton, where he could make a retreat and reach a final decision.

The old part of the building, a small Georgian mansion that used to belong to the Earls of Bessborough, was stately enough, and he had often seen its pillared portico across Richmond Park on his walks from Temple Grove. The additions were simple and businesslike: the parlours, with their aspidistras and oleographs, appalled him, but the Long Gallery reminded him vaguely of the back corridor at Allestree. The novices seemed to him insipid; the Juniors, or young Jesuit students engaged in studying the classics, science or mathematics in view of a university degree, struck him merely as noisy. He knew he wanted to be there, but did not want to be like them. The Minister, Fr. Kelly, impressed him by his sheer kindness and would have taken him to Southwark Cathedral for confirmation by Bishop Bourne, but the arrangement fell through. The Rector, Fr. Daniel Considine, his future novice-master, was described as a saint.

On his arrival he was given to read Rogacci's *Christian Reformed*, but found it unhelpful; he had not been the kind of sinner to whom the book was addressed; and then the life of St. Stanislaus Kostka, which he judged an ill-written fairy-tale: Stanislaus was presented as a clay-figure on whom tedious moralisings were draped. In fact, apart from the life of St. Aloysius, all other saints' lives repelled him.

The days were hot and heavy. The Jesuit Rule, when he read it now for the first time, appeared to him platitudinous. Being principles more than precepts, it threw no light on the way Jesuits actually lived. The retreat was dull. The method of making an 'election' or choice of life, as he understood it, left the retreatant with no choice. Anything that he could call a vocation had come long before this retreat. What he sought now was an abdicated life. It was to be in the Society because he did not see where else it could be. He was drawn by St. Aloysius, not by the retreat or by Manresa House or by Bournemouth. Later he was glad of this. None of his family could justly talk to him about glamour or influence or following his likings. He returned to Bournemouth little changed. Had he been told he had not a vocation, he would have been lost.

After a week with his family at Walberswick, where they had taken a house, he went to stay with his aunt Sophy at Derby. For the first time for months he now enjoyed palatable meals. He was still enchanted, as he had been in his childhood days, by the exquisite veils Aunt Sophy wore over her auburn hair at dinner. With her he went to Nottingham and was confirmed privately by Bishop Bagshawe at the Catholic Cathedral. He took the names Mary Aloysius. In the garden after the ceremony he caused the Bishop evident annoyance by shaking his hand without kissing his ring. When Aunt Sophy kissed it, he ascribed her action to her characteristic graciousness.

Although Lourdes had now ceased to be an obsession, he wanted to visit it in order to make sure that his vocation was to the Society of Jesus. With him went Aunt Sophy and also a curate from St. Mary's, Derby, Father Thomas Byrne, a man of high character without any imaginative sympathy on whom later a hard crust of ecclesiasticism was to settle; but at this time he was all that was expected of a jocose, pious, efficient young Irish priest.[1]

At Paris they visited Notre Dames des Victoires. Here, as always on later visits, Cyril was infected by the atmosphere of prayer that clung to its walls. When he caught sight of the Lourdes Grotto from the train, he knelt down in the carriage to the amusement of the ticket-collector. The hotel in which Fr. Byrne had booked rooms for the party was too far from the shrine for Aunt Sophy to cover the distance on her small feet; the proprietress offered them a carriage, but Cyril considered it shameful to be driven to the grotto, even in company with his aunt. They moved to an hotel overlooking the esplanade. Lourdes suffered for being too like the pictures he had seen; the three superimposed churches were manifestly gimcrack; he was distressed to see how low French taste, which he had so much admired, could sink.

On the verge of a decision whether to enter the Society, his mind was taut. Instinctively his scepticism asserted itself. He prayed not to see a miracle, for he knew he would at once struggle to explain it in natural terms. Unsuccessfully he tried to stir himself into an artificial fervour. He funked the cold and dirty baths. Once, over-

---

[1] Later his aunt Sophy gave a window to the Lady Chapel at St. Mary's, decorated the chapel and put a statue of Our Lady of Lourdes there.

powered by the smell of the peasants in their best clothes, he fainted in the crowds at the grotto. He positively sought disillusionment, from a dread of fostering unreality in himself.

But there were also moments of genuine interior worship. And he endured an agony of apprehension. He asked himself not merely whether he intended to change, but wondered whether he could. He entered a mirage: was there a real 'I' to change? The thought occurred that it might be better to drown himself in the Gave and get it all over. But no more than on his Scottish holiday with his father, did he have any real intention of committing suicide; he knew that if he did leap into the river, he would swim. Yet he saw that the only escape was to leave God to work the change in him if and when He pleased. This notion of abandonment took such strong roots that it grew into a principle of his spiritual teaching. He passed some hours of the night behind the large candles at the very back of the grotto. In silence, interrupted only by the rushing of the river and the wax falling from the votive candles, he ceased to speculate and experienced peace.

His observation of the brancardiers helped to define his vocation. While he admired their devoted toil, he knew that their work was only an interlude in their life. For him there were to be no interludes. He had seen Lourdes shorn of its gilt and had not lost his devotion to it. The Society of Jesus had no gilt; it 'had no beauty that he should desire it', and for this he was grateful. He was not going to Roehampton because he thought he would like the life he had chosen.

There was one strange episode.

The balcony of his hotel overlooked the street. On the far side of it was a hedge, and beyond this the Esplanade through which ran the canal. Early one morning he was woken by screams. He saw nothing and returned to bed. There were more screams. Two passing women leapt to look over the hedge, threw up their arms in horror, then ran away. Putting on his dressing-gown he ran down the stairs. By jumping up, he could see a man apparently drowning in the canal. Although the hedge was about his own height, he vaulted over it (he never understood how he did this) and hauled the man out, then found he could not get back over the hedge. He had to return by the gate, a short distance away. Later he was sent for by the mayor to make a deposition. The man was a pompous little anti-clerical, who sat sipping an iced drink. He questioned Cyril for a long time, then read out a rhetorical account of the incident which he finally asked Cyril to sign. This he refused to do. 'You will return tomorrow,' the mayor ordered him. But Cyril's novena was finished and he proposed to his aunt that they should leave at once for Biarritz.

At Biarritz he went to Benediction at the Dominican church. The sermon seemed a banal and empty declamation and at its climax electric lights leapt up around altars. In Paris he went to confession at St. Augustin, where the priest was as chill and fashionable as the church. To compensate himself he returned to Notre Dame des Victoires, believing still there was a hair's-breadth between total self-renunciation and the opposite extreme.

Back at St. Joseph's, Bournemouth, his health caused alarm. When the doctor undressed him, he smiled at the clinking cuirass of medals and the network of scapular strings that adorned him. Cyril then rid himself of all except the miraculous medal and the brown scapular. On the morning of 7 September 1897 he travelled to London, and, in the early evening, went on to Barnes and Roehampton. This was the real break in his life: his reception into the Church had given only formal recognition to what, in fact, he had been for several months.

2

His mood was again fatalist. Deliberately he closed his eyes to his future. When other newcomers joined him he made shy efforts at conversation. He was tired and dazed, but relieved to be there.

On 8 September the novices who had completed their two years took their vows. The suave waltz tune of the hymn customarily sung on this occasion stirred some remains of romanticism in him. A few hours later he felt that a thick wall of glass had been built up between him and all that had passed outside the noviceship. He could not conceive of it as a time of trial during which he might leave any day he chose, yet he could not imagine anything beyond it. The meals

Mary Martindale, daughter of John Martindale. A portrait (1782) by Romney, now at Kenwood House.

Ben Hay and Elizabeth Martindale.

Sir Arthur Martindale.

Cyril Martindale, photograph taken at Ryde on his third birthday.

were more substantial than he had been accustomed to, and he thought that if he was expected to eat as much as others did, then he could not possibly die in the noviceship.

The novice-master, Fr. Daniel Considine, a priest of widely acknowledged holiness, both within the Society and outside, was too shy or deliberately remote to gain the confidence of Brother Martindale, as he was now called. He appeared chill and enigmatic, and there were few novices who came to enjoy a warm and natural relationship with him. Possibly at this time his methods were tentative. Some believed that he was following his own theoretical system in the training of novices, but for the most part, they were baffled though deeply respectful.

At first Martindale retained a kind of double mind, one critical, even sceptical, the other unnaturally simple. He tried not to condemn artistically the pious shrines in the Long Gallery, which he knew were squalid, cheap and vulgar. When certain fellow novices impressed him as coarse, he closed his mind to any judgement. There were others, like himself, who were shy and nervous, and with these he found a loose bond of companionship. But no matter how hard he tried, he was unable to meet in conversation the more robust, efficient and hearty types. It was to be expected that in the artificial atmosphere generated by a novitiate, few real friendships should be made. The constant warning against 'particular friendships' that were injurious to community life inevitably translated itself into an attempt to feel the same towards all. While, in one sense, he was never alone, in another he was always so. Nevertheless, there were with him at Manresa a number of Jesuits who, in the more natural climate of other houses, became close and lifelong friends. Among these were Br. Chichester, later first Archbishop of Salisbury, Rhodesia, who arrived at Roehampton on the same day; and Philip Garrold, a recent convert like himself, who joined on 30 October.[1]

Only at football did the novices really become alive. Once Martindale, as an exercise in self-humilation, tried to play, but on finding himself continuously in the way, he decided it would be more charitable to discontinue. But what worked most against sociability was

[1] Cf. C. C. Martindale, *Richard Philip Garrold, A Memoir* (Longmans, 1921).

his misreading of a passage in Father Tyrrell's *Nova et Vetera*,[1] which he had brought with him into the noviceship and had been allowed to keep. He had understood Tyrrell to say that men were arbitrary symbols of God, and that, in daily conversation, all that was personal should be eliminated in order to reach the immanence of God in them. Of course Tyrrell meant the exact opposite, but Martindale did not have a sufficiently easy understanding with his novice-master to obtain the guidance he required. Even at this time he felt that there was something in Tyrrell's teaching that did not taste right.

Externally there is little of interest to record. Only one letter of his survives from the period, in which he stresses at length that he is exceedingly happy. 'I think I told you my hopes before,' he wrote, 'but the reality surpasses them altogether.' After his experiences at St. Joseph's, the menial duties of the noviceship were no trial; the relaxations left him exhausted, particularly the immoderately long walks. He took everything Fr. Considine said literally and never experienced the real friendliness which he reserved for his more wayward or mercurial novices, like Francis Devas[2] and Dominic Plater. Once Considine made him let down the blinds in his room and then draw them up again; Martindale had already been told stories of novices being ordered to sweep leaves against the wind and revealed no surprise. A trivial incident indicates that there was no instantaneous alteration in his character. Allotted the title of *Our Lady, Refuge of Sinners*, as the subject for his sermon in the refectory, he inserted a sentence that was intentionally directed to his novice-master. 'How,' he asked, 'shall men love the King, if the ambassador be so cold and hard?' Fr. Considine ignored the barb, but later told Martindale that clearly he would have no difficulty in producing purple passages. This admonition struck home. He never again attempted rhetoric in the pulpit, but adopted always with his

---

[1] George B. Tyrrell, *Nova et Vetera : Informal Meditations for Times of Dryness* (Longmans, 1897).

[2] Fr. Francis Devas later edited extracts from Fr. Considine's conferences in a series of three pamphlets entitled, *Words of Encouragement*, etc., which had wide popularity. Substantially they represent Fr. Considine's spiritual teaching, which is positive and inspiring. On the other hand, Fr. Devas told the writer, perhaps partly in joviality, that he had altered or omitted everything of which he disapproved.

audience a crisp, direct approach which particularly marked his broadcast sermons.

On the occasional days when novices met the Juniors for recreations, shyness overcame him. He was at once taken up and then dropped by Dominic Plater, who was in his second year's Juniorate. Later Fr. Plater's influence on him helped to alter the entire direction of his life, but at this time Cyril found him frothy and effusive. He took an instant dislike to him which never entirely disappeared and is faintly traceable in the official life he wrote of his saintly contemporary.[1]

Never did it cross his mind that he might leave the noviceship. Once on entering Fr. Considine's room, he confessed, 'I am afraid I have made a great mistake.' Considine leapt as though stung, thinking that Martindale meant he was mistaken in believing that he had a vocation. What Martindale meant to say was that he had misunderstood his novice-master's public direction concerning penances. When one novice did leave, Martindale imagined that it was the end of everything for him, that he had seen a soul walking out to damn itself.

Only one occurrence at Manresa left its mark on him for life. In early December, during the octave of Francis Xavier's feast, when he was kneeling before the saint's shrine in the Long Gallery, the realisation came to him that the Incarnation not only was, but is, true. Nothing led up to this; it expressed itself in no picture or idea, it generated no resolution and had no deliberately induced consequences, but from then on he saw the Annunciation as a greater feast than Christmas, and was able always to recall to himself by faith, not by imagination, that Christ was present in people and in himself. He made no attempt to explain this to Fr. Considine and, in any case, could not have expressed what he had experienced. It was never reproduced, though it altered for him his life, the world and religion itself. Something deeply human had entered his character for the first time.

The notes made by a novice are rarely of interest. Martindale would seem to have destroyed any he might have made. But if it is

[1] C. C. Martindale, *Charles Dominic Plater* (Harding and Moore, 1922).

asked what spiritual development occurred at this phase in his life, the answer is given in a later revelation of himself. Writing to his half-sister Helen, more than twenty years after the end of his noviceship, he speaks more intimately perhaps than anywhere else of what might be called his personal spirituality. This is perhaps the place to give an extract from it: the subject matter bears directly on his experience at Roehampton.

I suppose there are people [he writes] who aren't aware of more than their wishes and their plans. I have such a horror of my Self that I have a horror of its products: that is, my Self as isolated and substituted for God, or in danger of so substituting itself. In proportion as a man realises the possibility of this substitution, *and* the entire presence of God in this world and in himself, I take it his main effort is a negative one, i.e. not to interfere with God's action. I habitually, therefore, say in my mind to God: 'Don't let me be in your way. Act through me. I don't ask to be more than your unclogged channel. *You* act.' Then I am absolved, in the last resort, from thinking and trying. I offer a man a cigarette: I go to dinner: I say to God—'This is as good as an argument or a penance or anything good done by my intellect or choice, because *you* can act fully and as you please through *this*. If you do, it will *obviously* be your action and the result of yours.' Nor do I ask to see the results. Human eyes have no *claim* to see the divine. Sometimes God shows you the results: they are so preposterously disproportionate as to leave you in no doubt that they are His.

Well, a Saint, I know, gets far beyond that. He can be *positive*. 'God does the will of those who fear Him.' When a human will not only doesn't interfere with God's, but wholly and actively co-operates with Him, it is so united with Him that the two wills make one and it doesn't matter which issues the command. I am not there. I can't even do the negative part continuously. I set up the self-idol. Then one has to repent and re-begin. All my convert life I have tried (with huge crashes and constant absurdities and habitual panic—I fear everything) *not* to know, plan or try, but to let God work through me and (to alter the idea a little) to carry me to what He wants.

At Lourdes he had understood that the only escape from himself was to hand himself over to God. Now at Manresa, at the shrine of Francis Xavier, precision was given to this first grace. As far as was possible in these surroundings, he became conscious again of the beauty of nature, which he had deliberately shielded from himself since his entry into the noviceship. Trees, flowers, light, again enthralled him, but differently from the manner they had done in his boyhood. God shone through them rather than suffused them. Scripture replaced Longfellow; a fresh range of phrases intoxicated him mentally. His reaction was summarised in the prayer: *Ostende mihi faciem tuam : sonet vox in auribus meis : vox enim tua suavis est et facies decora.*[1]

His apprehensions remained. In childhood he could not see himself as the man his elders were or wanted him to be. At Manresa House he thought with horror of what might lie ahead; life in schools had no appeal for him. Once when the Jesuit students at Oxford came to play football he thought: 'I can never be like that—athletic, clever, cheery.' Although at the time he forbade himself any judgements, he later had justified criticism to make of the training he received. He thought it wrong that a noviceship should standardise mentalities, pretend that there was no world and no future save an ethical one. St. Ignatius, he insisted, had sent his novices out on long pilgrimages or into the Roman hospitals, knowing well what blasphemies and obscenities they would hear. Politics, which had never interested him, were not mentioned. No one directed the novices to meet the real difficulties they would encounter—jealousies, the possibility of idleness, disillusionment. While Fr. Considine was a gentleman and did not think on petty lines, he was essentially an Irish gentleman who had little notion of what English public-schooling was like. Still less could he appreciate the strangely mixed character that Martindale still was. Scarcely anything he said in his conferences seemed personally applicable to him.

Martindale struggled to be utterly different from what he believed himself to have been, but it was never pointed out to him that it was

---

[1] *Show me your countenance ; let your voice sound in my ears ; for your voice is sweet and your countenance comely.*

impossible to alter the substance of any man's personality. He roofed over his mind with a kind of cement which neither Fr. Considine nor his assistant novice-master, Fr. Roche, attempted to penetrate. In a sense he stunned himself and gave the impression of being a negative character. He never thought of the past, and when he thought of the future it was with an instantly checked shudder.

Through the winter his health slowly deteriorated. When Considine told him to stop fasting and to mortify himself in the quality, not the quantity, of his food, he consumed as much fat or gristly morsels of meat and skin as he could gather. In the early part of the new year he was judged neurasthenic owing to over-concentration on spiritual subjects and relentless self-suppression. His régime was relaxed. He stayed longer in bed, meditated in the grounds, and was exempted from duties in the scullery, where the smells nauseated him. In May it was decided that he should complete his noviceship in France. A fellow-novice, Br. Doyle, was assigned to accompany him.

3

On 25 May 1898, just three days after his refectory sermon, he set out for Aix-en-Provence. At Paris he was received by the Jesuits in the Rue de Sèvres with a warmth and generosity he never forgot. He became extremely ill and could recall only a visit to the textiles in the Musée de Cluny. At Lyons he had a day sightseeing and in the evening was again sick. He heard Mass in the chapel of the Jesuit College, and for the first time since his reception into the Church felt that there the Mass and Catholic faith were normal and the world Catholic, whereas Manresa House itself and the churches he had visited on his long walks, were all enclaves of Catholicism in an alien world. During the rest of his journey he was too weak to notice much, though he appreciated vaguely the heat, the acacias, the poppies and patches of bright green. This seemed his world: the scents, the smells, the dignity and squalor of the towns, the plane trees and tall houses, everything that made it up was all natural.

The Jesuit house at Aix had been built with simple dignity before the suppression of the Society, and occupied an island site formed by three streets. Inside was a Grand Cour containing a fountain. The church attached to it was in a chill late-Renaissance style with a large painting of St. Louis in a blue fleur-de-lis cloak over the high altar. On his first evening at recreation he was given the accolade by his fellow-novices. This seemed natural to him, but silly to Brother Doyle. His new novice-master, Père Louis Rosette, was a square-built man with a ruddy complexion, genial, quiet, sensible and much more English-looking than Father Considine; his assistant, Père Michel-Bent, pious, voluble and at times almost violent. The Minister, Père Denoyel, was a true ecclesiastical practitioner full of self-importance.[1] Among the old or retired members of the community were Père Louis Perraudin who innocently believed he met soldiers on their own level (he had a club for them near the barracks); a kindly old rustic, Père Royet; Pére Flandrin, very old, toothless and occupied with elegant ladies; and finally Père Henri Brémond, already suspect of modernism. He was wide-awake, but it was clear even to the novices that he was not altogether trusted.

Here in a more natural atmosphere Cyril made his first friendships in the Society. At once two novices became particularly alive: Louis Verny, a very simply born youth from the Ardèche, thin, vivacious, hardy and humble; and Frederick de Bélinay, socially from the opposite extreme, an ex-dragoon, handsome and talented; later he became a superb missionary in the Tchad area of North Africa and to the end of his life corresponded with Fr. Martindale. Others he found interesting and good men, who sheltered themselves behind a French armour of religious etiquette. It was de Bélinay from whom he sought advice about bathing. Timidly Cyril asked him what he did with the thick blue serge robe which the novices wore in their baths and the linen tent under which the wet serge was afterwards removed. De Bélinay answered that he bathed *tel quel*, and Cyril did likewise. The water was always grey, except after a thunderstorm, when it was red.

In the dedication of *Christ's Cadets* (1913) Martindale recalled his

---

[1] Fr. Martindale told an amusing story of this priest: how once, on his return from Egypt, where the Jesuits had a school, he passed a French ship. 'J'ai salué': then another, 'J'ai salué': then an English vessel, 'Je n'ai *pas* salué', he said, with a triumphant glare all round.

time spent with de Bélinay at Aix. 'Il y a déjà bien du temps que nous rencontrâmes sous le beau soleil de Provence, lorsque vous me racontiez des histoires de Saint-Cyr et du régiment, et me façonniez des chansons pour me faire rire, et que je vous prônais la grise Angleterre. A peu près tout a changé depuis lors, si ce n'est pas l'affection que nous avons eue l'un pour l'autre.'

These walks were less exacting physically. He was often in the cathedral, where at the Epiphany the *Marche des Rois* was played in good Provençal prancing measure. He made visits to Notre Dame de la Sedes, venerated in one of the parish churches of Aix, and sang there with other novices to the ecstasy of the congregation. The Poor Clares impressed him with the real poverty of their extern chapel, unlike the Carmelites, who were fashionable. For a month he did his hospital 'experiment' in the home run by the Little Sisters of the Poor on the north-west border of the town.[1] The asile was well equipped but, in spite of the Sisters' care, the old inmates were dirty and often anti-clerical. Martindale remembered vividly the visitation of the Mother Provincial. Her grey, clear, kind eyes made him realise that here was a real saint.

He fitted in with the French novitiate, or perhaps rather with France, more than with England or at least with Roehampton. Nevertheless it was a time of strain. Only much later did he learn how to be spiritually active and retain peace at the same time. There were spells in which he loathed the life in all its dull details: the spiritual books, prayers and customary exercises induced tedium, but at least he could speak freely about his revulsions to his novice-master without fear of being snubbed. The *vie des saints* nauseated him; he wanted to know how modern French Jesuits behaved and asked for the lives of Pères de Ravignan, de Ponlévoy and others. In the surroundings it seemed to him natural that Père de Lanversin, a royalist by instinct—he had succeeded Père Rosette as novice-master in September 1898—should exhort his novices in his first address to be *distingué*. He could never imagine Fr. Considine

---

[1] St. Ignatius, in laying down principles for the training of novices, prescribed a number of 'experiments', such as service of the sick in hospital, pilgrimages, etc., with the aim of testing the fitness of novices for the life ahead of them.

urging his English novices to be distinguished in the French sense. At Roehampton a sort of bluff commonsense prevailed.

It was on Quinquagesima Sunday, 1898, during his meditation, that he became conscious of 'serving God'. The realisation involved no new idea, plan or resolution, but the interior shock was so great that he was dazed by it throughout the day. He tried to explain it to Père de Lanversin, who merely said *Deo gratias* and seemed moved. And at the same time certain tendencies took personal definition through his reading of St. Teresa and St. John of the Cross. Constantly the notion of abnegation was at work in his mind, but in a positive manner, assisted first by the inspiration he got from his Manresa experience, and, now, from his acquaintance with the spirit of Père de la Colombière.[1] It haunted him on his visits to the Poor Clares.

Although the simple French cuisine suited him, the doctor decided that he needed English food, and prescribed raw beef, which he took in the form of dark violet tablets; and then tea, or rather a sweet ink-coloured fluid. He became extremely weak, and then was placed in the infirmary where he could take only hot milk. He perspired four or five times a day. It was even thought he might die. The sounds of people about their everyday business drifted through the windows from the street below, and he reflected, as he seemed to lapse smoothly into unconsciousness, that even if he recovered, his life would always be different from theirs. Then, mysteriously, at the very moment he began to improve, another sick novice, Pierre Lafont, went into a decline. The very day Martindale rejoined the community after his convalescence,[2] Lafont died. Frequently he told the story and understood that it was God's intention that he should live and that Lafont be taken in his place.

For convalescence he was sent to Le Thelonet, a small country house, formerly a farm, which the Fathers of Aix had acquired as a rest home. It was four kilometres out of the town on the road to Saint Victoire—a mountain frequently painted by Cézanne, who admired greatly the view from the Jesuits' villa. Here Martindale still

[1] Blessed Claude de la Colombière (1641–82), a French Jesuit, director of St. Margaret Mary and chaplain to the consort of Charles II at the Court of St. James.
[2] 31 June 1899.

77

suffered violent attacks of sickness, and worse headaches than he ever experienced later, save in Denmark during the second world war. But the solitude benefited him: he bathed early, sat outside eating dewy figs, slept in the pine woods, drank the good yellow *vin du pays* and felt that nature was working his recovery. With eyes that had been opened at Manresa, he contemplated his surroundings. The sunlight caught in peach and almond blossom, the aromatic shrubs, the red earth and grey rocks, the distant mountains, pine-covered or bare, the pools, with silver-blue water, the small green frogs that croaked at night. He absorbed all this with uninhibited pleasure. Far across the valley he looked towards the Sainte Baume and in his imagination pictured the Mediterranean that lay behind it.

During his illness, on 20 March 1899, a young Frenchman, who immediately became his friend, Pierre Teilhard de Chardin, joined the noviceship at Aix.

In the summer, when he was fully recovered, he made the pilgrimage 'experiment'. His companion was René Monterde, a man of unshakeable charity, and polite according to all conventions. The two novices were absent a fortnight. They went first by train to Aubagne, where, on opening a sealed envelope, they read their instructions to stay with the Marist Brothers. At Saint-Maxim the Dominicans were their hosts. They were poor, gave the pilgrims little to eat and showed them to an icy cell for the night. Next day St. Mary Magdalen's skull was brought out for their veneration: it had a patch of hair adhering to it at the spot where Our Lord, pushing her away with one finger, had allegedly touched it. Thence they climbed to the Sainte Baume: the cave-church associated with Mary Magdalen was poor and dripping with condensed moisture. They called on the Dominican nuns, who gave them milk and sweet cakes. Long afterwards one nun wrote in a letter, 'Nous avons vu la séraphique frère anglais.' Cyril was selfconscious in his long cassock and round clerical hat and once was rebuked by his companion for hurrying past a group of contemptuous young men: 'Nous sommes grands,' Frère Monterde told him, 'Nous sommes ambassadeurs du Christ!' As they neared the coast the churches became more elegant, rich and empty. At Marseilles, in a school run by the archdiocese, he saw young abbés, perched high at the back of the chapel, acting as *surveillants* over the pupils. Their destination was Notre Dame de la Garde, a madonna who kept pace with him throughout his life. At Le Thelonet and on his pilgrimage he had become aware of the anti-clerical mood of France, so soon to produce the fierce laws against religion. The countryside seemed already partly paganised; the little shrines were neglected, their paintings defaced. At La Thelonet the local men went to Mass for Christmas, for the first Communion of their children and for St. Cecilia, the patron of their band. Cyril took part in two processions; the second, on the Sunday following the feast of Corpus Christi, passed a cabaret. The men in the street outside continued with their bowls or dominoes and drinks; squibs and rockets were let off shatteringly under the nose of the Franciscan who carried the monstrance. At the altar of repose, just below the drawing-room window of a rich bourgeois' house, a lady emerged and sang the *O Salutaris* to the accompaniment of a piano, while her family remained indoors; at the end they called out their congratulations: 'Ah, mademoiselle! Vous étiez adorable! Quelle envolée de pieté la plus vraie.'

By contrast Cyril loved the upland churches, with their violently gilt busts of the saints and staring black eyeballs set in dead white eyes. It was no moment to judge religion in Provence. The atheistic movement in the government was about to reach its apex: *fiches* recorded whether an officer or official went to Mass, whether he did so merely to accompany his wife, and whether he carried a prayer book. The impression Cyril gained was that the Church looked for support to the rich bourgeois and suffered blatantly from its tastes.

4

In later years Martindale was not uncritical even of the French novitiate, which in its way and measure suffered from the defects general at the time in the training of novices. The instruction and reading appeared to him largely diagrammatic: too great emphasis was put on ethics, Scripture was read but not taught, texts were misapplied devotionally, and even the life of Christ was presented in detached pieces with appended morals. Nothing consecutive was given on St. Paul, still less on the Old Testament. Later he urged that novices should be shown a method for the reading of the Scriptures so that they might continue, under guidance, to read them intelligently during the rest of their training. The same held also of church history, so that later men set aside for special studies should not become merely erudite but learned. As for chastity, the approach was unreal and negative; a policy of funk and prudery prevailed. Martindale never accepted Fr. Considine's dictum that unchastity belonged to weak and soft characters. In France, Père de Lanversin had said to his novices: 'Mes frères, nous abordons. Quand nous sortons hors de notre demeure, que voyons-nous dans la rue? des statues . . . ah, des affiches . . . ah, des nudités . . . ah, mes frères, priez bien la Sainte Vierge.' Martindale's imagination remained frozen and stunned in France no less than in England, but this method of inculcating virtue seemed to him deplorable, especially for French novices. Later, in his booklet entitled *The Difficult Commandment*, he pioneered in England, at least, a positive and inspired approach to this subject.[1]

Finally, he considered that the noviceship had not prepared him for what was to follow, but only for more noviceship. Yet there was much he personally had gained from it, not only what he called later his 'first incarnational light' that enabled him to see God in created things, but also the impulse to serve God. This made him frequently halt and ask himself whether it was, in fact, God whom he saw or strove to serve. The two graces fused easily. Self-abdication was no longer the negative concept of his first months as a Catholic.

Whenever he caught himself acting contrary to these guiding ideas he became pharisaic and critical, tended to show off, and, then, to suffer a kind of mental paralysis. His portentous activity is an indication of how seldom this occurred. In a more practical assessment, the daily routine of the noviceship as much as its 'experiments', pain and even spiritual distress, taught him to endure the discomfort that was to form such a large portion of his later life.

[1] C. C. Martindale, *The Difficult Commandment* (Manresa Press, 1925). This book was translated into every European language, except Norwegian, and also into Japanese.

# 5
# *First Years as a Jesuit*

In August 1899 Martindale, in English lay-dress and bowler hat, travelled on the night-train from Aix to Paris, arriving on 21 August at Roehampton. There he made a retreat along with the English novices with whom he had entered the Society. At its conclusion, on 8 September, he took his first vows as a Jesuit. He felt a dullness of spirit, as he always did on occasions that marked a critical stage in his life, and answered woodenly to the congratulations that were offered him.

During the following days he visited his home. In a crowded railway carriage on his return journey to London, an old lady, leaning across to him, asked, 'Don't you love *The Imitation*? It is so true that only if you lose yourself, do you find yourself.' He blushed. Already he felt a perfect fool in his clerical suiting.

Later in September he arrived at St. Mary's Hall, Stonyhurst, a functional, barrack-like, but not undignified building in which the Jesuit students then did their course of philosophical studies. The artificially genial and condescending welcome he received from the Minister, Fr. Dinley, made him feel once again a new boy. For him this was not the north country, but nevertheless it was the land of *The Lancashire Witches*, and he enjoyed visiting places he remembered by name from his childhood reading. The near-by College made much the same impression on him as earlier it had done on Gerard Manley Hopkins. He could not help liking the Elizabethan part of the building, but the late-nineteenth-century addition struck him as florid and obese. The church was manifestly gimcrack, its huge altar altogether out of place and proportion.

It was an enclosed world into which he now entered, for the young Jesuits lived in isolation from the school. His Superior, Fr.

Coupe, was a man whose worth he slowly discovered and in the end greatly esteemed, though at first his pomposity concealed from many a loveable childishness. Fr. Boedder, a refugee German professor, Martindale revered as a saint. Fr. Joseph Rickaby did not cross his path outside the schoolroom; but Fr. O'Fallon Pope, who like Rickaby was to be with him again at Oxford, he saw frequently: then and later he found him a formalised man to whom he could explain himself even less than to Fr. Considine. With the Brothers he quickly established the happy relations that characterised all his years in the Society. His particular friends among them were Brother Byrne, a physical giant, who was believed to have strained his back carrying a piano down the stairs, a man noteworthy for an Irish picturesqueness of speech, and for certain physical compulsions that made him, for instance, always sleep at an angle, with his head pointing to the north. Then there was Brother Everard, the 'Prophet' as he was called, with a beard stretching to his stomach, an endearing character with whom Tyrrell corresponded in his last months as a Jesuit—'You plod on in your old ways,' Tyrrell told him, 'but some of us must follow our own.'

Among his fellow students, many of them from other countries, were young men who later attained the distinction that Fr. de Lanversin had set his novices as their aim. He found William Doyle, from the Irish Province, sarcastic and uncharitable; later, when he read his voluminous *Life*[1] he was unable altogether to shake off his incredulity. But this was the time of the Boer War, when the Irishmen at St. Mary's Hall manifested their nationalism by boisterous exultations over the British defeats. There were other foreigners, like the young Belgian historian, de Gellinck, who were marked personalities. But most of the men he did not know; for him they formed the masses, and he was happy in his shyness to lose himself among them.

Plater was a year ahead of him. In his biography[2] Martindale says that his recollections of him at this time were focused on the Shire-

[1] Alfred O'Rahilly, *Father William Doyle* (Longmans, 1920): other enlarged editions followed in 1920, 1925, 1930, and a shortened life in 1939. The movement for his beatification was not re-started after the second world war.
[2] C. C. Martindale, *Charles Dominic Plater* (Harding and Moore, 1922).

burn Almshouses, then situated above the College near the summit of Longridge fell, on the old Preston–Clitheroe road.

> Either I went up with Mr. Plater [he writes] during my first year, when he was 'catechist', or he, during his long vacation from Oxford, came up with me, when I shared that post myself. But I remember very clearly how devoted the little congregation was to him, how versatile he was in his methods—for the old men were very intractable at times—and, above all, his playing of the harmonium. We took it by turns, as usual, to give the instruction, and whoever did not give it had to play. Charles Plater, who had a real gift for the 'cello, could not achieve more than two tunes on the harmonium; one of these was 'God Save the Queen', which he performed with such astounding harmonies as to disguise it quite respectably; the other was a well-known song of Albert Chevalier's which he played with extreme solemnity and with ecclesiastical chords. The congregation either saw nothing odd about it or just accepted it as 'Mr. Plater'; but I used to find the effort to keep serious almost as exhausting as the tramp up the fells to reach the Almshouses.[1]

His philosophical studies, both at St. Mary's Hall and at Oxford, never interested him more than perfunctorily. His mind was not inclined to metaphysics: he was always certain of his own and God's existence and of the reality of the world outside him. This was simply due to his being unable to think otherwise rather than to arguments which seemed external to the subject. Had he been shown Descartes or Kant in three dimensions, and their place in the flow of history, he might have become interested both in the men and in their ideas. But this was not the method prevailing. There was no place then for the actual history of philosophy in the syllabus. Moreover, there was no tutoring and little sifting of talents.

In fact, the course hardly left a mark on him. No philosophy ever meant more to him than a way of looking at the world; and if a

---

[1] At this time the Shireburn Almshouses, a fine Jacobean building, were in a bad state of repair; later they fell into ruin, but after the late war were removed from their old site and reconstructed at Hurst Green by Fr. F. Vavasour.

number of principles were taken for granted, scholasticism seemed to him as good a way as any. He never developed a taste for philosophy. To the end of his life he was unable to see any flaw in the traditional arguments for the existence of God or for the soul's immortality. He never understood anything of space or time, nor indeed desired to understand. Because he knew he could never become either an agnostic or pantheist, natural theology was simply a subject to be learnt. Already he was committed to the concrete— to history, persons and their environment. Probably he was more integrated than most of his fellow-students. His two experiences in the noviceship were deepening in his soul. He knew then that the real part of his person was in touch with the Real that was beyond it yet within himself also. He had no temptation to become the pure transcendentalist or the pure immanentist. Then and later he was repelled instinctively by the modernist trends in the Church.[1]

On his arrival at St. Mary's Hall Martindale was put into the Oxford class, a select group of 'philosophers' who were destined, at the end of their course, to proceed to the University. At this time these men were taken for tuition by Mr. D. A. Slater, a master at Stonyhurst, who later became Classical Professor at the University of Liverpool. Plater, who was in the same class, had already formed a close friendship with Slater, and, for this reason, Martindale was never able to be as intimate with his teacher as he would have wished. Then, and later, he found it difficult to make friends, as he said, with someone on whom Plater had already laid hands. Slater was a brilliant teacher, and Martindale was always ready to acknowledge his indebtedness to him. He wrote of his influence at this time:

> It would be unfitting for me to linger on, and impossible to exaggerate, the devotion shown by Mr. Slater in continuing for so long to coach, both at St. Mary's Hall and at Stonyhurst College, men who could not give all or even more of their attention to his first-rate training; or on the manifold artistic graces, the whimsical charm, with which he enveloped his erudition; or on the ruthless courtesy of his corrections of the amateurish work that we all, I

[1] As the result of a complete misunderstanding, he was suspected many years afterwards of modernism, and suffered many irritations in consequence. Cf. inf. p. 140 sq.

Cyril and his aunt Alice.

Now darling aunt Day,
good bye.
                    nephew
ever yr very loving Cyril

End of a letter from Cyril to his aunt Daisy, written during
his first year at Temple Grove.

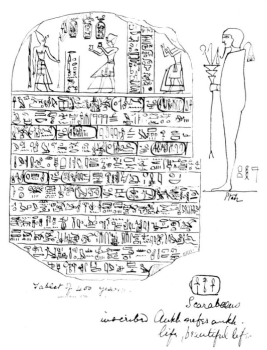

Tablet of 400 years.

Scarabæus
inscribed Ankh nefer ankh.
life, beautiful life.

A page from his Egyptian notebook compiled at
Temple Grove (aet. 12–13).

Cyril Martindale at Harrow.

confess, showed up to him. Enough to say that a unique encouragement, as well as a most forceful direction, was given by him to his class, the former undisguised, the latter so sweetly veiled that it was chiefly by perceiving your own improvement that you became aware of it.[1]

In his second year at St. Mary's Hall he was given to edit, in succession to Plater, *The Blandyke Papers*, collections of literary, philosophical and general essays, as well as verse, that appeared every months from October to May. He contributed a number of articles himself, and some facetious verse, and illustrated the whole of the May number with indifferent technique but a quality of imagination that he had revealed at Bournemouth and in France. Now, after three years as a Jesuit, he was slowly, but still only partially, recovering from his first paralysing shyness. He took part in plays, accompanied on the piano at concerts, and began to feel more in place than he had done at Roehampton. He enjoyed bathing in the Ribble, particularly in company with Plater, who, like him, was devoted to swimming and while in the water, as Martindale recalled, used to sing the most fantastic verses, or call out half a limerick, plunge, emerge gasping and finish it.

He celebrated his twenty-first birthday with his family. He was strung up and ill at ease and almost cringingly anxious not to offend his family. Although grim, St. Mary's Hall was now his home, and he was glad to be back. It was not until he was over thirty that he had an easy relationship with his father, and indeed got to know him for the first time and to respect him deeply. At present his father was still a remote figure, and when at Albury always overborne by Ben Hay. Cyril was glad to give him the assurance that he was going to Oxford.

Fundamentally he was as serious as when he first entered Manresa House. Twice he wrote letters to Père de Lanversin on spiritual subjects, but knew from his answers that the advice he received was inapplicable to English conditions. He got little help from retreats; often they served, as they had done earlier, to induce ridiculous scruples. Already in the noviceship an anxiety about wasting time

[1] C. C. Martindale, *Charles Dominic Plater*, 39.

had produced an irritating itch always to be doing something, and this, in turn, a restlessness of brain and inability to keep his mind quiet. His search for mortification, which he was still a long way from understanding, led him never to sit or lean back in a chair, so that, almost to the end of his life, he would perch himself uncomfortably on its edge. Once, however, Fr. McCoy helped him by explaining that the avoidance of particular friendships, on which such stress had been put during his novitiate, did not mean that he was to like or not like all equally. A casual word from Fr. O'Fallon Pope had unexpected consequences. The part of the day Martindale enjoyed most was after mid-morning coffee when he used to walk among the beeches and relax in a form of prayer of simplicity, which he feared might be inertia or distraction. Fr. Pope told him that this experience was due to the effects of coffee; and thus henceforth, Martindale was led more than ever before to distrust the consolations of prayer and their aftermath, and to seek first for possible physical explanations both in his own and in the saints' uncommon spiritual experiences.

He was still too shy to look on Oxford with anything but apprehension. He believed also that he was far below the standard of scholarship required by the University.

2

On 23 September 1901 Martindale left St. Mary's Hall for Oxford. Then, as now, the Jesuits were sent up to Oxford to get what their normal training could not give them. Their house, a small building leased by St. John's College, formerly a grange of the nuns at Godstow, was at the north end of St. Giles, adjoining the Lamb and Flag—a private Hall that took the name of its Master. In the year previous to Martindale's arrival as a freshman, Fr. Richard Clarke, its first Master, had died suddenly.[1] The Hall, being private, had then technically ceased to exist, but after negotiations with the Vice-Chancellor, it was reconstituted under a new Master, Fr. O'Fallon Pope. It now became known as Pope's Hall, after its Master, and not, as was commonly thought, by reason of the allegiance of its inmates.

[1] 10 September 1900.

The enterprise of a Jesuit house in Oxford, due to the vision of Fr. John Gerard, was still young, and its régime depended greatly on the character of the priest in charge. It is unlikely that Fr. Pope, a man as saintly as he was rigid, would have been appointed had it not been that the choice was necessarily confined to a small group of Jesuits, all converts from Anglicanism, who then held Oxford degrees. It was only five years since the English hierarchy had formally lifted its ban on Catholics matriculating at the universities.

Pope was a man of no academic distinction, nor had he the genius or personality of his distinguished successor, Fr. Martin D'Arcy, that would have made it possible for him to permit the students, without risk of laxness in religious discipline, to enter more fully into university activities. Under Pope the emphasis was exclusively on work. This produced a remarkable series of examination results and, at the same time, much strain, relieved partially during vacations spent in different houses of the Province. Walks and rowing were the only relaxations in term time. An enthusiastic oarsman at Pope's Hall, Mr. Edward O'Connor, later Rector of Stonyhurst, attempted to interest Martindale in his eight, known in the university as the hearse, for modesty (as the authorities in Rome then conceived it) compelled the Jesuits to turn out in long black shorts and stockings. But Martindale had not the strength for it, and he felt a fool walking down to the river in his clerical sports wear. Later he took up sculling.

He made some close friends in the Jesuit community. His afternoon walks were most commonly taken with Plater, Robert Monteith or Philip Garrold, all of whom had much influence on him, which he himself acknowledged generously in the memoirs he wrote later of these three priests.[1]

It was during these walks that I learnt to appreciate his power of metaphor [Martindale writes of Garrold]. I told him that it was sufficient for him to see or hear anything, forthwith to falsify it. A mutual friend used to play the violin for us; Garrold was especially struck by the Chaconne of Bach. I tried, rather priggishly,

[1] C. C. Martindale, *Memoir of Robert Monteith, S.J.* (for private circulation only); *Richard Philip Garrold, S.J. A Memoir* (Longmans, 1921).

I expect, to follow it as sheer music—almost mathematically. Garrold came away convinced that he had been listening to souls in Purgatory. He was relentless with me, and made me say, when we saw anything at all remarkable, what it *made me think of*. If it was, for example, Magdalen Tower, I expect I answered curtly, 'Magdalen Tower'. But he wanted it to be a Psalm or a Nun. Once we passed a red-hot furnace; he asked his usual question: I was too tired just then to want, even, to annoy him, and I answered with a certain amount of conviction, 'Hell'. He was quite furious, and asked me how I could descend to anything so commonplace, and said that to *him* it stood for love and sin (or perhaps hate) struggling in the heart of a saint.[1]

Often on rainy afternoons and at other times, Garrold, who was in the School of Modern History, made Martindale translate long tracts of Homer and Virgil, whole plays of the Greek tragedians and enough of any classic to give him a personal feeling for the author. During these sessions Garrold invented his system of studying history by means of symbols—crowns, axes, wigs and diagrams of all sorts. Martindale, as his notebooks show, adopted this system for Greek history and, later, for his study of the Fathers; and Garrold, on his side, adopted Martindale's system of assigning certain colours to particular trains of historical thought. Martindale, who was critical where Garrold was enthusiastic, was deeply affected by this utterly honest, affectionate and highly intelligent young Jesuit, and by his large-hearted sympathy for his fellow-men. Monteith's influence was of a different kind and was cut short by his tragic death as a chaplain during the first war.

Martindale's first term was passed in misery. He was appalled at the amount he was expected to learn and the quality of the knowledge required. In spite of Mr. Slater's brilliant teaching his instinct for Greek was not fully developed. In his first term he went for tutoring to Mr. H. F. Fox of Brasenose, a loveable, fierce man, who modestly judged that he could not take Martindale to the standard required for Schools and passed him on to Mr. Robinson Ellis and

[1] *Richard Philip Garrold*, 14-15.

Mr. Poynton. Ellis was, so to say, the last of the Renaissance scholars, save possibly for H. Munro of Cambridge, who knew all about Lucretius as Ellis did about Catullus; they were mortal enemies, and scientifically, could be astonishingly obscene. Ellis would invite scholars to high teas and, in one of the awful silences that characterised them, say, '*Mar*tindale, I have discovered a conclusive emendation for such and such a line of Catullus', and paralyse nervous undergraduates. By a deft touch or two he was able to transform his pupils' verses into beautiful Latin without re-writing them. In his special class, after reading out Martindale's verses and then those of E. A. Burroughs (later Bishop of Ripon), he would comment: 'Yes, but the impeccable Mr. Burroughs writes *in* Latin, Mr. Martindale *writes* Latin.' This was true. Later, discussing with Martindale a certain Latin usage he had come across, Ellis asked: 'Where can we find a parallel to this?' Martindale answered, 'You won't. The author was writing hastily and just made a mistake,' and he would explain that Cicero, for instance, had made an exactly similar mistake. He then showed that what Cicero meant to say was obvious, and also why he just missed saying it. This method, or rather intuition, he later transferred to his study of Scripture, particularly to the Apocalypse.

The sense not only of Latin, but of the Latin world, came through his reading. Always it was behaviour and persons that held him. Things military, legal and political he studied from necessity. He was interested in Emperors only as men, and by far preferred the earlier periods of Rome to the later. He revelled in W. Warde Fowler's *Roman Festivals*[1] and loved his dryness of expression. When he studied Apuleius he became intoxicated by its sensuality and Isaiac religion and by his realist and witch-haunted mentality.

His danger, of course, was to become a pagan in a pagan world. At Harrow, Virgil had brought Latin alive for him, yet in a mystic, almost Christian way: he had not been introduced into Virgil's world, but had brought Virgil into his. But now he walked about in ancient Rome with a double personality. Occasionally Propertius

---

[1] William Warde Fowler, *The Roman Festivals of the period of the Republic. An Introduction to the study of the religion of the Romans* (Macmillan, 1899).

showed him sheer beauty; Martial put him in touch with Roman reality. Anything Greek came later, though with a rush. So completely did he absorb himself in Rome that he might easily have lapsed into thinking that Christianity was a way of life on a par with religions past and future; but he was saved from that.

After a time it did him good to have entered so wholeheartedly into a human society. He always considered that he had been called to sympathise with weaker humanity without toppling over into its ways. Men, not abstractions, were to be his concern. Later he could imagine Francis Xavier staring with love, but not sympathy, at the paganism he encountered in India; now in the same way he himself looked at the Roman world.

This deep abstraction of mind and spirit in the classics explains his phenomenal, and yet almost accidental, academic success. Others at Pope's Hall had studied more intensely or were more technically proficient, but none manifested the same power to enter into the mind of the authors in his syllabus. When Ronald Knox came up from Eton in 1906, a year after Martindale had taken his final schools, he found that his name 'was still a legend among the people [he] knew—the amazing Jesuit who was a first in Mods and Greats, Hertford scholar, runner-up for the Ireland, got the Latin and Greek verse prizes, and the Derby scholarship, and then finished off rather unexpectedly with the Ellerton theological essay prize.'[1]

He accepted his successes with some surprise, particularly his first, the Hertford scholarship. When he learnt that he had won the verse prize, he was annoyed to discover that it was for Greek, not Latin. He considered that his work was little more than a pastiche of Homer, whereas his Latin verse was truly Latin and partly original. However, he won it in the following year: the subject was Sertorius. His first in Mods was again a surprise to him. In Greats he did not sink below alpha-minus and that was only in his Logic paper. At his viva the examiners showered compliments on him. One asked whether in a certain paper he had not left out something. Martindale answered that he could not recall anything. The examiner went on, 'The Eleusinian mysteries?' He replied, and then demonstrated, that

[1] R. A. Knox, 'C. C. Martindale', in *The Month* (May, 1959), 269–72.

they had no bearing on the subject. Afterwards three Colleges offered him a fellowship. In the history of the University few undergraduates could have made such an impression on their teachers.

At the beginning of this third year he had become not only stale but physically hysterical, and would shake at night in bed. The Provincial, Fr. Colley, the kindest of men, who was able to sympathise even when he could not understand, sent him off for three months to the Italian riviera, an experience that greatly affected him.[1] At that time in San Remo there was a Jesuit rest house, which not surprisingly was filled with an eccentric and international assortment of Jesuits, either mentally or physically sick. This was his destination. The Minister of the house was a mad German, Baron Egloffstein. Among his neurotic charges were a feverish intellectualist Frenchman, who insisted that boys should be educated in town in order to catch the *mouvement du jour*; a disdainful Roman, Locatelli; a childish Italian who was always screaming pieties about the house; an unbalanced Englishman, Fr. Lawless, and three Italian scholastics who quarrelled among themselves as violently as religious formulas permitted. The secular priests slunk about in dirty cassocks and black knitted shawls.

Here, in conversation with the Superior at table, Martindale's eyes were opened for the first time to the failure of the apostolic methods of the Church. He was shocked when he observed that no one came to Mass, and said to the Superior, 'Why not go out and talk to them?'

'But such men would probably be Socialists! They would be in mortal sin,' he answered.

'Then what about Our Lord's instruction, "Go, teach! Compel them to come in!"'

'They know the gospel is preached on Sundays. If they want to hear it, they can easily come.'

If this represented Italian Catholicism, then (Martindale thought) it should be revolutionised. The same Superior cautioned him never to visit an hotel in his cassock—it would be assumed that he was coming only to administer the last sacraments, and this would scare

[1] He left on 28 January and arrived back at Oxford on 21 April 1904.

91

the guests and infuriate the manager. In the expelled French Carmelite convent the Prioress had had herself photographed in a variety of ecstatic postures and later fell foul of the ecclesiastical authorities, but on the hills above the town there was an exiled French community of Benedictine monks who entertained him to dinner and speeches on St. Benedict's day.

Away from the house he was happy and relaxed. He painted a great deal, was at home in the Riviera churches, found that he could talk naturally with children, accepted beauty without inhibitions. He had seen it at Aix, but then it was through the lattices of the noviceship.

From San Remo he visited Florence, and returned by a devious route through Genoa, Milan, Padua and Venice. In the Jesuit house at Genoa, when the community was sitting at recreation, a very young intellectual priest raised the subject of Fr. Tyrrell, whom he described as a 'gran ballone gonfiato'—a great puffed-up balloon. Whatever Tyrrell was, he was certainly not a balloon.[1] An old Father joined in, and began to revile England: *inter alia*, Englishmen had introduced venereal disease into Italy. Martindale was riled and said icily, 'You interest me much, Father. You have seen so much more than I. Have you been often in England?' 'God forbid,' the priest answered, 'that I should ever go there.'

He did not care much for Genoa. At Milan he was shown the city by a young priest who claimed to know by intuition what parts of Homer were authentic. At the Jesuit house of studies at Chieri near Turin Liberalism was the only subject of conversation. When Fr. Schiffini, a noted theologian, inquired what subjects he studied at Oxford, Martindale judged it safest in the circumstances to answer, 'Aristotle'. Schiffini embraced him on his departure and presented him with his two heavy tomes on moral theology. Martindale did not feel justified in leaving them in the train and so toiled back with them to Oxford.

The effect this journey had on him was incalculable. It made him much older; it forced him to do things for himself. He had seen places he had previously only read about, absorbed varied beauty and

[1] Fr. Tyrrell left the Society of Jesus on 19 February 1906.

got into the mind of persons who did not belong to the classical world. But the Church in Italy had given him a considerable shock. In every Jesuit house he had met at least one priest who believed himself modern and was anxious to meet people, yet, timid as he might be, was considered audacious by his elders. In Venice, particularly, the Society seemed to be shrinking back into itself. Its church there, more like a mausoleum with its scheme of white and sea-green marble, was empty. His eyes had been opened, his mind stretched out to new horizons. The journey home tired him. On his arrival at Oxford he relapsed into melacholy and bitterness.

3

During his last term at Oxford his cousin and childhood companion Gwendolen Gisborne married Gerard Twistleton-Wykeham-Fiennes. Since Holme Hall was too small for the guests, the local hotel was emptied and the family, including Cyril and his father, were accommodated there. Early on the wedding morning Cyril went for a bathe in the river and on emerging unclad found the village children lined up to stare at him. The church ceremony was on a grand scale. The next day, SS. Peter and Paul, he went to Mass in the little tin hut that served as a church at Hadden.

At the reception he met Lord Saye and Sele, and travelled back to Oxford with him. He remembered the journey for a remark Lord Saye and Sele made to him. 'Here am I,' he said, 'in one sense at home in this sort of thing, and yet utterly out of perspective, and not at home. I can't live with the ancient aristocrats; I can't with the middle class. As far as instinct goes I am *sans-patrie, sans-famille.*' Gerard died young. Gwendolen, who was always extravagant, had then to sell Holme Hall. She kept in touch with Cyril until his death.

After his final Schools he stayed up for the Encaenia. That year Lord Curzon was Chancellor, and it was the first time for many years that the Chancellor had presided at the occasion. When Martindale appeared in the pulpit to read extracts from his prize compositions, Curzon looked at the programme, and turning to the Vice-Chancellor, obviously inquired who Martindale was. Thereupon Curzon firmly turned his back on him, and did not ask him to the Garden Party. Martindale knew that when his father had thanked Curzon for recommending his son for the diplomatic service and had afterwards explained why the recommendation would not be used, Curzon had said, 'Your son's choice is very noble.' Nevertheless he had disapproved and broken his connection with Arthur Martindale.

Neither then nor later did Martindale consider that the Provincial had acted incorrectly in asking him to decline the fellowships he had been offered. Both knew that, even if the question of domicile could be solved, the authorities in Rome would fence round his existence in College with a hundred restrictions. He himself felt that, even if he might be too worldly for the Society (at least, as he had seen it in France), he was not worldly enough for a College community; he still had little knowledge of affairs and no general conversation; his shyness would have paralysed him in the presence of other dons. But what settled the question for him was his own conviction that the life of research or lecture room was not for him. He was happy then that the decision was made that he should go down from Oxford and teach in a Jesuit school.

It is difficult to trace his purely spiritual development at Oxford. In spite of the strain his studies imposed on him, it would seem to have been continuous. Many of his vacations were spent at Manresa House, where he used to pray peacefully at the outdoor shrines. One at least was passed at Jersey, where the expelled French Jesuits had now established a house of philosophy. Another with the same Fathers at Canterbury, and a third at St. Beuno's in North Wales. At Jersey he met de Bélinay again, and also Pères Nicolardot and Poncel, who were shortly to run into the thick of the modernist troubles. On his way back he passed a night at Farm Street. Arriving late at night, he met no one save Tyrrell, who got him some bread, cheese and claret and then ran for his life. But it was at St. Beuno's that he had the only noteworthy spiritual experience of these years.

It cannot be dated or put into any accepted category. It occurred during a retreat, while he was facing a crucifix hanging on a wall. Suddenly the cruciffx seemed strongly and tenderly lit up as from within and transfused with an amber-gold light which conveyed to the soul a sense of incomparable beauty. It was unlike his novitiate illuminations, in which imagery had played no part at all; nor did the crucifix, as such, seem to come alive. It simply was there in the centre of the irradiation. It provided no new ideas, nor even an acuter realisation of the crucifixion (he was not in fact meditating on it at the time), but simply an understanding that the Crucifix was the most beautiful thing in the world. He did not pray, though he reflected afterwards that he should have asked God to keep his thought focused on Him while he was so excessively absorbed in the classics.

In the same retreat, but after this experience, he had an 'impression' of the Holy Family. It was not associated with any object or pictorial representation, and was not accompanied by any form of visualisation. It was simply a sense of his being present in the house at Nazareth with the Holy Family, but yet not looking at them. He seemed merely to be deluged with an awareness of incomparable beauty.

There was, as far as he could then see, no deduction to be made from either of these experiences. He was certain, however, that he had not fabricated them, that they had been thrust upon him as sharply and unexpectedly as anything that had occurred earlier in the noviceship or at Lourdes. Later reflection made him think that these graces had been granted him to compensate for the almost total lack of consolations he received in his regular prayers. All his time as a Jesuit he had been hampered by recurrent sickness and headaches; there was little relief in his life; the manner in which he drove himself in his studies had made him dread each new term as it drew near.

At St. Mary's Hall he had begun to write verses and continued this practice at Oxford, particularly in this third year, and later resumed it during his study of theology. The black notebook into which he transcribed them reflects his mood perhaps better than any letters. Neither outwardly nor interiorly did he deny, nor was he ever tempted to deny, his faith, but without question his verses betray an un-Christian melancholy and perhaps a flirtation with the

pagan world. He read them only to Philip Garrold, who was astonished, especially by the sensuousness of his Italian verses and the
sadness of some lines entitled, 'The Friar of Zurbaran', which end:

> *. . . surely the day is nigh*
> *When scourge and ecstasy*
> *And sickening doubt and sudden thrill of faith*
> *And this alternate death*
> *Shall be knit up into a single whole,*
> *And your exultant soul,*
> *Leaping from man to God, and God to man,*
> *Shall trace the manifold network of His plan,*
> *Knot by knot, mesh by uniting mesh*
> *Of spirit and of flesh,*
> *And seeing both made perfect into one,*
> *Find, in a death of each, the life of both begun.*

The mood, as will be seen, lifted only in the months immediately
preceding his ordination.

A story he had published in the *Oxford Magazine*, while he was
still at Pope's Hall, made him anxious to experiment in prose. As has
been noted, he was fascinated in childhood by gates and doors. *The
Gate God*[1] was strictly no story at all but a exposition of this fact,
evoked by the history of the cult of Janus. Others followed, at Oxford and at Stonyhurst, but since they belong to the Oxford temper
of his mind, they should perhaps first be touched on here. The second
story, *The Goddess of Ghosts*, which much later gave the title to one
of his three early collections, was the tale of a small Roman girl into
which he introduced all he knew of ghost-cults.[2] His style here was
influenced by Walter Pater and, in subsequent stories, by Meredith.
Finally, he tried to rid himself of all influences and write in his own
way. Several among the early stories are inartistic; their framework

---

[1] *The Month* (1904), 577–83.
[2] Cf. *The Goddess of Ghosts* (Burns, Oates, 1915), 137–97. The other two collections are
*In God's Nursery* (1913) and *The Waters of Twilight* (1914), both with the same publisher.
The stories first appeared in *The Month*, *The British Review*, and other magazines, some
of them under the pseudonym, Jean de Geollac.

is used to carry large tracts of book learning. But his progress in technique is steady. For instance, 'Red Magic'[1] is already much more truthful than the Ghost in 'Yonder'.[2] Here he was writing mostly of places he knew, Aix and Marseilles, and the central character of the story, the boy in Taurobolium, is largely himself. 'The Net'[3] was due to his real delight in *indigitamanta* or religious books prescribing the mode of worshipping gods. There is insight in this chapter, in spite of the artificiality of some of the conversation which he thought clever at that time. The boy's insomnia, escape and disillusionment were authentic, and clearly he was more conscious of the net than of the freedom it guaranteed. He was not exactly losing his faith, but learning it in a new way. 'Mors Immortalis', in what eventually became the same book, was written because he had to express the thrill given him by pottery in the British Museum and by a papyrus read in the Bodleian. It was the first symptom of his desire to bridge the centuries, or rather to find that everything in the pre-Achaean period was repeating itself in his day. It is perhaps the best chapter. The only really weak stories were 'Guardian Angels' and 'The Twenty-Firster'. Here he was showing off. He wanted, no doubt unconsciously, to demonstrate that he was in contact with modern times and persons. The former contained a short description of Gwendolen's house in London, the second of Allestree.[4]

The interest of these stories now is the indication they give of his development. He was becoming aware of ordinary people, and even of the poor, and he realised abruptly that the roots of his love of life on the old scale were not dead. His first conversion, at Bournemouth, had as it were been a turning to what he wanted. Now he was learning not to turn away from it. In the story entitled 'A Conversation',[5] which expresses some of the colouring of his San Remo visit, the two characters, Hugh and Arthur, represent the conflict in him between the ascetic and the hedonist. But perhaps more significant still, were the words he put into the mouth of the boy, Menandrion, in 'God's Orphan'. At the end of the story he made him say, 'I will go back and

---

[1] *In God's Nursery*, 47–67.  
[3] Ibid., 85–107.  
[5] *The Month* (1906), 49–61.

[2] Ibid., 1–20.  
[4] Cf. sup. p. 35.

live with the Christian.' He realised that the boy could not have become a Christian then any more than he himself could have done at that age, had not God taken the matter out of his hands. He knew that had this not happened, it might well have been with him, as with Menandrion, a choice between Christianity and suicide.

# 6

## Ordination

In September 1905 Martindale began his first period of teaching at Stonyhurst College. A contemporary of his at Oxford, Cuthbert Lattey, had prophesied that he would never be understood by boys, but he found his class docile and among his pupils made a number of friends with whom he corresponded on intimate terms to the end of his life.[1] During his year there he was not unhappy or unsuccessful, and it was for reasons of health and not for any failure as a teacher that he was given other work.

After his first class he was appalled by the low standard of Jesuit teaching at the time. He found that his pupils could not scan ordinary Latin verse, whereas at Harrow, at the same age, they would have been set to write Greek epigrams, and quite possibly in dialect. But he was quick to see the potentialities of his small class. He tutored them individually and strove to make them think. Early on he set his class the Benediction hymn, *O salutaris hostia*, to render as an unseen. Two boys translated *hostia* as enemy, and half the rest thought that it meant one who invited guests. Already he reflected that sheer ignorance was at the root of many apostasies. Latin prayers were not understood, and consequently much of the services held no meaning for the boys.

Then, and later also, he was fiercely critical of the religious instruction given both in non-Catholic and Catholic schools. In a letter, written two years after leaving Stoneyhurst to a pupil of his at that time, he summed up his observations:

A Protestant school usually says, 'Don't meddle. If a boy is going to be religious, he will be; if not, he won't.' That is fatalism

[1] His letters to Mr. E. O. Ryan have been put at my disposal, and, after the letters written to his family, have been of the greatest value to me.

and denies free will in man, and, above all, the love of God. It accordingly hedges the boy round with a *very* few slight safeguards and then says, 'Let him fight it out for himself.' The most powerful influence in such a school is the public opinion which happens to animate the school, the house or the set in which the boy is. It's a gamble, really; the odds are a little in favour of heredity, family, education and temperament, but not much.

Now we, if we are really to educate a boy, must assume baptism and grace; hence the boy ought normally to develop religiously. Obviously, then, we ought to inquire what his past training has been (we do exactly the same for Greek and Latin; we don't start all boys in the same place exactly, but we inquire) and modify our treatment accordingly. We should start by training the whole character, and not merely the pious side of him. And his religion, if it is to be 'pervasive', should be put to him not merely piously, but intellectually and morally, not just tacked on outside and likely to be stripped off directly the strings that tie it to the school are snapped.

As to the moral side, I believe we must educate, instruct and develop, not merely shelter, protect and keep innocent.

This he found lacking in the religious teaching at Stonyhurst early in the twentieth century. The penal approach to moral misdemeanour, as he clearly saw, did not build character and would have no lasting influence.

He started his third term in a state of extreme fatigue, and within a month of the year's end he was in the infirmary. After the summer vacation he was assigned the lighter task of teaching classics to the young Jesuit students at Roehampton. 'Even at Stonyhurst,' he wrote in 1954, 'I never felt myself a master. I was shy, amused, bored, liked (occasionally disliked), very tired, with a sense of huge responsibility.' He knew that some of the boys trusted him. To one he wrote towards the end of his life: 'You were the first, I think, who taught my isolated, shy self that I could be friends with anyone.'

2

His next two years at Roehampton were less exacting. He was happier here than he had been at any time since entering the Society. He got on well with the Juniors, enjoyed teaching Greek by his own methods and attempted to humanise their recreation room. Under his direction one of his pupils modelled a superb Mycenaean house, furnished with authentic devices and a movable roof that revealed both the men's and women's quarters. At the monthly scholastic exercises he arranged parts in sung Greek chorus and organised Greek dancing. At this time also he won the Ellerton Theological Prize Essay on Comparative Religion, but failed to get the Latin Prose Essay Prize on the pagan mystic and magician, Alexander Abonoteichos, a failure which he ascribed to the fact that the examiners were unable to discover the order of his thought, so that the essay gave the appearance of being thrown carelessly together. Nevertheless, on the strength of his academic record, he was now awarded the Derby scholarship. His former tutor, Robinson Ellis, suggested that he should take Ausonius, the fourth-century Roman poet, as his subject. He was to edit his works for the Oxford University Library.

The task involved collating all the existing manuscripts and editions of Ausonius. While working in the Ambrosiana at Milan, the librarian came up to him: it was Mgr. Ratti (later Pius XI). After a few courteous remarks he paused to ask Martindale what he wanted. He knew instantly where the Ausonius manuscripts were, fetched them and went off without wasting a word and without abruptness. At Rome he stayed at the Gregorian University, where he saw a great deal of Father (later Cardinal) Billot, who had leave from the Rector of the house to eat through two complete suppers.[1]

Martindale's stay in Rome was interrupted by a visit to Perugia for a single manuscript. There he found all but a few of the local

---

[1] Billot at this time was professor at the Gregorian University. In 1911 he was created a Cardinal by Pius X. He had a very great reputation as a theologian and was said to be part author of the Encyclical *Pascendi*, condemning modernism. In 1922, under pressure from Pius XI, he resigned the Cardinalate because of the attitude he took to the condemnation of *Action Française*. He died in the Jesuit noviciate at Galloro in 1931.

clergy had been excommunicated for modernism. A broken ankle
prevented him from visiting Assisi. Back in Rome he asked for an
audience of the Pope. He was granted a public one, at which Pius X
appeared deadly tired: his hands were inert and cold and he gave the
impression of being sulky and morose. Later he saw the Pope again
in private audience. As his ankle prevented him rising from his
genuflexion, Pius got up, lifted him by the elbows and asked, 'What
are you doing in my house?' 'Collating manuscripts of Ausonius,
your Holiness.' 'Poveretto,' said the Pope smiling.

The audience impressed him. Martindale felt he could catch the
holiness and recollection of the Pope even through his smiles. Many
years later, in 1925, he referred back to this occasion, contrasting
Ratti, who as Pius XI had recently received him, with St. Pius X:

The Holy Father [Pius XI] was really extraordinary. He seemed
to have as much wise humanity about him as a man could. He was
simultaneously regal, scholarly and priestly, and, as it were, a man
of affairs. If you say, what more could one want, well, I will tell
you one small incident. I had collected about half a dozen chauffeurs and was giving them a glass of wine in a small trattoria. I
mentioned the Pope and they all showed great enthusiasm (they
weren't at all a religious crowd)—he was so erudite, so wise, so
courageous, so able to touch on every part of life properly, so
fatherly, so gay, so affectionate with children, etc. Benedict XV,
who reigned just during the war, had disappeared from their mind:
I think he struck no one's imagination, poor man, and I hold him
to have been a real martyr and in God's Providence right for that
time, but no one will ever know about him. Then I mentioned
Pius X, who died just after the first horrors of the war. 'Oh,' they
all cried with one sort of gasp, '*That* one, a *real* saint!' As someone
said to me later on, the intuition of the Romans is something most
puzzling. These were not pious people, they could not have seen
anything of Pius at close quarters, yet they knew. So did I, during
my audience with him in 1908 or so, but I would be as puzzled as
they, were one to ask, How do you know he was a saint? I think
they would just answer, *Si vedeva subito!* You saw it at once. That

doesn't mean that Pius XI isn't a real Christian. You feel, This man is good all through. But all the more does one touch a certain difference—goodness and *holiness*. Something looks at you from behind the eyes. Anyway the note of conviction in the chauffeurs was unmistakable.

I shall store this up against the day of his canonisation, when all the papers will say, Oh yes, a good man, none can doubt it, but how narrow, how peasant, how nothing of a scholar, of the diplomatist.[1]

Martindale forgot what subjects, apart from Ausonius, made up his conversation with Pius X.

On the same visit he was introduced to the General of the Jesuits, Fr. Wernz, at the German College. He had dinner there and, sitting next to the General afterwards at recreation, pointed down the table to a young mouse-like frail-looking priest, and said as a joke, 'Paternity, that is your successor.' It was Fr. Wladimir Ledochowski. Long afterwards he told this story to the new General, who was not amused but, imagining that Martindale might be flattering him, made inquiries whether he had ambition for high office in the Society.

At Paris, on his return journey, he stayed in the flat occupied by the small group of eminent French Jesuits, Pères de Grandmaison, Lebreton and de la Servière. In a scrap of autobiographical writing, he described a day spent with de Bélinay, whom he now met again at Paris.

We made an expedition to St. Germain and the Fôret de Marly and sat under trees and breathed an air of purity. It was curious to be conscious (without need of words) of how far our minds had moved, without change of ultimates, from the noviciate, which had been for me an escape, but for him one long discomfort. From that St. Germain terrace we could look down towards that Paris where he would have been so brilliant and so lost. His personality was imaginative, vibrant; its steely determination was disguised by

[1] Pius X was canonised in 1954, just nineteen years after this letter was written.

the delicate iridescence of his style, and not all guessed the meaning masked by the elusive humour of his symbolism.

It was in Paris, sitting in a café, that he read the whole of the Encyclical, *Pascendi*.[1] He felt that the bottom had been knocked out of everything in his world. The curial *stylus* infuriated him. He returned with iron twisted in his heart. Another visit, this time to Leyden, completed his research. He went to St. Beuno's to begin his theological studies without being given time to write his book. After ordination he judged he could spend his energy more profitably on other things and, eventually, handed over all his Ausonia to the library at Heythrop College.

### 3

In October 1908 Martindale started his theological course at St. Beuno's in North Wales. He knew the house from the vacation he had spent there, and liked it. Moreover, he had friends in the community and was more ready now to make others. On the whole, his years there were happy. He loved the countryside, played tennis, sang at concerts. 'I doubt whether any house anywhere has a more friendly atmosphere than St. Beuno's,' he wrote in his life of Plater, who had started the course the previous year. 'There is a warmth of geniality there that makes all the undercurrents of life grow happy: and over it broods the thought, emphasised year by year, of approaching ordination.'[2]

The beauty of the setting of St. Beuno's never palled. The features of its landscape are described in *The Wreck of the Deutschland* which Hopkins composed during his theological studies there. Martindale himself writes:

> The scenery is of great beauty. Rhyl and the sea are away to the right; Denbigh to the left looms on its crag; the heavy tower of St. Asaph Cathedral lifts itself from among the trees some four miles distant; and beyond the hills on the far side of the immense

[1] *Pascendi Dominici Gregis*, 8 September 1907.
[2] *Charles Dominic Plater*, 100.

valley, yet other hills float upwards till behind them all you see the crest of Snowdon.

The College itself . . . taken as a whole, it has no little dignity. But behind it, a terraced garden climbs upward, in summer all bright flowers and dark pillar-like cypress-trees and hedges; at the top is a long walk whence the enormous view can be seen almost in its entirety. Many when contemplating those wide pastures and roads and farms and villages, and the old town and the spires, must have found no better 'composition of place' for St. Ignatius's meditation on the kingdom of Christ, when he bids you visualise Our Lord going forth through the synagogues, towns and homesteads to convert the land. I have liked to stand there with Charles Plater, and that thought was not far from his mind and inspired him with noble dreams.[1]

In theology, perhaps more than during any other part of his training, a great deal depended on the personality of his teachers. He always considered it his great good fortune that he had Fr. Albert Valensin to take him through the treatise on Grace. Since childhood he had been intimately, almost agonisingly, conscious of the supernatural active in himself, and now, under a stimulating teacher, he was able to study the workings of God in the soul. The long hours Valensin spent on St. Paul and St. John and on history in general inspired some of Martindale's own early books.[2] The parts of the treatise covering the quarrel between Jesuits and Dominicans shocked and saddened him: both sides appeared to him to express the relationship between free will and grace in terms of mechanics. His notebooks witness the seriousness with which he studied, in spite of the laboriousness of many lectures, which he relieved with scurrilous verses. Fr. Slater, the professor of moral theology, was unsympathetic to him; in fact a mutual dislike showed itself early. On his side Slater suspected Martindale of heterodox views he never held, while Martindale judged that Slater was unfair to a Jesuit friend and was responsible for his leaving the Society. Only later

[1] *Charles Dominic Plater*, 99–100.
[2] *St. John the Evangelist* (1920), *St. Paul* (1924) (Burns, Oates).

when Slater, now a blind man, was passing his last years in the confessional at St. Francis Xavier's, Liverpool, did he and Martindale appreciate each other. Then Martindale sought his guidance on the Marlborough case.[1]

Although he was anxious to learn Hebrew, he never got very far with the subject, for it was ineffectively taught by the erudite and lovable Rector, Fr. Townsend.

Like many others, he found the method of teaching theology unsatisfactory. Since relatively few men could be students, fewer still metaphysicians, subjects had to be taught in the schoolroom rather than studied in private. At the time there was no tuition or individual direction, and no provision was made for the further work on sections of theology which particular students might show themselves eager to assimilate. This was in part inevitable in a system which aimed at equipping all-comers, regardless of their ability, with a basic minimal knowledge of their subject.

One incident indicates the seriousness with which he prepared himself for the priesthood. From his childhood he had always recoiled from the sight of blood. Madame Tussaud's, and the pictures above the barrel-organ played by the two white-coated men in Bayswater, had given him nightmares. Now, as he approached ordination, he arranged with a doctor friend to watch one of the worst operations in St. Bartholomew's Hospital, London, lest, as a priest, he should have to witness some similar sight for the first time. He survived, and in fact claimed afterwards that he was alone among those present who did not turn green, although he quailed when an enormous growth removed from the patient was passed round the students in a bucket. The only thing that really sickened him were the brown rubber gloves worn by the men round the table.

While he was at St. Beuno's his Catholic aunt, Sophy Gisborne, died. It was the end of an epoch in his life. When Cyril arrived at Holme Hall, she could only gasp a few words and hold his hand. Cyril asked her where she wanted to be buried: she was the third wife of Henry Gisborne. 'Beside him?' he suggested. With her in-

[1] Cf. inf. p. 157 sq.

domitable realism she answered just audibly, 'He's got two there already. That's quite enough.' On his way back from Bakewell to Scarborough, where the theologians were on holiday, he felt very bitter about his own selfishness to his only Catholic relative, who had stood by him always and helped him into the Church. She was the last of her generation. He believed mournfully that the autumn of his life had begun after a very uncertain spring and no summer. His serious verses became more melancholic. He wrote lines on his mother, *Caro loca numine complet*, first in a theological notebook, then later transcribed them into a book that he kept for verses he considered worth preserving. They conclude:

> *In the big white bed you lay*
> *Dying gently, mother May,*
> *Wide, wide eyes that fought the mist;*
> *Lips a-tremble to have kissed*
> *Husband far away—and I*
> *Just alive to see you die.*
> *I to you and you to me*
> *Stretched weak arms at Allestree.*
> *Even so, too much. The red*
> *Stained the whiteness of the bed . . .*
> *Babe and mother, by Death's art,*
> *Scarcely might be known apart:*
> *'It's a miracle,' they said:*
> *'For certainly she is dead.'*

This mood recurred intermittently. There are verses of the same date that recall the death of his young half-brother, Geoffrey S. Martindale, who lay buried in Greystoke churchyard. This year, 1910–11, accounts for more than half his verses.

It may have been Aunt Sophy's death that inspired the *Rhyme of Aloysius*. He refers to it in a letter on the following 21 August: 'By the way, it occurs to me to enclose a recent *Month* article[1] which was meant to show the fighting side of St. Aloysius, a person whom I

---

[1] *The Month*, August 1910.

love and whose lives I detest. They were thought to be very irreverent by some people, but it was forced through, and *The Tablet* had a column and a half on it.' Certainly, to judge from his verses, he was reflecting almost morbidly at times on his childhood and early days as a Catholic.

For reasons that were never explained to him, he was sent, at the end of his second year of theology, to the house of the exiled French Jesuits at Ore Place, Hastings. The excuse was that he would be under Père Condamin for Scripture and that the sea air would brace him. Certainly, as he admitted himself, he was nervy. Nevertheless he was reluctant to leave St. Beuno's even for a French house where he already knew many of the Fathers. As it turned out, the stimulating intellectual atmosphere of Ore Place immediately revived him. The professors included Père Bouvier, who taught Apologetics, an erudite, gay, humane and evidently holy man, whom he regularly consulted.[1] He appreciated Père Condamin as a scholar but gathered little from him in the schoolroom. The lectures of Roiron, a fellow-novice of his at Aix, were marked by a mixture of French and German exhaustiveness. In the same house were his former novice-master, Père de Lanversin, now a shrivelled old man, and de Bélinay, who was his refuge in difficulties. The barrack-like, gimcrack building, run up as a temporary dwelling for refugees, swayed in the gales and was full of fleas. He found difficulty in eating and was put on the *table des malades*. As ordination approached he wrote some verses on the Mass, which he considered good enough to reprint at the head of one of his chapters in his biography of Plater:

> *I lift this Bread*
> *And lift therewith the world, myself and Thee.*
> *Hast thou not said :*
> *'I, lifted up, will draw the Universe to Me' ?*

---

[1] Martindale paid tribute to him in *African Angelus* (1932), 300. 'I once had for friend and professor of apologetics, one of the acutest critics that I have known, Père F. Bouvier, S.J., killed in the war. He might have been called "le petit caporal" with deeper affection than ever was Napoleon. Such humility, such humour, such piety and sympathy, so much erudition and sagacity and wisdom—all of which are perfectly different things—and such *largeness* of soul in his little body.'

## Ordination

*O heavenward Cup!*
*The drops that redden in thy tiny bowl*
*Could swallow up*
*The oceans undulant from pole to utmost pole.*

*O no demur,*
*Weak fingers, to exalt the enormous load.*
*Thou Christopher!*
*Thy God sustainest thee who sustainest God.*[1]

In the last weeks before Martindale's ordination the English Provincial, Fr. Browne, unaccountably wrote to say that since Martindale had been two or three times to London, to the British Museum, in order to gather material for a pamphlet on the Virgin Birth,[2] he had not spent the decreed time in the theologate, and that his ordination would therefore have to be postponed. The French Fathers considered this absurd and protested to the General of the Society, who, of course, upheld them. Martindale was not well, and the shock to his nerves was considerable. He went on with his preparation for the priesthood in a stunned condition, assisted greatly by the retreat given by Père de Grandmaison, who was serene and powerful and nursed him through to the ceremony itself.

During it he was torn between the finality of the priesthood and the will to receive it. He kept on saying 'I intend to be ordained', so that retrospectively he could have no doubts. The next day he offered his first Mass at the convent of the Holy Child, Mayfield. Daily for many years he had read through the words of the Mass; they were so familiar to him now that it did not seem like a first Mass at all.

Undoubtedly he was happy with the French Jesuits. 'Had France,' he once wrote, 'given me nothing but the friendship of these men of my own age, and of those older men, so kindly, wise, humorous and spiritual, my debt would have been past reckoning.' It was his last meeting with de Bélinay, who later was to create the great French

---

[1] Cf. *Charles Dominic Plater*, 99. Here the verses appear under the pseudonym, J. Harvey. In the notebook they are dated June 1911.
[2] *The Virgin Birth and the Gospel of the Infancy* (C.T.S. 1911, republished 1951).

mission of Lake Tchad, and whose last years (he died in 1958) were clouded with ill-health which prevented him from returning to it.

Nevertheless, Ore Place did not suit him, and he was sent to complete his theology at the house of the Irish Jesuits, Milltown Park, Dublin. He had been there only a short time when he became aware that those he found easiest to get on with were the Irish-Australians. Most of the others were openly anti-English. The Rector, Fr. A. Power, a fussy, suspicious man, but good at heart, assumed that a young very English priest would be at odds with the Irish or at least stand aloof from them. After Martindale had served his turn as chaplain to the Hospital of the Incurables, Power remarked, 'I am amazed that you seem to be liked there: that you, as an Englishman, can have any sympathy with them.' Actually, his work there showed him how he could win the lasting affection of simple and unsophisticated people. It was his first experience of priestly work and he was able to test his behaviour when confronted with the worst kinds of lupus and cancer. Many years later Fr. Power, then Rector of the Newman College in Melbourne University, apologised to him generously. 'I must have made you suffer a lot at Milltown. I have learnt a lot since,' he said to him.

Of the other professors, who had attained some distinction as theologians, Martindale could remember only Fr. Finlay, seemingly to him a rather clever man, and Fr. Taafe, who was very adulatory towards him and mildly sarcastic about others. The older Fathers in the house appealed to him in their old-fashioned way: they struck him as cultured, courteous, gentlemanly. The diocesan priests who took over the place once a month for their alleged days of recollection shocked him profoundly, with their glossy top-hats, fine, velvet-collared overcoats and slim umbrellas with gold rings. Wherever he went in Ireland he found them travelling first class. He was disheartened by their frequent greeting: 'Oh, you are English, Father. I hope you have not arrived too prejudiced against Ireland.'

Martindale was ready now to make friends, but the Irish only accentuated his extreme shyness. He discussed his problem with Fr. Fagan, the Spiritual Father, who had complained, 'Sometimes, when members of the community speak to you, you smile after a while and turn away.' When Martindale pointed out that he was often so tired that he could think of nothing to say, Fagan answered not very helpfully, 'Imagine an Irishman not saying anything because he had nothing to say!'

The rough food, the shabby house, the strange hours of meals and the nationalistic temper of the younger Irish brought on strain and ill-health. But his pessimism had lifted. With his daily Mass he had no need to write moody verses: the last in his notebook are dated the November following his ordination. He was glad to be sent back to St. Beuno's to prepare for his final exams.

4

St. Beuno's was his real home, but from the point of view of his health, his return had been delayed too long. He became almost too weak to walk. Feeling faint one day in his room, he went out for help, collapsed in the corridor and crawled back on all fours. Then he got shingles, starting on his left eyelid and ascending in a half circle over his head. He found it impossible to sleep. Finally he was afflicted with headaches and constant sickness, as bad as anything he had suffered since the novitiate. Unofficially but very kindly the professors told him that if he stood for his exams immediately, before he was scheduled for them, he need have no anxiety about passing. The Rector, Fr. Townsend, approved, but again the Provincial, Fr. Browne, intervened on behalf of legality. He suggested that Fr. Martindale should come to London for a week-end holiday, return and stay the last six weeks of the course. When the Provincial met Martindale, he sent him in alarm to two specialists, who advised an immediate rest for at least six weeks.

Without returning to St. Beuno's, Martindale was sent to the Nook nursing home in Hampstead. He felt immediately that this was what he required; the nursing was discreet, the decoration of the house in good taste, the food palatable, and he was left alone. In his first months as a priest, he had felt pushed around too much, and he was beginning to lose heart. But he treasured a letter from the Dublin hospital: 'The "Incurables" in Dublin,' he told a friend, 'have all met in the biggest ward and forwarded to me, through a rabid Nationalist, a unanimous and affectionate note of sympathy in my illness and incarceration. Now that, Sir, is a thing that makes me frightfully happy and content. To be remembered, to be liked, and to have gratitude, in spite of the useless tyke one feels oneself to be.'

His mind was still feverishly active. During the next six weeks he wrote the study of St. Aloysius that later appeared in *Christ's Cadets*. From Aloysius he was led on, first, to Stanislaus Kostka and John Berchmans; then, later, to *Captains of Christ* and *Commanders-in-Chief*. This new-style hagiography was certainly his first and perhaps among his greatest services to the Catholic Church in England. He revered the saints before he loved them, and was anxious to present them shorn of the untruths in which they had been clad for edification. He was not afraid to relegate to minor significance the miraculous events around which their lives had been constructed. When the first volume appeared, he wrote to his former pupil at Stonyhurst:

> Delighted that you like *le petit* Stanislaus. I can never realise that he lived to be seventeen. I don't think he developed really. You would laugh how relieved people are to find that persons like Aloysius were not really the prigs they believed them to be . . . I'm delighted that you like the book. The dedication isn't meant to flatter you or anything else of that sort, though I am charmed that it has 'a swank value in this life and a passport value for the next,' so to say. But I gave you the book because there is no pleasure in life like giving things to people one is fond of.

Either at the Nook or while he was waiting to enter it, he was interviewed by two, if not three, hypnotists (this was in the days before psychoanalysis). One of them was specially deputed to make him sleep; all agreed that he was a rare case of an 'unhypnotizable person'. Jointly and separately they hinted at a total mental breakdown, and advised him to leave the Society immediately. One, more wise than the rest, added, 'It is no good telling you to leave, because you would be back again the next day.' His friend, Lord Braye, wrote to his father, counselling the same course, and also to the Provincial. Nothing came of his letters.

From the Nook, Martindale went to Lord Braye's house near Windsor to convalesce. In a long wing which had been added to his Queen Anne house, there was a chapel, built in perfect taste. With Lord Braye was his daughter-in-law, Mrs. Verny-Cave. Although Martindale was well cared for, he found Lord Braye intolerant and extreme both in his views and conduct. He soon relapsed, then went for a time to live with the Davies-Cookes at Lady Delaware's house, Inchmery, on the Solent.

Mrs. Davies-Cooke was a remote connection of his, a cousin of his cousin Laura. Gradually she and her daughter Beatrice, then about forty, developed a great affection for him, as he did for them. Also at Inchmery was her son Aubrey, a very sick man after his service in the Boer War with the 10th Hussars.

It was now, rather more than a year after his ordination, that Martindale took his part in the first of countless Catholic enterprises he was later to inspire, guide or encourage. During his stay, Beatrice Davies-Cooke acquired a farmhouse together with a large thatched barn, with carved beams, at Hartley, near Dartford, in a part of Kent remote from any Catholic church. An early chest altar and pre-Reformation vestments were acquired, then a medieval statue of the Madonna; finally, cottages and schools were built and a Catholic centre established. After Beatrice Davies-Cooke had adapted the farmhouse, Martindale often stayed there. Later, after her death, the whole settlement was handed over to the Carmelites. This was the real origin of the return of the Friars to Kent, and indeed of the great development of their work at Aylesford, which was founded from Hartley.[1]

Later in his stay at Inchmery George Maude and Mr. D. J. Walker visited the house. Martindale knew Walker slightly and had contributed articles to *The British Review*, which Walker edited and financed. Maude, an ex-parson, was a stranger to him. The two friends had planned a visit to Algeria and invited Martindale to join them. His doctors advised against the trip, but Martindale protested

[1] Hartley is now the Residence of the Prior Provincial of the Carmelites.

that he would prefer to die under a warm sun and blue sky than sit on a lawn by the Solent eating Sanatogen. In the end he gained his point. At D. J. Walker's house in London, while preparing for the trip, he met the two Chesterton brothers; they were both equally scorned by the intelligentsia for their definite views; Martindale judged that Cecil had the finer intelligence or, at least, seemed quicker than G.K. at reaching conclusions.

Walker, Maude and Martindale were joined by David Kelly, who mentions their holiday in his Autobiography.[1] For Martindale it was his first direct experience of so much that he had imagined. The beginning was untoward because he did not greatly care for Maude. He found him a very 'classy' and unhappy man, but later he became more reconciled to him. In a chauffeur-driven scarlet Mercedes they went via Dieppe, Rouen, Chartres and Orléans to Brionde. At Chartres he made a fine sketch of the cathedral.[2] Not until he reached Brionde did he feel he was in the heart of an undiscovered part of France, but he was whirled along too rapidly to assimilate details until he came down into Le-Puy-en-Velay. Here the landscape was too glorious for him not to be affected. Many of his impressions he worked into his short study of St. John Francis Regis[3]—the red earth, the brilliant green plain, ringed by black and purple volcanic mountains, and the fantastic formations of the rock, their jets, cones and cubes, on which the old town, known to Francis Regis, was built, the houses fastened like barnacles to the cliff face. Then over the mountains to Provence, and the scents, flowers and sky associated with his noviceship. At Nîmes he went to a bullfight at which he was irritated by the faked enthusiasm of Walker who threw his hat into the arena, and then wished he had not. At Marseilles they were held up by a dock-strike.

He judged that Sir David Kelly had exaggerated his reminiscences of their expeditions into the underworld. In a letter, sent to a former Stonyhurst pupil after his return he wrote:

Following my instructions to make the change as complete as

[1] Sir David Kelly, *The Ruling Few* (Hollis and Carter, 1952).
[2] Cf. illustration, p. 148.
[3] *Captains of Christ* (Burns, Oates, 1917), 99 sq.

possible, I was attired in pale grey flannels, a straw hat on one
side, a classy soft collar, an unutterable tie (I confess it was black),
and a most natty motoring coat. I had to shepherd this youth
(G.M.) through scenes more lurid than any I have been in for a
long time. There was indeed one scene which I can't even convey
to you in writing, though I'd tell it with such dramatic effect.
Suffice to say I rescued him from their claws just as he was about
to succumb (he is a blond youth) to the ecstatic remark, *Voyez-
moi ce teint, ces cheveux dorés, ces sourcils.* We left the 'bar' very
virtuous men (this was at Marseilles). However, I had better be
honest and say that I don't think a priest, even in pale grey, etc.,
dare remove his landmarks too far. One gets into false positions
easily.

At Algiers Maude became sick and returned to Europe. The rest
of the party continued to Bougie, then inland across the Atlas range
to Biskra, on the edge of the Sahara. Here (he wrote in the same
letter):

> I felt better than anywhere . . . I went for a long camel ride and
> spent the evenings in horrible cafés drinking delicious coffee and
> listening to drum and hautboy music (monotonous but very
> exciting) and watching extraordinary Sahara girls dancing (heavily
> caparisoned, please observe) in thick dresses and a chain armour
> of coins, etc.

Then back through Batna, Constantine, Tunis, Palermo, Rome,
Munich, and Nüremburg. The journey provided him with much
material for a number of stories which eventually formed *The
Waters of Twilight.* Later he maintained that the Dolly of these
chapters stood for the perfect non-intellectualised man he would
have liked to be, and the 'I' largely himself as he believed he then
was: a tormented person, suffering the conflicts of an artist puzzled
by the struggle in himself between faith and reason, between good
and bad behaviour, ultimately on the side of the angels but at great
cost to himself. There are fewer affectations in these stories than in
the earlier group, no tracts of erudition or learning drawn from

books. Many of the conversations are textual. The description of El
Kantara is exact in all its detail; Ain Saf is Biskra; the Moorish café,
the girls, the prayer, the suffocating night are just as he remembered
them. The Old Testament meditation on St. John the Baptist
occurred as it is written. At the head of the second chapter there
was a quatrain which some condemned as pantheistic:

> *Fear not! Love's fire burns only in My Name*
> *Who am the Hearth, the Fuel and the Flame.*
> *I am the Source, the River and the Sea;*
> *Needs must thy cup be Mine, and given to Me.*

The chapter 'Two and Two Make Five' does not belong to this
journey. It opens with an idealised portrait of Charles and Christopher Vaughan, whom he met with their grandmother, the Duchess
of Newcastle, before he started for North Africa. The last part, with
its quotation from Hopkins' *Windhover*, gives the key to his own state
of mind: the first person is now seeking the proper place for reason
in matters of faith. When his friend Robert Monteith read his
description of the Vatican[1] he wrote in alarm to Martindale, saying
that he would certainly be misunderstood and that he was already
badly enough suspected of modernism without writing 'parables'
that could be taken two ways.

However, the Algiers trip worked out of him any melancholia that
remained after his ordination. On his return he was examined by
his doctor, and wrote:

> He [my doctor] would not consent to give me any advice unless
> I would consent to leave the Society. I said I couldn't possibly.
> He said I wouldn't last long if I didn't. I said I wasn't keen on
> lasting. He said I ought to be, to do things for the Church which
> did things for me. So at last he gave in and insisted that at least
> I must give up all idea of work, mental and physical. I am told
> that he gives me ten years as things are. Of course doctors talk a
> lot of rot and probably things will be much better than that; but it
> means the sacrifice of a lot of dreams and ambitions, of course,

[1] pp. 135 sq.

not that that matters much really. If you want to know what cheers me up especially, it's what you said in your last letter about feeling 'bucked up' by me and so on. Well, if that's really so, it more than compensates for the rest. It's a human sort of thing, and, after all, books and reputations and all that sort of thing are rather humbug . . . I shall consider life a success if I've made some friends who value the fact of friendship as I do.

This was written on 8 October 1912. The Provincial, on the doctor's orders, assigned him no work for the next twelve months. He stayed again with friends, with Lord Braye, the Vaughans, Lord Denbigh, the Lovats, and others. Occasionally he was at Farm Street. He corrected proofs of his books, continued his studies on the young Jesuit saints, wrote some reviews for *The Month* and other journals, and completed a few more stories that he included later in *The Goddess of Ghosts*. In the early summer of 1913 he gave a lecture at Oxford and five at Cambridge; he spoke also to the boys at Eton. He was still very weak. 'I seem to get along all right with my own species,' he told his friend, 'and, in fact, to meet quite a lot of interesting people. It is curious how a fact like that does not alter one's subjective impression of uselessness and loneliness one atom . . . I go to a quaint specialist who tries to send me to sleep by crooning little sermons to me and nearly does. But it doesn't last.'

In August 1913 the Provincial proposed that he should return to Stonyhurst. 'But what to do there I've no idea. The main point is that the antique padres in this house [Farm Street] think me a fast, impertinent young man, incapable of taking care of myself and making an undesirable number and sort of acquaintances. If it wasn't for them (I mean, the outside acquaintances) I would be as lonely as you or more so. As for my soul, well, remember the poor rickety thing in your orisons.'

In the ten months since his return from Algiers he had discovered that he was liked by others and had formed a circle of friends which was to expand continuously. Among his brethren he was still almost psychopathic in his shyness.

# 7

## *The First War*

At Stonyhurst, Martindale was given a scholarship class in the school and was appointed at the same time assistant to Fr. Roy Steuart, the Prefect of Philosophers, a rather grand title given to young men, many of them foreigners, who, on leaving Catholic schools in England or abroad, followed a course of higher studies as a substitute or preparation for the university.

It was now that he formed a lifelong friendship with Fr. Steuart. From their first meeting he respected him greatly. 'I could not but admire,' he wrote in his memoir of Fr. Steuart, 'the lightness and the firmness of his touch with these young men who were well aware that they were no longer schoolboys but not so very clear as to the frontiers of discipline and emancipation. His inherited and acquired culture made him able to ask not too much and not too little.'[1] Fr. Steuart was also Martindale's immediate Superior and treated him with the same deft touch.

Martindale was now more self-possessed and knew better what to expect from boys and young men. Most of them, of course, were to be killed in the war, though some, like the Trappes-Lomax brothers, survived and remained his friends for life. In the school he discovered quickly that the standard of studies had greatly improved; he found also that the boys were anxious to learn. Moreover, during his year at Milltown Park, in preparation for a return to the schoolroom, he had reflected a great deal on the responsibilities of a master.

> Well, real *education* [he had written from Dublin] is the most fascinating and terrible and intimate and eternal thing . . . fancy having one's fingers at work moulding the very essence of another's

[1] C. C. Martindale, *The Two Voices* (Burns, Oates, 1952), 45.

life—his soul, his character, his outlook, his judgements, choices, self-appreciation, hopes. For education is nothing less ... One realises it in proportion as one manipulates dexterously or awry the evolving, living germ-soul. One can evolve one bit at the expense of another; one can starve one part owing to one's private fads; selfishness, jealousy, laziness, conceit in one's self, all drives me, inevitably almost, into twisting and distorting and suppressing and irritating the poor little soul entrusted to me. 'Horrid, austere, discouraging Thing,' you very properly are saying at me. But don't. Because provided one approaches these souls to be educated with, O, infinite respect, affection, slow study, self-distrust and, more than all else, prayer (because left to oneself, one will remain a clumsy, meddlesome mischief-maker to the end of one's days), well, provided all that, to *educate* is the very greatest work a man or woman can possibly undertake. It means causing souls to live with more life—you supply them with a greater vital power of assimilating truth—that is, of getting into touch with and absorbing reality; you lead them to have a wider world-life instead of their narrowed and inward-looking and hence *false* self-life. But alack! How true must be one's own interpretation of life and the world and God to enable one to dare to offer it to another.

His correspondent was about to begin educational work: this was his guidance to her. He excused 'so portentous a letter' on the ground that hers had 'flicked awake' an interest which was rarely dormant in him. Several times in later letters he returned to the same subject. His own day-to-day routine at Stonyhurst never appeared to him drudgery. Each moment of the day had fresh interests unlike what had gone before. All the time he saw himself brought into contact with 'the quivering, innermost soul-to-be-educated; with its raw wounds, sometimes, to be touched, or its exquisite beauties to be wondered at; and, in both cases, God to be invoked and thanked.' He described his day:

6 a.m. I rise on a gratified world; 6.45 I hear boys' confessions daily till 7.15: sometimes they make me laugh and sometimes sigh

and always increase my affection for the adolescent human animal
with its queer sprouting soul . . . At 7.15 I help to distribute Communion which now lasts long. 7.30 Mass. 10 till 11 Latin to a
younger Chichester-Constable, a huge Australian and a convert
from Charterhouse. 11.15 to 12.15 Greek to a scholarship class,
two Philosophers and five boys. All work like niggers with me and
not at all, by compensation, with their other masters. Afternoon
empty: I write reviews, articles, letters and earn money for the
Philosophers' Library. Then for an hour or so a schoolboy comes
for a little private coaching, then a 'Philosopher' for Greek of
sorts. Then amiable conversation and supper. After supper, the
smoking-room or my own.

Philosophers came to his room as they wished, boys when they
had 'difficulties' to discuss with him. At these times, over a surreptitious cigarette with the senior boys and often a teeth-chattering confession, he made many friends. He was sailing in quiet waters. To a
former pupil of his first period at Stonyhurst, he wrote, 'I'm pacific
and demure and out for nothing except all that is most correct . . . It
is, however, true I got on Farm Street's nerves. I do on lots of
people's.'

He owed his happiness at Stonyhurst in large measure to Fr.
Steuart, who did not inquire into his extra-regular activities. Everything was going well for him, and there was something genuine in
the spirit of the 'philosophers' that widened his horizon; he realised
also that he could help them, no matter what their background and
former schooling. He wrote lightheartedly: 'An awful decree is im-
pending over me, forbidding me to ride on the back of a motor bike.
But it's not yet officially promulgated, and I'm lying low.'

He acquired four yards of ribbon about an inch wide. 'I am re-
forming my picture gallery,' he explained, 'and am making one long
line of picture-postcard-size photos with a strip of ribbon along the
top to finish them off neatly.' This gallery, constantly increasing,
travelled with him to Oxford, then to London, survived two wars
and adorned his room at Petworth at the time of his death.

His letters to his half-sister Helen during this year (1913–14) show that he was thinking on serious subjects along the lines he was to develop later both in his sermons and books.

It was now that the teaching of the Fathers on the mystical body of Christ was being re-discovered.

So in the vine. Branch A doesn't borrow from branch B, but one sap pours up and round through the many branches, giving them a vital and organic unity though they're many. In the Greek our Lord's meaning is clear: I am the vine's trunk, you the divergent branches. But the whole of 'being in Christ', which is Christianity, implies that His Spirit or Blood or vitality is in us, and that the total Christ is He plus *us*. He without us is as incomprehensible as we without Him.

Grace he defined in the same letter as 'the knitting-up of the innermost self with the linking Self of Christ.' In the 'stupidest and clumsiest ignoramus' (to take another phrase from the same letter) he found, on these Christian premisses, an ineffable addition to the fulness of his own life.

Moreover it was now that he was learning to know and love his father and, also for the first time, to rediscover his family and explore new and natural human affections. In a letter to his half-sister Helen he expressed his genuine happiness at entertaining his father at Stonyhurst.

Among the 'philosophers' at Stonyhurst were two sons of the Duchess of Bourbon-Parma. She chanced to be on a visit to the College when the news of the Sarajevo assassination came through. Instantly she bought every paper that was to be had in the village. 'Do you think this is the end of a dynasty?' Fr. Steuart asked her. 'It is the end of our world,' she answered. And so it proved to be. It was the end also of the world in which the young Fr. Martindale was discovering his authentic vocation.

2

Immediately on the outbreak of war Martindale offered his services as chaplain. He was disappointed not to be accepted. He philosophised to comfort himself, in a letter written on 30 August 1914:

I have no luck. If only we could meet and talk, I should sing you the praises of being 'useless and ignorant'; provided one wants not to be. The consciously useful and expert person *can* be awful . . . The realest things are spiritual. I constantly feel more 'really and nearly' in touch with people when I simply sit and grin and listen and haven't an idea what to say and probably do say nothing except 'poor old chap' or 'Jove!' Then they give in, hands down. The supreme thing is, not to interfere with the action of God. Sometimes he uses one as his instrument. The thing is, not to wiggle in his hand, nor to lunge out on one's own.

Already, before the opening of the September term, his old pupils were back at the school on leave from Sandhurst. Typically and instantly Martindale noticed that no one, himself apart, seemed to appreciate that they might want to confess after their new experiences. At ten o'clock, when the community retired, he would invite them for a last cigarette in his room. When the moment came, as invariably it did, he would suggest confession. The next morning they received Communion at his Mass. Afterwards he kept in touch with them by letter, purveying both news and advice until they were killed. In a number of cases, for years afterwards, he wrote to their parents. Typical is a letter he wrote to a pupil of his first period at Stonyhurst:

But, dearest and respected Sir, I do beg of you not to marry, in or out of church, a girl who is not your class or, at least, is not absolutely certain to be a lasting help to you. Having watched these things, I do grimly beg of you not to do it, for the sake of your entirely bald and almost toothless Poetry Professor.

I shall shortly send you a photograph of *me*. I have been elected to the *Société Archeologique de France*, and this involves my sending these people a photo of myself in cap, gown, hood, etc. So I went off to Manchester with T. Trappes-Lomax, B. Chichester-Constable, T. Spencer and C. Sellier, whom you must remember as kids at Hodder, but who are now Bloods, dear Sir, the supreme and finished article.

He now began working on more stories later included in *The*

*Goddess of Ghosts* and on his vast biography of Robert Hugh Benson.[1] The two essays, 'The New Narcissus' and 'Unchanging Lakedaimon', were inspired by his experiences at Stonyhurst. He insisted that 'Lakedaimon' was not in the least degree a study of homosexuality as some persons took it to be. He was keenly interested in Spartan education and was now interesting himself in Jesuit education.

He had undertaken *Benson* in January 1915 at the joint suggestion of the family and of Cardinal Bourne. It is not difficult to see in it the close control he had to keep over himself. He did not really like Benson and did not dare to explain how Benson constantly recast his memories and dramatised himself, but he did hint at the extent to which Benson became thoroughly hysterical towards the end of his life and believed that no form of literary composition was beyond his talents. This was his first effort *à longue haleine*; it enters every detail of his subject's life and analyses every book he wrote.

This work took him to Mirfield, Cambridge, Buntingford and Tremains and introduced him to many interesting persons. Of Mrs. Benson, R.H.'s mother, he wrote after a visit, '[She] is, I think, too diplomatic for my taste, and rather too exacting. You *couldn't* play the fool in that house—you may be brilliant and chaff people and make epigrams and be intense, of course; but even serenity there has to be rather like that of an Archangel off duty, so to speak. She is very much the wife of an ecclesiastic and distressingly aware of the *dessous* of Anglican church politics: and while I admire her and enjoy her, my affection would probably always be temperate.'

At Mirfield he found the community stiff. During supper, while they were speaking of their theological course, Martindale tactlessly interjected, 'Benson and others of you keep talking of the number of confessions you manage to hear on missions, but I can't remember your mentioning doing moral theology.'

'Yes,' said one of the Fathers, 'that is rather a gap.'

Martindale pressed: 'When you come across a really puzzling case, what do you do?'

[1] *The Life of Robert Hugh Benson*, 2 vols. (Longmans, 1916).

'We tell the penitent to return in a week,' came the answer, 'and meanwhile we will have talked it over ourselves.'

His distaste for Mirfield may have accounted in part for the lack of warmth he displayed in his first encounter with Ronald Knox, when he went on to visit Lord Halifax. Also he felt suffocated by what he described in a letter as Halifax's 'little court of ex-governesses and clergymen'. He referred at the time to many incidents of this visit, without mentioning Knox by name. The meeting has been described from both sides in Evelyn Waugh's *Ronald Knox*.[1] For interest and record it is worth setting out two other accounts of their exchanges. Much later Fr. Martindale wrote:

> On the last evening, just as we were going into dinner, Ronald Knox and Mr. James appeared. Ronald Knox rushed up and said to me, 'Can I speak to you?' I said 'Later, when I am packing.' They arrived at dinner superb in cassocks and ferraiuolas. He came up: 'I want you to receive me into the Church.' 'Why?' 'Because I don't see that the Church of England has a leg to stand on.' I said, 'Perhaps the Roman Catholic Church hasn't either. That's a mere negative reason of yours.' 'Do you mean to say that you won't receive me, etc.' I said, 'Not till you have some positive reason.' I think this impressed him, and I rather think that after some time I wrote and said that he ought by now to be ready.

Evelyn Waugh takes Knox's version of the conversation from the *Spiritual Aeneid*, which Martindale judged 'fairly accurate'. Knox has also another account, similar in all essentials.

> In those days, if you were a high Anglican with what one used to call Roman difficulties, one of the people you were sent to see was Lord Halifax . . . He was a very wonderful old man, with every sign of holiness about him. He asked me to stay for the week-end at Hickleton, the place where he lived in Yorkshire; and I went there with a friend, another High Church clergyman. It was really impossible not to feel at home; the whole household was such an exact replica of a Catholic household; and I still remember going

[1] pp. 146-7.

down to dinner dressed up in a cassock and ferraiuolo and heaven knows what (I used to like dressing up in those days), and feeling there couldn't be much wrong with a Church in which you could wallow about and enjoy yourself like this. And then I was introduced to the other guest who was staying there, a very thin clergyman with a face that looked like an extremely animated skull; not dressed in a cassock at all, but in a rather seedy frock-coat which didn't fit him too well; and I think I knew in that moment that this was the real thing . . . I went and talked to Fr. Martindale that evening while he was packing up to go somewhere else . . . and he was just sufficiently discouraging to make me feel I was caught.[1]

Martindale enjoyed his stay with Lord Halifax, who gave him the use of his secretary, Miss Grace Wellington, a Catholic, 'because', as Halifax said jokingly, 'he could not trust the Anglicans'. He found Halifax himself 'the dearest old man, as always, full of old courtesies' . . . 'a fascinating talker living in a world of dreams'. His wife was 'quite kind and stately and played the most pathetic out-of-date tunes on a piano'. However, Martindale was distressed to find that the Anglican chaplain, without Halifax's knowledge, administered the sacraments to the Belgian refugees and wounded in the neighbourhood. One day he was taken to Garrowby where, after a picnic lunch on the terrace with 'three delightful grandchildren', he was shown some priests' hiding places. As the housekeeper handed him his coat, he remarked, 'They are quite unlike what I imagined such things to be, and they look so new.' 'Of course,' she answered, 'his Lordship had them all put in himself.'

From Yorkshire he went to Cambridge and to Hare Street, Benson's house, which was now Cardinal Bourne's country residence:

The house was like a stage *set* for R.H.B.; and not only was the actor, who alone justified the scenery, not there, but the incongruous Cardinal and his secretary were, and I felt a fool all lunch, being not only a guest, but explicitly there to observe, criticise and *write*.

[1] Introduction to an Oxford Conference given in 1936 and printed in *The Month*, May 1959.

Then later:

> Yesterday I tea'd with Thackeray's sole surviving daughter, a
> slender, straight old lady of about 85, I suppose. Her house is also
> one huge reliquary—every picture has its history and that in itself
> is a weariness of the flesh.

The biography gave satisfaction to the family and, surprisingly,
was a financial success.

### 3

Shortly after the outbreak of the war it had become clear that the
Philosophers at Stonyhurst would be disbanded: Catholic boys were
entering the army immediately at the end of their school course.
Early in 1916 the remnants were disbanded and the priest in charge
of them, Fr. Steuart, went to the western front as a chaplain. Martindale was ill at ease living in comparative comfort, and gladly responded to the suggestion of Fr. Plater, Fr. Pope's successor at
Campion Hall, that he should join him at Oxford: Plater promised
Martindale an abundance of work, and arranged the transfer. Martindale insisted always that he had never requested to be sent to
Oxford, but merely showed himself ready and glad to go. Later when
Fr. Henry Keane, Plater's successor, reproached him for trying to
plan his career, Martindale was emphatic that he had never proposed or sought any destination for himself in the Society, except
possibly his return from Ore Place to St. Beuno's, which indeed had
been promised him by the Provincial, should Ore Place not suit him.

Many of Martindale's Jesuit friends believed that his move from
Stonyhurst to Oxford was the making of the priest that they knew
in his middle years; that hitherto he had been a kind of eremetical
scholar, aloof, undemonstrative, uninterested in others; that at
Oxford he discovered himself and his power of winning and retaining
human affection. This is only partially true. Oxford was the occasion
of a further, and, indeed, very rapid development along lines already
well established.

What wartime Oxford did was to give him greater freedom in

displaying the immense affection that inspired his work and accounted for the immeasurable good he did as a priest. His personal
affection for others, as he was already well aware, constituted the
greatest problem of his life as a priest. Since his entry into the
noviceship he had passed his years mainly among his fellow-religious
or, in a small measure, among schoolboys or young men. With boys
he had always to be on his guard against even the appearance of
favouritism, let alone inevitable likes and dislikes. Consequently he
found it difficult to feel affection for any of those he actually taught.
That he liked most of them, neither they nor he doubted, while his
breeding prevented him from betraying any aversions he might have
formed. To all he showed sympathy when they were in difficulties,
and he understood their problems as well as any schoolmaster. Thus,
while they were in the school, the beginnings of affection, on both
their side and his, may have taken root; but it was only later, when
they were at Sandhurst or subalterns, likely to be killed before they
were many months older, and when there was no risk of misunderstanding or misinterpretation, that he gave his affection full rein.
After the war, among those who survived, he gathered many devoted
friends.

In the Society itself he was on easy enough terms with others, and
close to some like de Bélinay, Monteith and Garrold. His active
dislikes, even when they were not suppressed, were never imple-
mented. But, partly owing to his extreme shyness and partly also to
his misunderstanding of Fr. Considine's warning against 'particular
friendships' and his inculcation of 'manly' virtues, it was hard,
indeed almost impossible, for him to feel, still less to exhibit, affection for his fellow Jesuits, no matter how greatly he might admire
individuals among them. When younger members of the Province
and, more rarely, priests older than himself came to him with their
difficulties, he felt instantly humbled by their courage and often
on the verge of affection. But then he was naturally impeded by a
correct, even scrupulous, interpretation of priestly confidences; this
compelled him, after conversation in or out of confession, to act
towards those who had sought his help as though nothing had occurred. Many years after this period he advised a young Jesuit, who

had recently taken his first vows: 'Go easy about "feelings". They are human and no human thing is negligible, because God-made. They have not to guide us: but you do not want a shrivelled heart. We need *fully* to love people, if we want to do them any good. A technical apostolate is perfectly barren.'

At Oxford, now largely converted into a military hospital, the situation was altered. From men of all classes and antecedents he received unfeigned affection, and, for the first time, felt free to return it. Most men he met he was unlikely to see again. He found that he could spontaneously feel affection for them, and at the same time convey it in a hundred different ways. Often he could reach them even without words, gestures or expressions. And this discovery was a new, real and most important element in his life. Only when he went to Australia for the first time ten years later did he realise how enduring were the attachments he then formed. For the first time in his life he was spontaneous almost to the point of being unreflecting. On his visits to the Oxford hospitals he found himself holding men's hands. Never before had he seen so much pain, and it was his way of seeking to transmit part of it from the sufferer to himself. There were some who were shocked, but he knew that when he made this gesture the men felt relief.

Nevertheless he was always on his guard against entering too intimately the lives of others. 'I have the greatest difficulty,' he wrote in a letter early in 1918, 'in preventing the younger officers I take out from making over their whole and quite inmost life and secrets before they or I are really ready for it. I have a terror of taking a *selfish* interest in other people. To be really at the roots of a person's soul ought to be reserved for God unless you're simply pushed into it by Him. Yet it may happen instantly and yet rightly.'

On his arrival at Oxford he was given work in the Sub-faculty of *Litterae Humaniores*. He lectured on Latin poetry to small groups in Colleges that were willing to lend him a room. He also did some private tutoring. But as his work for soldiers became more absorbing, these lectures became steadily fewer and in the latter part of the war he gave none at all. They did, however, invest him with a university status which he found useful.

From the outset wartime Oxford provided him with exceptional opportunities for apostolic work which, he was quick to appreciate, would pass with the return of peace. As he himself wrote, 'never before, perhaps, had men been available in such large groups so easily; never, it was to be shown, were their minds so susceptible to influences good or bad; never were the ultimate issues of life so forced upon the attention of the dullest, the most frivolous, the most preoccupied; never were the doubts, desires, spiritual hungers, questings, loneliness of men's souls to admit such intimate approach and sympathy.'[1]

Plater was the first to understand this, and Martindale quickly learnt from him. Martindale himself acknowledges it:

[Plater] not only gave his best and his inmost to the men themselves, but his heart positively bled if he thought he saw that here or there their needs were unrecognised, and invaluable chances, never to recur, were being neglected. It was agony to him to hear of hospitals unvisited, camps unchaplained, souls unshepherded. Often enough I would deliberately refrain from telling him of the distressing instances of this . . . lest he should at once seek to add another field to his labour, or, if clearly he could not help, pass nights of desperate insomnia during which his imagination would present to him the work he could not fling himself upon.

This was the priest under whose inspiration Martindale was put to work. First Plater asked him to visit the wounded Catholic officers in Somerville College. Luckily he hit on two who were good Catholics and, through them, got to know the others whom he used to wheel about in spinal carriages. Then he was directed to the other hospitals—the Town Hall, the Examination Schools and Headington, the Workhouse up the Cowley Road. Everywhere he found that Catholics did not know one another. Only when he announced in each building that he was coming to say Mass, and got promises from each individual Catholic to attend, did they discover themselves as a body. In the Examination Schools, the surgical section of the

[1] *Charles Dominic Plater*, 216.

hospital organisation, he sometimes feared he would disgrace himself. He never forgot his experience there when a young soldier, with his leg amputated above the knee, was about to have the stump dressed. As Martindale was passing, the soldier asked him to hold his hand. He did, and had the illusion that time, instead of being over in a flash, appeared to lengthen itself. But Martindale did not faint.

Some of his experiences here and in the Workhouse Hospital, where the cadets came to Mass, he incorporated into his instructional book, *Jock, Jack and the Corporal*;[1] other incidents were used in *Mr. Francis Newnes*,[2] particularly in the last chapter; most, however, went unrecorded.

Once, as he was returning from the military hospital at Cowley, he met a Catholic patient walking dolefully home. The man explained that he had gone into the Cowley Fathers' church, thinking from the Calvary outside that it must be Catholic. There was a number of people waiting for confession and they made way for him. When absolution was given, it sounded strange in the soldier's ears. He asked his confessor, 'Excuse me, are you a Catholic priest?' 'Certainly.' Still uncomfortable, he asked again, 'Do you believe in the Pope?' 'Oh well,' came the answer, 'I see you belong to the Roman branch of the Catholic Church, but we all are truly one.' The soldier, emerging from the confessional, called out at the top of his voice, 'What the hell do you mean by making me go to confession when you are no more a priest than I am?' He was distressed because he would have to make his confession over again. Martindale assured him he could guess what he would have to say and dealt with him in the street. The soldier had never been so happy and amused.

This story Martindale felt free to tell because the man, on his return to Cowley, ran round and narrated his experience to all his Australian friends in the hospital, and in this way brought many of them to the sacraments.

Martindale's reputation soared. He felt now that he was the kind of priest he had always wanted to be, loved by simple people and of service to them, understanding yet not condoning their sins.

[1] Burns, Oates, 1920.    [2] Burns, Oates, 1921.

In letters to a friend in Canada he described further incidents, tragic, amusing and pathetic:

One yarn pleased me because it was so unconscious on both sides. A friend of mine who smokes only Turkish, obtained from a tobacconist called Hoare, was offered a cigarette by another man. The latter said, 'Have a virgin?' My friend placidly answered: 'No, thanks, I always stick to Hoare's.' I was the first to see it and disgraced myself by a loud laugh.

Then, in a letter of April 1917:

My usual studge at Oxford has been mildly diversified by two or three stuntlets and my reputation is finally ruined. I have aeroplaned—only twenty minutes and only 3,220 feet up: still, worth it. I had only one qualm during a nose-dive and none during a spiral dive. I was very smart (take it from me) in khaki without which none may enter the forbidden precincts. I still wore it at night, luckily, since two Canadian R.F.C.s asked me to dinner. I went and had to fight one of them for twenty minutes on his drunken way home. Luckily he thought that someone else was hitting him and developed a fine hate for this innocent soul while he maintained his love for me.

And in the same letter:

At 7.30 one day you might have seen me hop from a taxi into a London flat attired in sandals (one of which came off), blue pyjamas, and a captain's British Warm. Such is the problem. Solution: I had spent the night with a man off the next day for France at 7.40. He kept me up talking till 2.30 a.m. I agreed to breakfast at 6.45 if I might go straight back to bed after it. But after that meal he said, 'Come as far as the lift.' So I came. Then he said, 'Do come to the front door.' So I went and shivered on the pavement. Then, 'Do come to the station.' So I went and, returning, had to effect the above described sheepish exit.

With his hospital work went the hours spent in the Cadets' Club, formed by Fr. Plater in a room in the Turl. His evenings there passed mostly in conversation while the cadets were dancing. Soon enough, however, he would suggest taking the fresh air, first with one man, then with another, and walking along the Turl, would hear their confessions. As this practice became known, a wan smile would greet his proposal but nevertheless the soldiers submitted. He saw a divine intervention on his behalf when two men who remained obdurate were immobilised, one with a broken leg and the other with 'flu, in answer to his prayer that they should come to the sacraments.

It was from men in this Club that he and Plater formed the first group of soldiers that were taken on week-end retreats. For this purpose Plater was given the use of Begbrooke Place, about seven miles out of Oxford. Usually Plater took the wounded and Martindale the cadets; later other groups were organised from among the Fusiliers, who were stationed at Oxford. There was one feature of these week-ends that all the men found most moving. As the Blessed Sacrament was not reserved in the house it was fetched processionally from the near-by Servite Church, all the men reciting the rosary on their way there and singing Eucharistic hymns on their return. That very act, Martindale wrote, 'transformed' the men. It took them in memory right back to their childhood days and knocked down their spiritual defences even before the first conference opened. At the start the number of retreatants was small, but the effect on the men, bewildered at first, enduring.

One incident, a chain of incidents, at a retreat week-end deepened his conviction that he was being used in a deeply mysterious manner for divine ends which he strove not to impede; it was so uncommon even in a priest's life that he long remembered its details. He recounted it for the first time in a letter written eight years after it occurred.

At a dance in the Club he met a drunken cadet, a Catholic, whom he persuaded to make a retreat. On his arrival at Begbrooke Place, the lad protested, 'I am here under false colours. I don't intend to go to the Sacraments. I'm married, I've left my wife and live with another woman whom I don't intend to give up.' Martindale told him to sleep on the question and to see him again in the morning. 'Mind still made up?' Martindale asked him the next day. 'Yes,' he answered nervously, 'but the other way. I will give her up, but I don't know how to, for it will break her heart.'

Martindale assured him that if God had helped him thus far, He would support him to the end. The cadet took Communion. Ten days later Martindale received a letter from a woman, saying that she knew he was familiar with a number of soldiers and might possibly have met a man with whom she was living; she wanted to leave him, but dare not for fear of causing him pain. This was the very woman. Each, independently, found the other ready to do right.

Two weeks before Easter 1925, eight years later, Martindale received a letter from a London priest: there was a man in hospital who said he would have nothing to do with the parish clergy but would see only Father Martindale. He visited him from Oxford. It was the same lad. Martindale confessed him and gave him the last sacraments, then asked a London friend to visit him in hospital. As this lady was about to leave town, she, in turn, asked a friend of hers to go in her place. Out of the entire population of London she hit upon the soldier's ex-mistress. Martindale had no time to stop the meeting. It was appalling, but it sealed the spiritual work begun at Begbrooke. The following Easter Monday night Martindale received a cable in Oxford and was able to reach hospital just as the man, recovering consciousness for a minute, exclaimed, 'The one person in the world I want to see! hurrah!' Then he died.

'I tell *you* this,' Martindale ended his story. 'Otherwise I just keep it to remember with happiness. I hope he prays for me.'

The climax of his Oxford work came with the influenza epidemic of 1917. It was said that Oxford was worse hit than any other town, save possibly Portsmouth. To minimise the funerals and reduce panic in the city, four or more coffins were frequently placed in the same hearse. The strongest among the young men, often Australians, fell the easiest victims; they would be playing Rugby at three in the afternoon, fall sick at five, and die from two in the morning onwards. Strangely Martindale found that he could tell by the scent (his sense of smell was always acute) whether a man had contracted the sickness, and at once would inform the doctors or nurses. Nevertheless, the patients usually died.

After a time, some of the non-Catholic clergy either caught the infection themselves or feared for their families, and consequently Martindale, with other Catholic priests, was left to do what he could for dying men of all creeds. He prayed that he might not catch it till the very end. One Sunday he woke and felt that he had it. He was too weak to walk. There were no taxis available at that hour, yet the Examination Schools were full of men seeking absolution and Communion. It was unthinkable for him to leave them defrauded. He made himself some inky tea with much sugar, said Mass, consecrated the hosts he thought he would need and managed to reach the hospital. He then went into New College Gardens and spent the morning in a tent with six cases. Three died. He sat between two of them, both delirious. If he held his hand to the men's chests, they were quiet; if not, one thought he was playing rugby, the other wrestled. About one o'clock he could endure no more and returned to bed. One of them died, the last victim of the epidemic in Oxford. The fear that others also might die without his ministration haunted his own 'flu dreams.

In his next letter to his friend in Canada he wrote cheerfully: 'The only news is that I have tried to peg out with the 'flu and failed. Everyone at Oxford was dying of it. I simply fed on germs until I went down myself.'

The instruction of cadets continued to the end of the war. 'Many of them,' he told a relative, 'declare that their experience leaves them no choice but to become Catholics. I never mention the subject, or anything like it, till they do.' Then he recommended a book for his father's attention: 'If Daddy cares to, he might get *A Spiritual Aeneid* by R. Knox, the son of the Bishop of Manchester: he is an impossibly brilliant person and his book is very funny. Still, I'd die rather than write an autobiography! But it might amuse Daddy, as I occur up and down it.'

It is difficult to date the exact time he received an offer of work from the War Office. He referred to it only after the end of the war:

Ridiculous as it seems, I can now tell you the War Office offer. We ended, last year, in being able to pick up all the German wireless giving the actual orders in the field (e.g. hour and place and quality of attack and movements of troops, etc.): all in code, of course (quite unsystematic), and a code which changed monthly. Our de-coding staff consisted of three with six subordinates, living at Paris-Plage (if that's right): you had to do the de-coding wholly by intuition as there were no rules and you had to do it *at once*. (The only thing you could start from was numbers, and two or three groups of letters which recurred near the numbers and stood, e.g., for units which you knew.) A naïve War Office decided, as I told you, that I was a fit person to 'intue' the inner meaning of these mysteries and bombarded me to come along and do it. I said (i) I'd do it badly, (ii) I'd need an *overwhelming* sense of duty to make me give up Oxford. *They* said I could have a month's trial in London and could have every week-end in Oxford . . . I was just going to say No, definitely, when our big push began and the German plans all went west.

Then I was to have been sent to America to improve their minds, camouflaged as a Bishop's Secretary (!!!) but over that, as I said, a muddle occurred, probably at this end. Also I could have gone to Spain, to do ditto, on the pretext of representing England (also as some sort of secretary) at the Bi-Centenary of Suarez. But no . . . The only thing I did do (most reluctantly) was to edit those propaganda letters, which (as the F.O., where I called, optimistically assured me a week ago) were very effective, especially in South America, Spain and apparently Holland . . . Here is my bill of offence.

Martindale admitted with his 'usual perversity' that he never felt so sad as he did on Armistice night. He knew the disillusionment, the drabness, the broken homes that awaited returning soldiers. For himself it was farewell, as he thought, to his Australian and overseas friends. In the Oxford hospitals he had discovered his priestly vocation and, in a true sense, himself. Peace time would bring different work for which he judged he was less well fitted; the change was unwelcome.

I am still at Oxford [he wrote shortly after the war] and

gradually overcoming my repulsion for the elegant, sophisticated, analytical, inconclusive young men who gather here. The terrible thing is that the bloody athlete beats them at their own game and has lovelier, more delicate, more spiritual things at the back of his soul, which he is too shy to look at, than they have ... The Exquisite is always going in for a sort of spiritual self-abuse. Sorry, but so it is. When the athlete plays rugger, he is somehow in love with God. When I say 'athlete' I mean also clerk, policeman, navvy, taxi-driver, porter, sailor. But it survives middle age, the period of sins against the spirit, with difficulty. So, for God's sake, remain kiddish. Really, I'm rather clumsily quoting Christ, now that I come to think of it.

Until the summer of 1919 the Oxford hospitals were still full. Martindale was also lecturing twice a week on Roman poetry: 'There's no book on the subject,' he wrote, 'and I have to make it all original.' He did this conscientiously, but without enthusiasm.

He believed that he had been faced with no deliberate choice between the life of scholarship and that of a people's priest. It had been made for him by the course his life had hitherto taken.

# 8

# Aftermath of War

From 1918 until 1925, when he was transferred from Oxford to London, Fr. Martindale's life ran, for the most part, smoothly. It was made up mainly of writing, some university work, frequent retreats to working-class men and the inter-university Catholic movement. In this period also fell the 'Aloysian' year, several expeditions overseas and the Marlborough divorce case in which he was concerned. After leaving Oxford there was little change in the character of his activity, except that in general it was more broadly national; the expeditions took him farther afield and some fresh interests added to the old which were never abandoned.

During this later Oxford period it is easy to trace a plan behind all his writing. In his war-time excursions from Stonyhurst and Oxford he had found himself instructing many soldiers. To make certain that they remembered what he had said, he used to write a skeleton outline of each lesson on a half-sheet of paper. This was kept, and if lost by the catechumen, it was immediately replaced. The task of preparing these sheets became increasingly exacting so that before the war closed he had them printed, on one side of the page only and on perforated paper. This was the origin of his *Words of Life*, a catechetical pamphlet that has not been superseded to this day. It was intended not as a replacement of the Catechism (he always took his men through that book to satisfy the law), but as a presentation of the fundamental truths of the Catholic faith in an harmonious theological framework. Hence he emphasised all that the ordinary man had forgotten or had never learnt, and all that the Catechism presumed he knew but did not. Stress was put on the supernatural life; grace was explained in terms that anyone could comprehend.

Out of *Words of Life* came *Jock, Jack and the Corporal*, a book
planned to put the pamphlet into conversational form. As he proceeded, the characters got hold of him, especially the Corporal, who
was drawn from life, even to his red forelock. The Australian also
was an exact portrait. The author can be seen growing all the time
in his affection for these men so that he has constantly to force himself back from the story to the instruction. As a piece of catechetics
it was too long; the Cockney argot is dated; but the book, like so
many others he wrote, served its purpose. Often he had it read
during his retreats to working-class men who would cry when Jock
died. Significantly he tried, but failed, to keep the story unsenti-
mental.

With *Jock*, two other books written at this time form a trilogy.
*Mr. Francis Newnes* was intended as a catechism for the Catholic
Social Guild, founded by Fr. Plater. At the beginning is a description of the Octagon which Plater had hired for his social courses.
But Martindale was less interested in social studies than in the
subsequent career of the Corporal who remained unconverted at the
end of *Jock*. He had now started giving retreats to other groups than
soldiers, and this work acted as a hinge for his story. He found himself unintentionally dwelling on the love affair of the principal
character: though the girl's conversation was drawn from her actual
words, she did not come alive. Exaggeration, particularly in his
sketch of Cecil Rougham, a smart, religious youth, tilted over into
vulgarity. The behaviour and thoughts of the characters were, for
the greater part, drawn from his own. An exception was the parson,
who was based mainly on an Oxford ecclesiastic, Canon Streeter.
To a close friend he wrote: 'I warn you that you have to think what
I think about it [*Mr. Francis Newnes*], because in parts it's me in the
raw, and to flick it, is to flick a skinless me.'

The third of the series, *Albert Alfred, P.C.*, began as an attempt to
sketch the character of two policemen of his acquaintance. It is the
weakest of the three, for the plot, such as it is, was inserted late into
the book. The most interesting feature of it is the accuracy with
which he depicted New Zealand before ever visiting the country.
There is manifestly less zest here than in the other two books; he

was sharing in the general disillusionment that followed the armistice.

Much later, but in a similar vein, came *Bill*, which was due to his happy association with Poplar. It marked a renewal of his zest. He always maintained that the stranger the things written by Bill, the more probably they were the actual expressions he used.

Both during the war and, more acutely, after it, he saw the need for yet two other categories of books: first-class works on religious questions, and a second grade, not specialist yet scholarly and able to satisfy the averagely educated and intelligent person. The first, for lack of knowledge and time, he considered himself unable to satisfy, but the second he judged within his reach.

This was the idea that lay behind the series, *Catholic Thought and Thinkers*. He himself wrote the Introduction and the volume on St. Justin; Mr. Maurice Wilkinson contributed a ponderous essay on Erasmus and Miss E. M. Wilmot-Buxton one on Alcuin. The series got no further. He was unable to find collaborators that were both learned and lively; and, moreover, the publishers, Harding and More, assisted in wrecking the scheme by their insistence on specially carved initial letters which forced them to price the books out of the reach of the public for which they were intended.

Many of his own books written in the after-war years carry serial titles that need explanation. *The Household of God* series, for instance, contains two first-class essays, on St. Paul and on St. John. Another group, *Upon God's Holy Hills*, containing essays on Anthony, Bruno and John of the Cross, never had other contributors. It was not that he did not seek them, but he himself was experimenting in a new *genre* of saints' lives, which was to supersede permanently in style the hagiography fathered on the Catholic public by the Oratorians and others in the nineteenth century. He explained his plans and their progress in a letter dated 25 May 1919:

> As for me, my lectures on St. John are being printed in U.S. and will reappear as a small book here. General title of the series, *The Household of God*: sub-titles of groups of volumes, e.g. *Princes of His People* (e.g. St. John—Gospel finished, Apocalypse almost

finished), (St. Paul; perhaps Matthew, Mark and Luke in a lump);
*On God's Holy Hills* (e.g. monks, men-mystics: very likely again
sub-divided thus: *The Guides*, St. Anthony of Egypt, St. Bruno of
Cologne, St. John of the Cross—finished), *In God's Garden* (nun-
and other women mystics), *In God's Army* (three volumes, you
know); and others on students, bishops, beggars, etc. If I live till
eighty and refrain from premature dotage, I may finish about half
of it; as a whole it will represent Catholic spiritual life as a psychological and supernatural continuous fact.

More than half this scheme was, in fact, completed in the next
three or four years.

His work on St. John brought him into a painful controversy with
an American Jesuit, Fr. Drum, a professor at Woodstock College,
Maryland. In an article in the American Paulist monthly, *The
Catholic World*, Martindale had written that there was no reason to
suppose that the fourth gospel was *not* written by St. John, son of
Zebedee. Unfortunately, in the process of printing, the negative was
omitted. Fr. Drum immediately pounced on this. He attacked
Martindale's entire article, and also his book on St. John, although
the omission of the 'not' made nonsense of his whole argument. His
philippics were printed first in *The American Ecclesiastical Review* and
then in its rival journal, *The Homiletic and Pastoral Review*. Drum
loathed the English and the English Church, which had been so unfortunate in its converts: Tyrrell, Benson, and now Martindale. An
inflexible, wild, emigré Irishman, he received, unaccountably, a
hearing in Rome. Martindale remained silent, baffled, unable, save
at the close of the attack, to get an American review to print his
explanation.

About the same time Martindale was denounced to Rome for an
article he wrote on St. Margaret Mary in *The Tablet*.[1] He described
the saint as a melancholic, at least in comparison with St. Gertrude;
and worse, he told the story how, after Margaret Mary had performed a singularly revolting penance, Our Lord rebuked her: *que
tu es folle à faire celà*. On this the Visitation nuns at Harrow, in their

---

[1] 'St. Margaret Mary Alocque', *The Tablet* (1920), 681 sq.

turn, denounced him to Rome for repeating a Protestant calumny. Luckily for him the nuns at Paray-le-Monial had just then published the saint's authentic writings: *'folle'*, not *'bonne'* as the Harrow nuns maintained, was in the original and had been altered to 'bonne' by a copyist who considered the story disedifying.

Nevertheless for a long period, on the instructions of Rome, he was equipped with four censors,[1] even for *minima*. Modernism had always repelled him and he was both distressed and bewildered by the suggestion that his work was tinged with it. But the habits acquired in the noviceship remained with him throughout his religious life and he made no attempt to defend himself. Moreover, he interpreted *minima* to include letters and postcards, which he submitted with maddening frequency to his Superiors. In the end elucidation was sought from Rome, and he was told nothing smaller than a pamphlet came under the Roman instructions. After Fr. Drum's death these restrictions were relaxed.[2]

There were other misunderstandings that led Martindale to be suspected of modernism, but he was unaware of them.

At this time, when any priest who had been at Oxford was watched with suspicion, his own career had been unusual enough to invite criticism from those who did little else than criticise. Certainly he never disguised his own ineptness for scholastic theology. Its insistence on the analogical nature of man's knowledge of God led him to give others the impression that he believed no knowledge of God was possible except that due to His direct gift. The emphasis in his writing was on Christianity, not deism. He certainly maintained that all knowledge of God that really mattered in life came through Christ and that it was in Christ that we are to see God. He was never capable of using his imagination about spiritual things or states, such as heaven or angels or hell. Moreover, he was prepared to suppose that the essence of a vision was purely spiritual and that the recipient supplied all the colouring material. Throughout his books and

---

[1] The Society of Jesus insists on two censors for any work written for publication: a third is customarily appointed for work on certain subjects, e.g. Scripture.

[2] Cf. *Homiletic and Pastoral Review*, vol. 21, 390, 509, 607, 722, 813, 904, 1021, 1124; and vol. 22, 754, 'How to Read the Fourth Gospel. A Rejoinder's to Fr. Drum's criticism'.

articles of this period it can be noticed that he always accepted with greater ease the reality of spirit than of matter. When he wrote of John's visions and, later, of Lourdes or Fatima, it was not in order to debunk a story, but to penetrate as deeply as possible into the core of it. He was struggling always to get away from the emphasis that traditional hagiography put on the abnormal at the expense of truth. What he wrote in appreciation of his friend Fr. Thurston elucidates his standpoint: 'I think he was so zealous for the idea of holiness that he wanted to get rid of all that might have distracted attention from the substance to the occasional concomitants. Thus he seemed almost angry that he could not resist the evidence for St. Joseph of Cupertino's levitations and the liquefactions of San Gennaro's blood.'

In purely theological questions Martindale made no secret of his dislike of arguments *ex convenientia*: as, for instance, that it was *right* that the Mother of God, in consideration of her dignity, should have been conceived immaculate. He held that men were no judges of what God might or might not consider suitable. Would men, he pointed out, have argued, before the event, that our Lord's life and death were suitable for the Son of God made man?

At the same time it must be said that he took pleasure in shocking those he believed were his friends. He would talk lightheartedly and at length on the parallels between Mithraism and Christianity in a way (as he well knew) that far outstripped the evidence. But the commonplaces of today were the scandals of fifty years ago, particularly in the field of Scripture and ecclesiastical history. Always he was irritated by the defensive attitudes adopted by apologists for the Church and their desire to make a case. Few even among his friends understood what was a puzzle even to himself, that the invisible was more close and real to him than the world of sense.

Two larger books belonging to this immediate post-war period engaged him for continuous months: the life of Fr. Plater, who died in Malta shortly after the end of the war, and his Memoir of Fr. Bernard Vaughan.

The former was particularly laborious, although he was assisted by Plater's voluminous diaries. Many fellow-Jesuits who greatly admired Plater resented or criticised the book. Certainly it was unfortunate that he embarked on it immediately after Plater's death, when Plater's moods, resulting from his ill-health, had jarred on his own frayed nerves. It is perhaps more a portrait of a great priest in his days of physical decline than in his achievement. In any case, Martindale had perhaps been too close to him to draw a well-balanced portrait. As his health failed Plater, like Benson, became at times almost hysterical, and started work that was certain to have no issue. When his blood-pressure was high and his life in danger, he was pleasant, gay and voluble; when it was low, he was often glum. In both conditions he made life difficult for those close to him. The biography is perhaps more an analysis of him in this condition than of the man himself. Nevertheless Martindale was always eager to confess that he himself would never have contemplated, let alone begun or persevered in his work for soldiers and miners had it not been for Plater, who pushed him along the grooves that he himself had already made.

*Father Bernard Vaughan* was a Memoir, not a biography. Martindale knew Vaughan only slightly and found him in every way the opposite of himself. His sympathy with him was largely intellectual. While he admired Vaughan's work, he abominated his methods. He himself could never go in for the play-acting that was so much part of Vaughan's repertoire, yet he was able to realise, paradoxically, how sincere this play-acting was. He appreciated also the way Vaughan, until the time of his last illness, was always able to laugh at his own performances.

In spite of their shortcomings, both these books are documents of interest for the historian of Catholicism in England in the early years of the century.

*Father Bernard Vaughan* became an immediate and outstanding success. Martindale wrote:

> If a Memoir of Fr. Bernard Vaughan comes your way in Winnipeg, you ought to glance at it. It went into a second edition in two days and has had the most unanimously good press that could be had. . . . It was rather fun writing an absolutely honest life of B.V., whose preaching I simply could not stand, and to find that

not only the book made people laugh etc., but made them *like* him better than before, and recognise his tremendously high ideals to which he never played false, his humility, and, above all, his simplicity. I assure you that simplicity is a very difficult thing to describe, precisely because it is simple. You can't elaborate it.

On 26 December 1921 he wrote:

The world staggered lately under an upgush of *four* books by me in a fortnight; but I must confess that one was very small and none very large. [The letter was written *as from Campion Hall*, but] in reality drinking tea in bed in London, where I am lying doggo and having a quiet time and not a single show and not a single restaurant—well, there will be *one*, I hope, on Thursday, when I propose to administer a meal and a music hall to a prize-fighter, a Whitechapel tea-shop man and an artificial limb-maker living with his non-wife, though by no means out of wickedness: she and I nursed him through double penumonia, one on either side of his bed. In fact they are all pure gold though slightly crusted and unglistening.

2

During every period of his life his books were written in intervals between other activities.

Most of the retreats he gave in the after-war years were to men. Occasionally he accepted with reluctance, or at least with lack of enthusiasm, an invitation to give a retreat to the ladies at Grayshott. Half these retreatants, he found, were regular attendants. There might sometimes be seven who really needed a retreat, and, among these, three to whom it marked a recovery in their lives. He felt also that he could not talk to women; he was irritated by their frequent tendency to make a relationship 'personal', and he lacked Fr. Steuart's desire to teach high methods of prayer. His own method always was to follow the retreatant, or rather the Holy Spirit in him. Never did he believe that he himself had something special to impart.

The greater number of his retreats for men were given at Birmingham or Swadlincote, and the rougher the individuals who gathered for them, the more at ease he was. His visits, particularly to Swadlincote, were happy, and due in the first instance to Mr. Harold Ward, a young industrialist, enthusiastic, shrewd and inventive, at times wildly idealist, at others blackly despondent. It was through Ward's persistence that the miners were organised for retreats. Martindale was his instrument, irresponsive at first to Ward's effervescence, but later incapable of resisting it.

The work took him at week-ends through Derby and Ashby-de-la-Zouch. From the train he would catch sight of the silhouette of hills where Allestree was. He noticed that a row of poplars had been felled since his last visit for Aunt Sophy's funeral. As he passed he saluted his mother's memory, and asked and re-asked her simple prayers for such an unexpected sort of son. The world he re-pictured in his childhood memories was now twice or three times removed from him.

On his first visit, the irrepressible Ward introduced him to the Ashby fire-brigade, whom he found heroic, loveable, amusing and respectful, as he was told, to the 'representatives of religion'. Photographs were exchanged over supper.

At Swadlincote he stayed usually with Fr. Parmentier, a Belgian priest, audacious, childlike in spirit, imaginative, realist and gifted with an uncommon power of perseverance. Being frail and shy, he was regarded as a kind of mascot by the miners, who took care of him, did all he timidly asked of them, built his church and spent hours of their leisure assisting him.

When in a sentimental mood he first wrote about miners, Martindale described them as massive men; when he met them working underground and unclothed, he was struck by the slightness of their build. They were wiry and hard, of the stuff from which swift and darting footballers were made. On Sundays they dressed smartly, but the comradeship among them was such that a dressy young man did not mind being seen with one who neither wore nor owned a collar.

His sentiments at the time are distilled into a few pages of *Albert Alfred*, but he was never in danger of thinking that the work of miners was the worst in the world. In fact, he readily admitted that he knew only a hundredth part of the men's lives in the sense that Dr. Brett Young did. Indeed, as earlier with soldiers and later with seamen, he felt both 'close' to them and, simultaneously, separated from them by a chasm of experiences. When the men told him, 'You understand us so perfectly', he wondered how much, in fact, he did understand. He did not have to live their life and could only imagine the drudgery of it. But he did share with them a fatalistic attitude to life that, in some measure, made the condition of their work appear natural to him. Thus, when he went down a pit for the first time, he was able to imagine that he had been down pits all his life. It was the same in Kent, Co. Durham, Kimberley and Johannesburg. Often he confessed he was frightened.

There was no doubt about his love for miners themselves. He found them immediately and easily likeable men, with no reason for erecting any barriers of pretence. He was compelled also to admire their generosity. Later, in Co. Durham, in an allegedly 'red' district that was no more than pink, he found the cold intense during a coal strike and slept in his clothes in the unheated presbyteries. Nevertheless, the people would bring their priests pieces of coal wrapped in brown paper. The priests would keep them until they had enough for a fire, and then take them to some family where hardships were more acute.

One Sunday at Swadlincote he saw a man he did not know and who, by exception, was robust-looking. He was no miner at all, but an ex-marine who supported his mother by handing round his cap after fighting the men as they emerged from the pit. Martindale invited him to luncheon; then afterwards sitting with him on a heap of bricks, he pressed him with a series of questions. The prizefighter had said his own occupation was not a man's job.

'What is man?' Martindale asked.

'A creature.'

'No, everything is a creature of God.'

'Well, a creature what appreciates beauty.'

'What is beauty?'

In answer the man plucked a piece of rank grass:

'There's some that call this a mere weed, but I say it's beautiful.'

Pressed to explain, he went on, scowling with the effort to express himself:

'You look at this stalk, so thin and weak, and this great thick head on the end of him. You'd expect him to double up under that. And yet he doesn't.' He took delight in the delicacy of the stem, then continued: 'Well, it ain't a stalk. It's a hundred little threads all separate yet all joining together to make this what you might call a stalk.' He paused, adding triumphantly, 'All separate—and in between, it shines.'

The man had touched on something that took Martindale back to his early experiences at Manresa House. Here was a poet and philosopher talking of the one and the many, individuality and the whole, the mysterious shining forth of the being 'that made it to be what it was'. Often the man wrote him letters which cost him much effort and witnessed to the affection he had for him. There was always a sentence or two that made them worth reading. Martindale never broached with him the topic of the Catholic faith; he visited him when he was ill and helped him to pray when he was dying.

The priest who succeeded Fr. Parmentier discontinued the retreats at Swadlincote; the Bishop of Nottingham, Dr. Dunn, did not see why the practice should become normal. After two years, therefore, Martindale ceased to go there regularly. He had been greatly impressed by what he always described as the 'innocence' of miners. It was the same epithet he applied later, in a different context, to seamen, and this innocence, paradoxically, was noticeable even when they were ill behaved. A large number seemed never to commit any grave sin at all, others put up a genuine fight; most succeeded, some were desperate at their own weakness. But there was very little malice or planned wrongdoing among them; no blackmail, doing a man down to get his job, long-drawn-out seductions, cruelty to children or boys. It was these virtues, perhaps negative, that attracted him, and he found them all the more striking because they existed in such surroundings. Their lives were hard, their towns hideous, their Sundays grim. Sexual Reformers were then beginning to teach 'safe' methods, primarily to girls, and this gave them their only opportunity to escape with trivial expense from the universal squalor.

147

At the same time Martindale understood how these men frequently deteriorated when they got power.

He admired the girls and women belonging to the miners' families, but others in the district disheartened him, particularly young girls who were more imitative of cinema fashions than were the boys. He wrote: 'They can retain extraordinary skill and self-consciousness during amorous passages, even while letting themselves float on a flood of sentimentalism. I don't believe a young man knows how to do this; anyhow he doesn't. He may be a nasty young cynic, very well aware of what he is up to, or he may go romantic and have the blood in his head.'

It was at this period, understandably, that Martindale became interested in psychology, but he avoided the danger of regarding miners and other working-class men as cases. He always considered it something close to sacrilege to manifest curiosity over the souls or the characters of others, and to imagine that he could heal anybody. Some of these men's oddities, he soon discovered, had a sexual basis. He was often confronted with adult homosexuality. He was aware also that his own nervousness with women led some to say that he confined himself too strictly to men's society.

His small and most successful book, *The Difficult Commandment*, later translated into almost every language, developed from a conference he gave to miners. He had sent it privately to a friend for censorship to assure himself he had made no errors; not only did the censor approve but he urged him to print it. Martindale protested that he did not want his name associated with sex-books, but he eventually agreed to have it published anonymously. When it was generally recognised as his work, he put his initials, then finally his name, to later editions. It was his positive approach to the problem of sex that made the book so deservedly popular. He was perhaps the first priest in England to denounce in print as execrable the dogma that an ingrained habit must necessarily have begun guiltily.

Two early drawings by Cyril Martindale.

A retreat group *c.* 1917. *Seated centre*, C. C. Martindale; *seated left*, Fr. Charles Plater; *standing, third from left*, Fr. M. C. D'Arcy.

At Broadcasting House, 1935.

3

In retreat work Martindale followed Plater's lead; his inter-university work, which later produced the University Catholic Federation, was due exclusively to his own initiative.

Even before the end of the war it was obvious that the universities would be fuller than they had been hitherto, and that all would have a fair percentage of Catholics. After Catholic societies had been formed in the universities, it was Martindale's plan to federate them in order to produce a stronger Catholic corporate opinion and sentiment. Oxford gave a chilly welcome to the scheme; Cambridge, under its chaplain, Dom Bede Camm, was openly hostile, but a staunch supporter was found in Professor Bullough, a man 'fastidiously cultured, yet fiery, far in consequence from being always understood, no less intolerant than elegantly courteous, able to cope better with active men of half a dozen nationalities than with even one lethargic Englishman.'

In the younger universities the response was more generous.

At the start, local activities of the Federation fluctuated but Martindale managed to visit each group once a year, and inspired the foundation of an inter-university Catholic magazine. It started as a one-man job in 1919 and gave publicity to the movement. 'Space is so limited,' he wrote soon after its inauguration, 'that one must cut out padding and merely laudatory epithets. Manchester, which laments its cuts, has had lectures from G.K.C., R. Knox and Shane Leslie, and no one has a notion what they were about. If instead of saying "Fr. R.K. delighted us" in four keys, they would put, "Fr. K. said there were eight assassins among the British bishops", that would be worth hearing . . . I find that St. Thomas did physical jerks and exulted in feats of strength. Some patron.'

Eventually the magazine expired: it could not be made sufficiently interesting or useful to get undergraduates to buy it. On the whole the Bishops of the day were uninterested in the work, indeed even in university education. They appeared less concerned in producing better-educated Catholics than in saving the students from the dangers of university life. However Martindale found most loyal lieutenants among the laity. A large part of the organising work was done by Professor Hugh O'Neill, of Manchester University.

The association survived, and later formed links with university groups in other countries. But the impulse for this international university movement, later called the *Pax Romana*, came originally from abroad.

In connection with this work Martindale made an extensive visit to the Continent in 1923. In August he lectured at Mürren, then at Interlaken before going to the Eucharistic Congress at Zagreb; thence he continued to Budapest and returned via Innsbruck and Ljubjana.

It was his first foreign excursion as a priest. The state of the Church in these countries depressed him as much as it had done before the war. In Zagreb a young Jesuit remarked to him: 'We have never taught the people anything: we have relied on their immemorial devotion.' At Felsögöd his Hungarian friend, Colonel Bozoky, was building a church: Martindale had helped by raising funds in England. This was shortly after the Bela Kun revolution. The country was impoverished, the food uneatable, but the church was built and three stained-glass windows inserted. In the rose window he and the Colonel were commemorated.

In the next year he visited Hungary again, for a *Pax Romana* Congress at Budapest, and on his way he took in Berlin, Warsaw, and Czestochowa. These travels, and a third visit to Budapest, were described in a series of articles.[1]

In so far as the Congresses took him out of England to places of beauty, he enjoyed them; but usually he returned depressed. Both politicians and clergy wanted a return to the past which was irretrievably lost. Priests lamented the severance of Church from State and the loss of their own grandeur. There had been little change of heart, and the gulf between the great abbots and the parish clergy appeared to him infathomable. Back in England he was dismayed by the almost total lack of Catholic interest in the condition of the Continental Church.

[1] *The Month*, vol. 142 (1923), 497–504; vol. 143 (1924), 35–41; vol. 144 (1924), 308–18; 428–37; vol. 145 (1925), 38–46.

Not long afterwards Martindale ceased to be active in the *Pax Romana* movement, partly perforce, because he could not undertake all the travel it involved; partly by choice, because he recognised, as he said, that almost anyone could organise better than himself. Yet while he was associated with it, the English branch, under his inspiration, undertook much charitable work, particularly the relief of students in distressed countries.

Meanwhile, John Eppstein, who was striving to inaugurate the Catholic Council for International Understanding, sought Martindale's help. Unfortunately Eppstein had a mania for theoretical planning: endless divisions and sub-divisions were formed before the organisation barely existed.[1] Martindale began to have doubts about the effectiveness of the work. Moreover, he could seldom attend the multiplicity of meetings that were arranged. Also he was realising, perhaps for the first time, that he was exhausting himself as well as dissipating his energies. He felt that his rôle was now to diffuse ideas, here and there, on occasions. England was still rebuilding its parochial life and could not look beyond it: only an heroic few, among priests, were capable of seeing the importance of international work. Martindale felt that he could achieve little; and always, when this was proved, he quickly tired of talking. The confusion of his life and the variety of his work in these years is shown by this letter. It is undated but belongs to this time:

> I shall be giving the Swadlincote retreat, I hope, for Passion Sunday week-end, and then I hope to come to Manchester till the Friday a.m., when I go on to Liverpool till the Monday or Tuesday after Palm Sunday. That week-end I shall be giving a women's retreat at the Wavertree Cenacle. A solid cheque and bales of cloth have gone to Austria. Belgium has just written to inquire how Campion Hall manages its gym, its boxing and football, and who finances us, and would we finance Louvain also. And a Czech Spa write to ask if I will find, for a Hungarian Doctor of Philosophy, a post in a London hotel for a waiter, so that he may learn English.

[1] John Eppstein, born at Reading 1895; educated at Wellington and Hertford College, Oxford; private secretary to Viscount Cecil at Geneva, 1929–33.

And an Italian duchess writes to ask for a musical M.A. who likes literature, that he may be a companion to an idiot Duke. And Hungary writes to ask for photos and accounts of the more noted British pilgrimage centres where there are shrines of Our Lady. Zagreb wants an exact account of the various sorts of Anglicanism, and Poland a statement of the educational position, system, and outlook in England. America has professed willingness to publish any amount of 'classical' yet Catholic stories on the lines of *The Goddess of Ghosts* in a new Catholic magazine. . . . Also this week I have had to lecture on Eastern religions to our 'Heretics' society; on the Jesuits in the hub of C of E-ism, Keble—it began at 7.45 and ended at 11.30; on St. Paul to our respectable congregation, and tonight I am to talk on Mind-Healing to the Irish Society, of which ninety-five per cent is Black Protestant. My condition was that I should be given a fish dinner beforehand. Also I expect to have tea with a blind atheist, and to receive a girl who has taken a super-fine first in English into the Church tomorrow, when moreover an artillery officer is coming to Oxford to explain why he has broken off his engagement, and to be condoled with. Do not therefore rebuke me for prolonged silence.

In February 1925 he summed up the major failings of the Church as he saw it in many places in the years following the war:

Permit me to go off the deep end myself. The Church of God, which is the body of Christ, is suffering from five wounds (all but bleeding to death, but it can't do that):

1. Identification of Catholics with partisan politics.
2. Frightful ignorance of their religion: a traditional belief minus instruction cannot survive the modern press and cinema.
3. Hopeless confusion as to what is or what is not socialism, so that tens of thousands of honest lads are damned as Bolsheviks when they are only asking for the social reforms that Leo XIII says are strictly just.
4. Alienation of the clergy in thought, talk, and behaviour from ordinary decent folk.
5. Making religion an affair of correct keeping of rules instead of

the love of God which makes you *want* to do things that the rules order you to. That is the wound of the Heart.

And schismatical nationalisms dislocate Christ on a new cross.

4

On 2 February 1924 Martindale, after a nominal tertianship and 'farcical' exam, took his final vows as a Jesuit at Stonyhurst. He had been a priest thirteen years; he had now, as he said, 'sealed, please God, for always the choice that I made at the same time as the biggest choice of all, I mean the choice of serving God (if he would have me) as a Jesuit, which I made when I first became a Catholic'.

He was in a condition of exhaustion when relief came, either by accident or the design of his Provincial, who in 1926 appointed him to organise in England the celebration of the bi-centenary of St. Aloysius' canonisation. It was work certain to appeal to him. For a full year it engaged his total effort. More for ecclesiastical than historical reasons St. Stanislaus, another youthful Jesuit saint, was linked with Aloysius in the commemoration.

His genuine happiness over this assignment surprised only those who did not know how deeply devoted he had remained all his life to the saint of his own youth.

At first he was left a free hand, though directions later began to arrive from Rome. He was asked to purchase and distribute an untold quantity of excessively sentimental pictures illustrating St. Aloysius' life. He protested. Then he was given posters in the same repellent genre, and told at the same time to collect money for a mysterious object called an obol. Again he protested: he was not sure what an obol was and guessed that the bishops, in whose dioceses he was expected to solicit collections, would be equally uncertain. Finally he was sent a mass of blank paper, on which boys were expected to sign promises that he judged impossible for them to keep. He pointed this out and insisted further that an identical form of words was unsuitable both for seamen and for schoolboys.

However, with the Provincial's backing, he adapted the Roman directives to suit English taste. He had his own picture made, which he used later as the frontispiece of his book, *The Vocation of St. Aloysius*.[1] In each place he visited, on special paper headed with the Gonzaga and Kostka arms, he wrote a very short affirmation which he judged that particular group could sign with sincerity. Then, taking his line from a letter written for the occasion by Pius XI, he addressed himself to audiences ahead of his arrival:

> The Holy Father in a letter which may be quoted has recently made his mind quite clear. He says he was so impressed by the multitude of young men who visited him during the Holy Year (1925) that he could not but reflect what they might not do in the world, if they were personally and solidly convinced of certain principles and prepared to act according to them with the full strength of their will. For this they needed inspiration and direction, and he seized the occasion of this bi-centenary which enabled him to provide them with both. For here are two young men who, in circumstances of far greater difficulty than any in which we are likely to be, displayed, as he says, 'alert intelligence, strength of will, vigour of character, energy of action and high-hearted disregard of self'. All this they used to extricate their lives from incredible entanglements, and to consecrate them to the service of their fellow-man and of God.

His aim, as he told, for instance, the Catholic Society in Manchester University, was to stress the primacy of the soul over the body, obedience, not only to conscience, but to the official Ministers of the Church. His message was framed to actual and British needs, and the response was perhaps more remarkable and enduring than in any country of the world.

From Aberdeen to Devonport, on a carefully planned itinerary, he visited every school, seminary, college, society, sodality, larger parish body, men's organisation in the chief provincial towns, the colliery areas, and training ships.

I do not see [he wrote to Manchester Catholic Society] how I

---

[1] Fr. Ledochowski, the General of the Jesuits, criticised it as being 'typical of modern restless art': his ideal, like Pius XI's, was the statues of the saints in St. Peter's; but unluckily Pius XI shortly afterwards became enthusiastic for icons, and the General instantly adjusted his tastes.

can reach every one of our University Societies this year, but I must certainly do so before next June, and I want as full a meeting of each as has ever been known. And I hope that each Society will send a letter to his Holiness the terms of which I shall suggest on each occasion for approval. Oxford has already sent theirs. I may say that I believe you will like the lecture. I have tried it, for example, on a hundred young mechanics during a short retreat in an Air Force camp: only the other day three hundred Blackpool men listened to it with great benevolence; in fact, since the evening of Monday 28 June to the evening of Thursday 1 July, I got in ten lectures between Blackpool and Preston, including one to seven hundred schoolchildren, a very panicky experience. I am actually at Edinburgh, where I am to address, I believe, the Police itself! After Edinburgh I go to Cardiff and the neighbouring towns, where I shall have dockers and colliers to see. In fact, with the exception of August 3 to 13, I seem to have a minimum of two lectures a day till the end of Lent, if all goes well.

In the mines the signatories left oily fingerprints on the embossed paper and this gave him particular pleasure. At the end of the year he arranged all the documents according to dioceses and placed them in a large plain wooden box with the initials S.S. carved on the lid. This was instantly called the 'Baby's Coffin'. However, the Jesuit General, when he saw Martindale on the pilgrimage that concluded the celebrations, was pleased. 'How English! You must show it to the Holy Father,' he said. 'Of course,' Martindale answered, and asked to have a private audience arranged for him.

However a general audience had already been fixed by Mgr. Hinsley, then Rector of the English College. When Hinsley introduced Martindale, Pius XI exclaimed, 'Questo nome e conosciuto—e bene conosciuto—da Noi qui a Roma.' A private audience followed.

Martindale had been told that it would be improper to show the Holy Father the grimy letters, but he insisted that these were just the ones he was anxious for the Pope to see. On his arrival at the Vatican a footman inquired contemptuously whether the 'Baby's Coffin' contained objects to be blessed and, on learning that they were letters, produced a massive silver tray on which the box was carried into the Pope's private study. Martindale slunk in after it. At once the Pope tumbled all the letters out onto his table. Momentarily forgetting himself, Martindale corrected him, 'Oh, Holy Father, you mustn't do that! They're all arranged according to dioceses.' 'Quite right,' came the Pope's answer, '*Nil sine Episcopo*'. Then Martindale asked him to look at the dirt-stained letters. The Pope delighted in them and in the variety of men and boys who had sent them. On seeing the package labelled Leeds, the Pope went on: 'We remember Leeds. Our train was to wait four minutes. We descended to buy two sandwiches at the buffet. When we came out the train was already *en marche*. The guard's van was still open. We leapt. En ces jours-là nous étions plus élastiques ... Your countrymen applauded.' 'Of course,' Martindale explained, 'they would have thought it sporting.'

Instead of the designated thirteen and a half minutes, he was kept three-quarters of an hour. The Pope told him he had done well not to make St. Aloysius a little nun. 'Era voluntaristo,' he said and thumped his desk, repeating the phrase more emphatically.

Martindale summed up his impression of Pius XI in a letter written on his return: 'Simply a superb person, most dignified and yet extremely friendly and without one atom of pose: extremely alert and full of questions to the point. I talked chiefly about university students and working men, especially colliers. I also saw my General for one and a half hours and got tactfully ticked off and, I hope, better approved of.'

Inevitably he reflected on the Papacy.

'On the whole, if you are to be a universal father,' he wrote, 'you have to complete your self-abnegation more than anyone in the world.' He observed that every single person approaching the Pope ordered his life in subordination to him, 'so that I imagine the only moments in which a Pope can be perfectly happy are those when he is going to confession and his confessor speaks to him simply in the name of God, or when in prayer he can abdicate mentally all that his Headship of the Church implies.' After this audience he saw the Pope as a solitary, looking out over a world spread out before him, in gross and in detail, and viewing it from the opposite point to that which it naturally took of itself. Peter had been crucified head downwards and there lay the lesson for his successors.

As for *The Vocation of Aloysius Gonzaga*, Martindale meant exactly what the title implied: not a life, which he never intended. It was the result of scholarly research and painstaking writing; in fact, the most satisfactory of his manifold books. The Introduction contains his avowal of faith in the saint's intercession.

I conclude [he writes] by praying a Saint, who has always been dear to me, and to whom I am grateful beyond measure, to prevent me from inserting in this book any merely personal ideals, any subjective interpretations that are not warranted by the truth; and I ask him to further a difficult task, for the difficulty of which, after all, it is he who is responsible . . . I trust, therefore, within the accidentals of time and place, to indicate, with his help, why young men who read this story will wish to ask him for friendly help in their own circumstances, sure that he will understand them and have the experience indeed to succour them.

He studied the Gonzaga background in the British Museum and so thoroughly that anything he later discovered made no substantial difference to his work. It was a successful, perhaps unique, study of a boy and young man in a turbulent Renaissance setting, of his mental as well as his physical environment. Within this setting he examined how his calling to the religious life developed. The result certainly was something very different from what had previously passed for the standard lives of the saint. He had struggled to release Aloysius from the mawkish presentations that had made him almost repulsive to the post-war generation of schoolboys. He preferred to see him portrayed, as he was in the Jesuit College of St. Michel in Brussels, almost like a red-Indian, rather than as an hermaphrodite.

5

It was during his years at Oxford that the Marlborough affair occurred. In 1920 Consuelo Vanderbilt, after an ill-matched and unhappy life, had divorced the Duke of Marlborough. In the next year she had married M. Jacques Balsan in the Savoy Chapel Royal. The Duke then married Miss Gladys Deacon and shortly afterwards expressed a desire to join the Catholic Church. Through Mr. Evan Morgan he was introduced to Martindale at Campion Hall. After learning from the Duke the circumstances of his marriage with Consuelo, Martindale had no doubt whatever that it was null, viz. that no marriage had been contracted, since Consuelo had incontrovertibly been forced into the match. However, the Duke and Martindale had agreed that the Vanderbilts would never provide the evidence on which the case hinged. Martindale, nevertheless, undertook to instruct the Duke, which he did over a long period at Campion Hall, not at Blenheim, for he was anxious to shield himself from any suggestion that he was pursuing the Duke. Once, however, he accepted an invitation to dinner when the King and Queen of Portugal were staying at the Palace. It was an awkward evening. He wrote after this visit:

> I didn't know anyone there except the Duke of Marlborough and his wife and Winston Churchill a little: still the dinner was pleasant up to a point, though I was dead tired after the afternoon. When the ladies went away, it resolved itself into a tête-à-tête between Dom Manuel and me, and I got a dose of international politics from him such as I have never had before. I concluded that he really could discriminate and knew a lot. . . . He told me at one point that something I said was in an un-Christian spirit! I said that it was true, anyway, and that Christianity didn't clash with truth, to which he said that so many Christians told lies that one was apt to forget it. . . . He is a very pious creature and horribly lonely. When I told him so he said it was a great compliment. This shows that the iron has entered pretty deep into him. I said that one had, half the time, to set one's teeth, and he said that his were worn away with setting them. You remember he was, as a boy, in the carriage with his father and brother when they were assassinated.

Later in the evening the Duke asked him to sit by him. The Duke then showed him his jewelled crucifix. He was a lonely and sad man.

The evening, perhaps, was spoilt for Martindale by his own state of fatigue. Earlier the same day he had preached from a table in the open market-place at Princes Risborough to a small group of Catholics encircled by a fringe of true Baptist elders with 'top hat, black tie, shaven lip, good old grim scowl'. At the end, he reported, 'they were thoroughly approving, nodding and finding it quite evangelical'.

Three years went by. Then the Duke unexpectedly announced that the Vanderbilts were ready to provide the evidence for the nullity. Consuelo found that she had not been received into French society, whereas her brother-in-law could introduce his wife anywhere. If she could get her marriage with the Duke declared null, she and her husband would be considered properly married. It was she, not the Duke, who applied for her case to be tried by the ecclesiastical courts; she also paid the costs. The Duke paid his fare to and from London to give his evidence, but no more. When a nullity was finally granted on the ground of coercion, an exact statement was drawn up jointly by the Duke and Martindale for the press. Then, at Farm Street, at a luncheon given to the laity on 8 December 1926, Bishop Brown of Pella, the Auxiliary Bishop of Southwark, called out, 'The Duke of Marlborough has got his annulment.' This was doubly false. The Duke had 'got' nothing; and the case was for nullity, not annulment. Instantly the press pounced. The explosion released the worst anti-Catholic British prejudices. As Sir Shane Leslie wrote: 'The cases of the Empress Josephine, of the Princess of Monaco, or of Signor Marconi were politically and historically of more importance, but none rocked society alike in England and in America as this one did.' The Duke became a prisoner at Blenheim, besieged by reporters at the Palace gates. Martindale received as many as three hundred press cuttings on a single day.

J. L. Garvin, in *The Observer*, was particularly venomous. He urged that the declaration of nullity implied that the children of the marriage, the Duke's elder son and Lord Ivor Churchill, were illegitimate and that neither could inherit Blenheim. When Martindale wrote to *The Observer*, pointing out that the editor knew nothing of

Canon Law, that the children of a marriage *thought* to be valid were not regarded or treated as illegitimate by the Church, the editor refused to publish the letter. With other papers Martindale pleaded that they did not know the evidence, that if women were to be forced into marriage, as Consuelo undoubtedly had been, this was tantamount to treating them as cattle, that all the evidence for the declaration had been provided by Protestants, who had sworn to the facts: hence the outcry implied that it was they who had all conspired to perjure themselves. *The Times* published letters from both Catholics and Protestants. Eventually when the fragmented facts found their way into the press, the controversy died. Winston Churchill stood by his friend and cousin; later he wrote:

> After his divorce in 1920 he [the Duke] was denied the Sacrament by the authorities of the Church of England. This is not the place to discuss the propriety or wisdom of such decisions. The need of contact with the sublime and the supernatural of which he was profoundly conscious, led him to the Church of Rome. He asked for sanctuary within that august and seemingly indestructible communion, against which his ancestor had warred with formidable strength. The shelter and protection were accorded, and the last years of his life were lived in a religious calm which fortified him against the troubles of the world and the errors we all make in travelling through it.[1]

When the press was quiet, Martindale agreed to visit Blenheim. He stayed there for ten days and completed the Duke's protracted instruction. He was assisted by the Duke's love of hierarchy, by his sense of authority and discipline and, in a lesser degree, by his attachment to pageantry. Instinctively the Duke searched for an order in divine things: 'No wonder that he should be grateful should he find that God had infallibly revealed to man His immutable Truth and unchanging moral law; and to these he tried—since for all human creatures it involves a struggle—to subordinate himself.'[2]

---

[1] *Charles IXth, Duke of Marlborough, K.G.*: Tributes by the Rt. Hon. Winston Spencer Churchill and C. C. Martindale, S.J. (Burns, Oates, 1934), 9–10.
[2] C.C.M., ibid., 15.

It was during this visit that Martindale drove to Heythrop with the Duchess. 'I don't believe you are English,' she said. 'Why?' asked Martindale. 'Well, because you are so flexible,' she answered. Martindale said: 'I don't see how. But we have never yet come up against a principle, or, at least, against a principle you don't like. If we did, you would discover rigidity quickly enough.'

Before the Duke's reception a fresh storm broke. The Westminster canonists had declared the Duke's second marriage valid because the first was null; Southwark, incorrectly and perversely, that it was not, because the first marriage was at the time thought to be valid. Finally it was decided that facts took precedence over opinion. On 1st February Martindale, after hearing the Duke's confession at Farm Street, went with him and the Duchess to Archbishop's House where he was received into the Church in the presence of Cardinal Bourne. The witnesses were Lady Gwendolen Churchill and Lady Abingdon. Afterwards the Cardinal congratulated the Duke who then knelt for his blessing. The Duchess gave the Cardinal her ring. He blessed it and, after due remarks which elicited a renewal of their consent to the marriage, he returned it. A note was then prepared for the press.

Until now Martindale had refused any offer of a present. On the day of his reception the Duke gave him his crucifix, probably the work of Cellini, which was later presented to Campion Hall. The Cardinal received a processional cross. In later years Martindale visited Blenheim on three or four occasions. Once also the Duke gave a tea-party for Poplar children at Carlton House Terrace. For the most part Martindale met the Duke quietly in London for luncheon or at Farm Street for confession. The Duke realised so vividly the meaning of the sacraments that 'after confession he became like an old man; he would lean upon one's arm; and after his Communion, he would be as it were dazed with the magnitude of the mystery to which he had been admitted. Technically accurate language in which to express it was not always his. But the fact was.'[1]

Moreover, the Duke had second sight. When in 1929 Martindale had a grave motor accident in New Zealand, the Duke called at

[1] Ibid., 16.

Farm Street to inquire whether anything had happened to him, long before any cable reached the press. During his last illness in 1934 the Duke refused drugs to relieve the pain of his cancer because, as he told the priest who attended him, 'I have joined the religion of which the centre is the crucifixion.' At his burial at Blenheim certain stanzas from one of St. John of the Cross's poems were read at his request. Churchill wept, and when the new Duke spoke without appreciation of the Requiem service, he rebuked and enlightened him.

The story of the Duke's marriage, as told in Consuelo's Memoirs, is inaccurate in many points and was corrected by Sir Shane Leslie in an article in *The Month*.[1] The 9th Duke was sixty-three at the time of his death. Shortly before his last illness he had arranged through his friend the Duke of Alba to retire as a layman into a Spanish Benedictine monastery.

[1] *The Glitter and the Gold*: an Autobiography, by Consuelo Vanderbilt Balsan, formerly Duchess of Marlborough (Heinemann, 1953). Cf. *The Month*, April 1953, 197–206.

# 9
# Farm Street

In 1927 Fr. Martindale left Campion Hall for Farm Street Church, which was to be the centre of his activity until April 1940.

While continuing the work he had begun at Oxford, he shared in the routine tasks of the community, heard confessions, took his turn as duty-priest, instructed converts, preached. It was the tradition of the house that the Superior governed mainly by co-ordinating the movements of the individual priests who each engaged in his own work; organisation was minimal. This suited Martindale and, on the whole, he was happy at Farm Street. The Superior was his friend from Stonyhurst, Fr. Roy Steuart.

During the next ten years he preached there, at Westminster Cathedral and in other churches several series of sermons later collected into books.[1] As a survey of the registers shows, the persons he instructed and received into the Church were mostly casual callers who happened to find him on duty. There were a few like Francis Fenn, George Tomlinson,[2] Lady O'Malley (Ann Bridge), Sheila Kaye-Smith and others who had sought him out personally.

Although he did not shirk confessional duty, he never formed, as other priests did, a clientele of penitents who sought his special direction. He did not believe he had any special message and he disdained the type of penitent who took in confession between the hairdresser and luncheon. 'I am rapidly emptying my confessional,' he wrote to a priest friend, 'by telling ladies to stop dissecting themselves and enumerating the sin-dust that flecks them, and to tell me whether they seriously try to do unselfish things for anyone else.

[1] e.g. *Christ is King* (1927), *The Kingdom and the World* (1928), *The Wounded World* (1928), *The Creative Words of Christ* (1929), *The Cup of Christ* (1930), *What Think Ye of Christ?* (1931), etc.
[2] Now Fr. Francis Fenn, S.J. and Mgr. George Tomlinson.

They then feel hurt and say that their conditions are very special and difficult; and that they cannot do much for others, but try to live with the mind fixed on God and can't manage it.'

To those who did not fear his advice he was practical in his suggestions:

If you really want a definite Lenten penance [he told a lady who assisted him often in his charitable works] go and see Mr. Jack F., recently de-appendiced at the Royal Northern Hospital, Holloway Road, unless your own recollections of the place are too dismal. When he is out of the place you might possibly ring up the Ministry of Pensions Hospital in Richmond Park (*Star and Garter* end of it) and see if Major French, D.S.O., is able to see anyone. He is in an appalling state and will die soon, please God, and you would not have to do more than just smile at him in a Catholic way and let him see that there is a little of the love of God going after all. He is half paralysed and often operated on. And then eight *Hail Mary*'s for the father, mother and six children I told you of. And I shall want lots of prayers for three retreats: one Miners, one Bookies, and one Beaumont elegants, who won't come without lots of help.

It was in the December following his transference to Farm Street that he visited Paris to address an ecumenical assembly on 'Reunion'. His aeroplane got considerably off course in the French mists and tumbled to a halt in a muddy beet-field miles from any road leading to Paris. While the passengers sat under an icy moon waiting for transport, 'I persuaded,' he wrote, 'the one girl passenger to produce a gramophone I saw she had, and a young man to produce some records I'd seen he had.' After the ensuing musical interlude, a bus arrived. He reached the Place St. François Xavier at eleven p.m. instead of four.

Martindale's Paris audience was controlled by the ideas of the Abbé Portal who had been shown Anglo-Catholic churches in England by the late Lord Halifax. His address, if not a failure, was a disappointment to Frenchmen who believed that only a few diplomatic adjustments were required to make corporate reunion easy.

Mother Madeleine Eugenie.  Jesuit Residence, Stenosgade, Copenhagen.

The Assumption Convent, Hellerup, Copenhagen.

Eightieth birthday.

He tried to suggest to logical French minds the average Englishman's attitude, not only to the established Church, but to the British Constitution itself. Could the French ever understand the English distaste for clear outlines any more than the English understand Spanish intransigence? While he gave proofs of his admiration for the old *pietas Anglicana* and the austerity of its ethic, he considered in his heart the newer Anglo-Catholics frivolous compared with the old Tractarians. In honesty he felt compelled to say that the trend among the few was to greater realism, and among the great majority to indifference; while nearly all were convinced that a man's religion, if any, was entirely his own affair. He had been invited as a person unlikely to be bigoted, but he was criticised as unbending. His concern was never so much with the Church of England as with the lack of Christian belief in the country as a whole. As a Catholic priest he believed it his duty to proclaim the entire faith, with no word of rancour or disdain, beginning, as Our Lord did, 'according as they could hear'. He judged that this meant starting from conscience, the difference between right and wrong and the human life of Christ.

Before leaving Paris he visited the church of Our Lady of Victories, where, in spite of the hustling crowds of working men and women, smart ladies, students and artists, he found it impossible not to pray.

To his old interests were now added the Holy Child Settlement at Poplar, International Eucharistic Congresses, work for seamen and for the Society of Perpetual Adoration. He also pioneered a new and wider apostolate through the British Broadcasting Corporation. His literary work, including his series of three books on the Missal, was inspired mostly by the enterprises he assisted.

Poplar was perhaps the best substitute London could offer for Swadlincote. He began by visiting the Settlement with great enthusiasm once or twice a week, until it was found that the club-rooms were built over an open drain and that the rotten ironwork of the roof was likely to collapse on the inmates. It was then that he undertook to raise £3,000 for demolition and reconstruction. But in more than material ways he was a support to Mrs. Spencer-Bull, the heroic warden of the Settlement. He also protected her and her assistants in their difficulties with the clergy.

From his letters written at this time it is clear that his visits to Poplar sometimes saddened him. He had already seen enough of material poverty not to be enduringly depressed by it, but it was the determined injection of East-enders with Communism and irreligion that made him feel helpless. As far as he could see, the clergy in East London were doing nothing to combat or counteract it. Yet little as the young men practised their religion or knew about it, Martindale would not have them called corrupt. Corruption, he believed, came in middle age, owing to success or despair. His impression was that the Catholic priests had an infinite capacity for being duped, not merely by beggars, but by their own flock. This was brought home to him when he attended the annual dinner of the parish Guild of the Blessed Sacrament. The priest, who had invited him, pointed out proudly, 'All these men make a monthly corporate Communion.' Martindale, after looking round at them, thought it unlikely. When he spoke to the Guild members individually after the dinner, one after another said sheepishly, 'To tell the truth, I ain't been to Mass not in months.'

The priests then in Poplar were to learn much in the war years. When Mrs. Spencer-Bull, the Warden, was invited to sit as a Catholic representative on the local housing committee, she was rebuked by the Canon, a kindly, hard-working Irish priest: 'Ah, what do you want,' he asked, 'mixing up with a lot of dirty Protestants?' His assistant practically preached class warfare: 'Let the West End keep to the West End,' was his jibe at Mrs. Spencer-Bull. In some ways, as his book *Bill* shows, Martindale learnt more from Poplar than from the war: how lightly, for instance, incest was considered in the East End.

In the new Settlement buildings he was able to conduct rather disorganised retreats. Then, and at other times, he would lead boys onto its flat roof, where he would hear their confessions. Once, in the middle of their tour, he took down the Australian cricket side. Every boy in the club was allowed to have one ball bowled at him by a star bowler, and to bowl one ball to a star batsman. He also brought the All Blacks, the New Zealand touring Rugby XV, to Mass at Poplar one Christmas. On another occasion he got a director of Arsenal to present a real Arsenal football to Limehouse; this produced jealousies for miles around. He described a typical evening at Poplar in a lighthearted way:

> Then to Poplar, a place in the Far East, where I go to fool about in a glum way with boys at a club (I also do this at Bow, another Far East drainpipe). I have sunk to the nethermost—I write songs, quasi-topical, and propose to sing them until the boys can do them for themselves. I coo to railway companies and they give me posters for nothing, and, having made a selection, I decorate brick walls with them, thereby kidding myself that I introduce a little colour into the lives of that grey race. I watch boxing, until I hear an unanimous criticism of what happens and then I too make it and am approved. . . . Hoarse hooligans suddenly say to me, 'Larst night, I went with one of 'em. Under a Arch. Thought I'd better tell you.' 'Feeling a bit sorry about it?' 'Ar.' Finally I return at late hours by 'bus and tube and hope I've not been a fool.

Some of Mrs. Spencer-Bull's assistants considered that he limited his influence at Poplar by showing favouritism to certain youths; however, his apostolate was necessarily individualistic. Boys in difficulties were usually shy of approaching him but sent their friends as ambassadors. 'Bill X says he doesn't believe in God no more. He's over there in the corner, waiting to speak to you.' Then the kind of dialogue, familiar to readers of *Bill*, would begin. 'Well, what's all this about not believing in God?' 'Ho! We all of us come from slime.' 'Who put the slime there?' Another would approach him: 'Heard about Jack? He don't believe in Jesus Christ. He's over there.' Jack was a very different type. Martindale noted his objection textually. 'Well, if Christ was the son of God, same as they tell us, how could God go and kill him? I could never kill the child of my own brain.'

It was soon after his transference to London, in a very long letter to a friend overseas, that Martindale revealed the spiritual sources of his untiring effort. After a small treatise on the difference between conviction and faith, he continues, first in a more personal way:

Now, when it comes, as you say, to loving and always expanding and deepening your love, I see that I could in myself combine a great deal of selfish love and indeed intense pity with cruelty. This is a frightful thing, and it is only the grace of God that helps me, as I experience that it does, really to love my fellow-man rather a lot, and to be prepared, save in moments of 'low vitality', spiritually speaking, to work myself to death for the sake of the unlovable, even humanly speaking. For I have only to think of man's lonely inside self really to forget everything else about him, even ungratefulness and lies and everything else. Sometimes men have said, 'I hope you are doing all this in a personal way, because you really like me, and not merely because you think it right, or because you love me in God, or something abstract and orthodox like that.' But they don't see that it is just when one remembers two things in the world, their self and God, that one can love them with all one's heart and perseveringly. Frankly, I simply don't know what I should do if once I forgot the love of God enveloping us all, and the human presence and simplicity of Jesus Christ.

He was writing to a close and old friend. He continued:

Now I think I see what I am likely to say when you, as it were, oppose the Church and her laws and the saints, etc. to God and Christ. Be as patient as Christ himself with human material. Poor Jesus Christ! What stuff He had to work with! The best of Christians is little more than a travesty of Christ! Yet compared to an average Christian what a colossus a saint is! Really unselfish, truthful, pure, simple, *all the way through*: no poisonous fibres writhing their way down between the marrow and the bone. But, anyhow, the thing is to discover Christ beneath the deepest disguise. *Adest!* But see the Church as Christ building up his own body slowly. As St. Paul audaciously says, Christ hasn't yet reached the full stature of his maturity. Not only has He to incorporate more and more individual souls into Himself, but He has more and more to transmute them till really there is but one life—His—in them all. But how slow! and what patience and gentleness He needs and shows! How ashamed of oneself one must be when one catches oneself getting angry with, or despising, or bullying, or neglecting a sinner, or even a dull or uncouth person, as one often does. One has steadily to look at that by which a thing—a man or an institution—lives, not that by which he dies, at what he is *becoming*, owing to the innermost push of the vital germ, which is nothing less than Christ alive with His Holy Spirit.

2

Martindale's interest in the Society of the Perpetual Adoration began when Mrs. Eyre, a wealthy Catholic lady, expressed a wish to build a church in honour of the Sacred Heart, but was instead persuaded by Cardinal Bourne to purchase a disused Wesleyan chapel in Horseferry Road, between the Cathedral and the river. This she did after an initial show of reluctance. The chapel ran across, but only partially occupied, an 'island' site filled with brothels and squalid shops. To give protection to the church, Bourne insisted that the site had to be purchased by a religious community who would demolish the old buildings and erect their own. In 1927 the nuns of the Perpetual Adoration, in order to get out of Balham, which was inconveniently situated for their work, complied with the Cardinal's wishes, but at the cost of living below Thames level and of a debt of £22,000. For a long time they were unable to get rid of their tenants.

This was their plight when Martindale came to their assistance. He was horrified at what seemed to him the barren money paid out in interest on their debt. When he told the nuns that they must pay it off at the rate of at least five hundred pounds a year, they complained with tears that in all the time they had been at Horseferry Road, they had not reduced their capital debt by fifty pounds. Although Martindale had no instinct or inclination for business, nevertheless, by providing method, an objective and determination, two thousand pounds were paid off the capital loan in the first year. He insisted that all the money he raised for the nuns should be devoted to the abolition of the debt. By the outbreak of the war he had achieved his goal; the squalid houses were being slowly demolished, and a fund had been opened for the building of a new convent.

Early in the second world war both the Settlement at Poplar and the Convent at Horseferry Road were demolished by German bombs, but Martindale was able to comfort himself with the reflection that both were free of debt and possessed a small reserve fund.

The Horseferry Road community had a special appeal for him because its principal work was to supply vestments and altar furnishing for missionary priests. His incessant effort on their behalf was chiefly responsible for turning his literary effort from general catechetical books to a series on the Mass, which he found time to write when he was invited to Australia to take part in the Eucharistic Congress in Sydney. On the voyage out he began and completed *The Mind of the Missal*, and, on his return, a better book, *The Words of the Missal*. Later, for the sake of completeness, he added *The Prayers of the Missal*. Of the three, *The Words* is perhaps the best, for it demanded more study and verbal precision. The motive that impelled him to write all three is the same: 'The only thing I cared about is the Mass and those who offer it.' So many Catholics either cared nothing for it or knew nothing of it: almost by ancient custom it was unintelligible to them. With deep conviction Martindale believed that, if priests made the effort to explain it, the Mass could be made intelligible to all, even in the Latin. He never campaigned for the use of the vernacular, but would have welcomed, without venturing to advocate, a number of simplifications in the Church's liturgy.

While Horseferry Road inspired the series on the Mass, there were also other impulses.

His lectures during the Aloysian year had taken him to many convents. Mass, so often, was presented simply as an element in school life with no bearing on anything outside it. He had found nuns in a condition of near-panic over the religious education they were giving, yet incapable of formulating a remedy.

He wrote:

Girls, the nuns frankly own, lead dual lives, one at home, one in the convent. Their religion is a well-fitting dress, but not a skin.

Hence rapid apostasies of the very girls who won religious doctrine prizes. I am lecturing, God help me, at Roehampton, Hammersmith and Notting Hill at their request, on these very points. The knowledge of religion turns into correct recitation of the catechism formulas, worship and piety into exterior cult, almost fetishism, and behaviour is according to a minimum legal code, not the free rush of love.

Later, he sometimes regretted that he had not carried on with this apostolate of the Mass. On the other hand, when he found that he had said in the main what he had set out to say on any particular matter, the desire to continue evaporated. Nevertheless, after writing these three books on the Mass, he turned to the Holy Week services: a series of several pamphlets followed on *Palm Sunday, Tenebrae, Maundy Thursday* and the other days of the sacred Triduum.

## 3

It is difficult to give an adequate picture of Martindale's incessant apostolate at this period. In a letter written in January 1928 he described a typical patch of his priestly work. At Hull he had given a conference to priests in the morning; that evening he addressed a meeting in a public hall on 'Man, Automaton, Ape or Angel?'; the next day he conducted a twelve-hour retreat for ladies; the following day, at Bradford, he spoke at the boys' school on St. Paul, and in the evening gave an open lecture on 'Man'. Then early the next morning he went on to Newcastle, where he spoke in a Church of England parish on 'What the Roman Catholic Church stands for'. In the train up to London he answered letters. From King's Cross he went to Poplar. Never, even at his busiest periods, did he employ a secretary or seek voluntary help. Often he wrote as many as twenty-five letters a day, all marked by his idiosyncrasies of composition and typing: some dealt briefly with engagements, others were compact little treatises on matters of faith or on the relation of belief to reason. Except when he was ill he never omitted to say his office. And there was a constant stream of articles, many of them in obscure periodicals edited by small religious congregations; there were also books, interviews, journeys. He confessed that he never refused a request for a sermon or an article if it was physically possible for him to comply. There were countless private pleas made among his friends for financial help in Catholic enterprises, especially for the building of churches and for the support of penurious academic societies. His activity and ubiquity became a legend in the fifteen years before the second world war. Yet his chronic fatigue never wholly extinguished the spark of originality that flashes in the odd paragraph or phrase even in his most hastily written articles or letters. There were frequent periods spent in hospital, but even then the pressure was seldom eased; only the travel suspended.

The secret of his resilience has already been suggested: the double illumination of his noviceship, the first at Manresa, on the immanence of God, and the second, at Aix, on the nature of work. Since his first reading of 'Rabbi Ben Ezra' sheer bulk of output retained for him something akin to vulgarity. He had discovered and developed a secret of his own. His was not a frenzied activity, but something like a spiritual servitude. In a long letter written from Bradford to a non-Catholic who remained most close to him all his religious life, he explained further the motives that impelled him:

Here [at Bradford] I spend hours in an icy confessional, thank God, hearing people who combine in some mysterious way the qualities of sinner and saint, and often are just saint. The town is all black and yellow snow, and the sky opaque gray. There is a vast difference between gray and grey, and this is gray. Emphatically. The people are so cold! They can't sleep for it.

Now, as for what you ask about detachment. It is very difficult to answer and I do not profess to succeed at my own method. There is an abstract appreciation of a fact or a type (this involves a mere cold, and in that sense detached, registration: this is no good) and there is also an emotional appreciation in which you are, as it were, aware of your emotion, almost trade on it, think you have achieved something special because you have been emotionally reactive to a person or situation, and emotionalise others by means of your emotion. This I think is no good. It just creates a corresponding emotion and the person concerned does not rise above *you*. Moreover, this is what uses up your resources in that line—nerves.

Then follow two paragraphs that reveal the development of his spirituality. The principles are those that had guided him from the days of his noviceship:

> Therefore, odd as it may sound, one must believe in God. I say (i) the only ultimate agent is God, and (ii) the results are to be due to God and known to God. Before a sermon or a talk or interview, etc., having prepared so far as time and intelligence and health allow, I say: I now abdicate. It is now up to You, God. Act! Let there be me only as a channel for You. I stand back. I rest no weight whatsoever on my feelings or wishes or ideas. I do not know what You want or how or when. Therefore I leave it to You, not as a *pis-aller*, not through cynicism—O, well, I suppose we had better leave the thing in God's hands, what's the good of me trying—but because here is Infinite Fact, infinite knowledge and power. Therefore I should never be anxious or perturbed.
>
> This appears to me to be a half-way state. A saint would know himself so completely united to God, at least he sometimes might, that he could say to God, 'I want so and so. Do it please'. *God doth the will of those that love Him.* But this is terrific. So are the saints, despite all their human elements, and despite our duty of showing those when we write their lives—as when one recalls that St. John of the Cross, a perfect miracle of detachment, liked asparagus and couldn't stand Andalusians, he being a Castilian. Now and again, so to say, it comes off. . . . I had lunch today with a priest for whom I have a colossal respect even humanwise, the original of Chesterton's Fr. Brown. He had given me a whopping lunch, part of which I liked, and part of which I hated, because it was such a lot. The grace involved, *In the Name*, etc., and the sign of the cross. I am sure that I truly adored God creating all those things, including the olives and the port, and was able to see them all as not out of harmony with the Crucifixion. Therefore I think that for a moment I saw God's action in the food, and also Christ's

complete will-for-sacrifice. See? Silly example, but the nearest one.

Then he touched on the obvious difficulty in such an approach: what to do when ordered to stop a certain work that one honestly believes to be God's will, and, from every human indication, is a work that others cannot or will not do and moreover, is important for the community or for an individual.

> Well [he asks], is God going to be defeated by someone else's stupidity? No. And one may be mistaken. But suppose one isn't. One still is not necessary to God. Now, what does one really want: that God's will should be done in this matter, or that *I* should be his instrument for doing it? Ah-Ah! That probes very deep . . . But what one sees, even all this life, is but a fringe of reality. Is one to suppose that God will accept a generous act on one's part and not be *at least as* generous? Ho! What an idea! And, moreover, who knows exactly what God wants? If a navvy says, 'The Rev. C.C.M. is O.K., but 'e do talk rot, an' me for the next drink and the next girl' . . . one can't tell that God wants anything else *now*. In fact, *In complete peace I will sleep and take my rest.*

But this acceptance of stupidity must not lead to indifferentism.

> Not from one atom of activity does this exempt one. Not even from going to see some schoolgirls act the *whole* of *The Gondoliers*, followed by speeches from several aldermen with Bradford accents, *and* the local Director of Education, who talked for half an hour solid, in a cold room, on the Rudder of Mind, the Keel of Character, the Wind of the Sense of Beauty and much more ungodly tosh, all of which I thought I ought to go to last night in order to encourage the local nuns of the Cross and Passion. Would you believe it?

The simple fact is that one ought to believe in God, in Christ made Man, and Grace whereby we are incorporated in Him, and the Holy Ghost who thereupon inhabits us.

## 4

On 8 June 1928 Martindale sailed for New Zealand on the *Rotorua*. He had been invited by Bishop Cleary of Auckland to give missions in his diocese for three months on his way to the International Eucharistic Congress at Sydney. He was now on the permanent committee of the organising body.

His actual experiences in New Zealand and Australia are given in his book, *The Risen Sun*, published on his return and dedicated to the 'Diggers'. He had kept the names of all the Australians he had known at Oxford, and at first he thought of listing them all, then their initials, in the dedication; but as both names and initials would be common to many, he settled for a more embracing word. With him on the *Rotorua* went all the photographs of his Australian and New Zealand friends taken during the first world war.

His book has interest now largely as a record of the condition of Catholicism in Australasia at that time. Autobiographicaly, it reveals much of his priestly spirit, a subject about which he reflected a great deal when he discovered that so little was being done for men at sea. Priests travelling to missionary posts, he quickly appreciated, for the most part left the crew to seek them out; they contented themselves with offering Mass in the first-class lounge for the Catholic passengers.

A seaman 'may be overwhelmed with shyness,' Martindale wrote,[1] 'especially if he has got for the first time into trouble. . . . I pray that the priestly spirit may be one that seeks, and that it be infinitely gentle when a soul is found. The fire of the Holy Spirit warms, and does not scorch: He came "not as an eagle, but as a dove".'

Already he had compiled a prayerbook for seamen which contained, along with devotions suited to seafarers, the first sanctioned form of Catholic burial at sea when no priest was available. There were also directions for assisting men dying at sea:

> Do not think this was uncalled for. Almost immediately after publication it was used for that very purpose. Again and again

[1] *The Risen Sun* (Sheed and Ward, 1929), 31.

men have written to say that they had hated 'giving their comrade to the sharks' without a prayer. Here is a true little story—raw comedy, if you like; but tragic as much such comedy is. A man had to be buried. The captain asked if any of the men knew a prayer. None did. 'Not even the *Our Father*,' he insisted. Not even the *Our Father*. Desperate that no homage, no hope, should be expressed by anyone, the cook came forward and sang: 'For he's a jolly good fellow.' Such a burial, I imagine, would have to be kept well secret from the lad's mother . . . If there is one thing that the Catholic mother wants to know, it is how her son died, and what she may hope about the boy's eternity. Not that the pathetic offering of that cook will have counted for nothing in the eyes of God, Who understands better than His human creatures do what is the meaning of man's own heart.[1]

His voyage to New Zealand was his forcible introduction to the sea-apostolate. In his book he does not reveal how in his shyness he postponed his first contact with the crew of the *Rotorua* until his conscience left him without peace. Then, unexpectedly, the approach was made easy for him.

One morning, shortly after three o'clock, he came up from his cabin to walk on deck. Without knowing it, he took a seat alongside the exit from the stoke-hold. The first three men to emerge were all Catholics. After that all was easy, although afterwards he still sweated with shyness every time he sought to make his first approach to a new crew.

On the spiritual care of sailors, both in the Royal and Merchant Navy, he had already thought a great deal. Almost by instinct he progressed from dockers to seamen, and later from seamen to men of the Air Force. Many priests, as he had already discovered, were temperamentally unable to deal with them; they either bullied or snubbed the men or left them, as they said, to 'come to the sacraments', should they feel inclined. Only the smallest percentage of men did this.

In the Army Martindale had found that many peacetime chaplains

[1] Ibid., 29.

never entered the men's huts. They maintained it was undignified. Others hardly knew two of their flock by name. As he saw the problem, it could be solved only by individual, unceasing labour; general notices or exhortations produced no result. Moreover, whether with soldiers or seamen, he was convinced of the need to show affection. 'I sail very near the wind,' he wrote to the Catholic port chaplain at Swansea. 'For instance, I hear their confessions in their huts, sitting on their beds as often as not. I usually make their confession for them, half chaffing and, having done that, I bring them easily to a good personal act of contrition and resolution.' In a church he would make them confess, not in the box, but in the sacristy, with their elbows on his knees. 'I know people exclaim, "Oh, how sentimental!" Well, it isn't. They need affection and they respond to it almost alarmingly.'

Of his voyage to New Zealand he wrote:

> I made acquaintance with all the officers and half the engineers, electricians, wireless operators, etc., and could have swum in the gin they daily offered me. I used to begin my rounds from about 11.30 a.m. till lunch, resume them at 4 p.m. and end them about midnight. The number of ex- or rickety Catholics I found, quite without looking for them, would stagger you. I am convinced that half the people on the globe are, have been, or in their hearts want to be, Catholics. Why, going out, I was told there was one Catholic steward: I found nine.

Before his voyage he had worked for sailors in London and other ports. He had been distressed to find that ship-visiting suffered from disputes between the two Catholic organisations—the Society of St. Vincent de Paul and the Apostleship of the Sea—who undertook it. To indicate his impartiality, he wrote his *The Seaman's Prayerbook* for the former, and, on his return, a pamphlet for the latter society. While he looked on helplessly at the quarrels, he offered a line of solution to those who might be in a position to act.

> I back the Apostleship of the Sea, too, and in a sense, chiefly. For I am sure (and now the Cardinal [Bourne] agrees) that until

there is one Society *ad hoc*, with no other job (the sea is a by-issue with the Society of St. Vincent de Paul) we shall make no progress. I hold that there is a work to be done and that it makes no difference who does it locally—if one finds locally the Society of St. Vincent de Paul, or the Knights of St. Columba, or the Catholic Young Men's Society can and will do it, by all means let them. But the thing should be co-ordinated under one title, and the Apostleship of the Sea is a Rome-recognised thing *ad hoc*.

For many years he had been collecting money to assist the Apostleship of the Sea. He was anxious to provide a central fund sufficient to cover the running expenses of the staff, so that, as with Poplar and Horseferry Road, any bequests or collections would be used to extend the work. Already he had gathered a large sum (one donation was for £500) when he found that it was being consumed piecemeal on day-to-day expenses. He began again. The same thing happened, though he was so explicit the second time that there could be no excuse of ignorance. Eventually his connection with the work was forcibly severed at the time of the second world war, though his interest remained. He was delighted to see the work prosper without his backing.

Soon after landing in New Zealand, Martindale was very seriously injured in a motor accident. Bishop Cleary of Auckland, his host during his visit, was reputed to be the most perilous driver in the Dominion. Indeed, as Martindale later learnt, both Archbishop Mannix of Melbourne and another Australian Bishop had seriously considered sending him a cautionary cable. Cleary always took his corners on the wrong side of the road. Usually, if Martindale saw another car coming towards them, he called out to the Bishop in warning. On this occasion their car was at the top of a gully; at the other end of it, Martindale could see another car approaching. He was too tired to say anything until they were at the bottom and the Bishop was already slicing off the curve to the right. Then he remembered and called out, 'God, the other car!' In a moment it was there, a few yards beyond and above them. The collision was head on.

He felt two gentle taps on his forehead. When he regained consciousness, he found himself deluged from head to foot in a pale yellow-coloured liquid. He imagined that a can of petrol had spilt over his head (not that there was one to spill). He did not at first recognise that it was blood. Gradually he was able to see the other car; the man was in hysterics and the woman lying in the hedge head-downwards. He realised he was bleeding profusely, and believed he was dying. He reflected that if he attempted to pull the woman to her feet, he would only bleed more but would be doing something decent. Then he began to see his blood as dark blue. He had two consciousnesses, much as he had experienced under morphia but, before he was able to distinguish hallucination from reality, the occupants of a farmhouse had run out, washed him, applied iodine to his wounds and taken him to hospital where somehow the Bishop, a leg and two ribs broken, had already arrived.

Only when his scalp was touched did he feel pain. He lay in hospital for a month. He complained of headaches and was re-examined. At the moment of the accident he had knocked a tooth with his knee into the antrum where it had lodged in the bone. An infection was about to spread into his sinus.

He crossed to Australia. No one realised how grave his condition still was. The part he took in the Eucharistic Congress is described in his book. Almost every day, sometimes more than once a day, he was called on for sermons, lectures, addresses, messages. Before the accident he remembered every detail of his activity; after it, none. The doctor, who had accompanied him from New Zealand, drugged him heavily before each occasion. Facing a vast crowd at the Town Hall in Sydney, he made a gaffe that instantly ensured his popularity. The Archbishop kept pushing a microphone in front of him. Martindale knew, or believed he knew, that he was everywhere audible. When for the third time he pushed it away, he said, forgetting the instrument, 'I hate this damned thing.' Before leaving for Brisbane he got influenza. At Melbourne Archbishop Mannix asked him to give two clergy retreats and the first men's retreat in the Archdiocese. He did the last but a second attack of influenza forced him to cancel the rest. Later he reflected that this was a blessing for he believed he would have totally misjudged the Australian priests.

He maintained afterwards that his accident permanently affected him, and that his work now demanded twice the effort it had done before. Nevertheless his output was not reduced though it was sometimes stimulated artificially. He would say that his head had never been the same since. On his return to London, in a letter of 3 August 1929, he wrote:

> I can't pretend that the fool accident in New Zealand has left no permanent traces: at least, they last till now, and are by way of having made my eyes older with a jerk—but that would have happened slowly anyhow—and to have tired my heart without injuring it, if you see what I mean: but the poor blighter got such a colossal strain that it remains fagged. But chiefly, I think, my whole *self*, and head in particular, are tired: and I can't put myself so hard at jobs as I could. And this is not merely due to advanced age, albeit it is advanced by now. Oh well, enough said about that.

More than physically, the accident was a crisis in his life.

In the autumn he was sent to Sweden to be examined by Dr. Holmgård, alleged to be the best brain specialist in Europe. Holmgård referred him to Dr. Busch in London. He was submitted to a deep X-ray of the brain, an experience he long remembered with horror. A wound was discerned in the *corpus striatum* of the brain, scarred over but permanent. When Dr. Busch cross-examined him on the effects of the accident, Martindale explained that for no assignable cause he suffered from recurrent 'black-outs'. He would be listening to what a person was reading or saying and be unable to follow any meaning. He could see clearly the number of a bus and not realise that it was a number, let alone the number he wanted. Often he would go to his table for a pencil and either not know what he was looking for, or pick it up, not knowing what to do with it. Sometimes a sudden lethargy would descend on him. He would feel it in his veins like a liquid and be unable to do anything at all. Dr. Busch warned him that precisely this would be the result of his injuries. He told him also that at such times he should not attempt to force the pace of work, and still less rebuke himself (as he often did) for laziness or self-indulgence. Later, more as a result of the accident than of age, he suffered from a recurrent inability to find words or even ideas, and therefore, to talk. In the last eight years of his life, which were passed at Petworth, his mind never ceased to be active; yet he was the antithesis of the garrulous old man—he welcomed especially any visitor who would relieve him of the task of talking. His worst wounds were on the left side, and at the top of his head, but, paradoxically, his inclination was always to lurch to the left. Less puzzlingly, his hair grew imperfectly on the right of his head and on that side, from his cheekbone upwards, the skin was harder.

Between the accident and his death there were to be more than thirty years of activity which cost him at times twice the physical and mental effort it had hitherto done. Moreover, his head, as he would put it, was weak; and inevitably this weakness quickened his reaction to the stimulus of any kind of drug or drink. Yet contrary to Dr. Busch's advice he did not reduce his output of work.

# IO

# *The Thirties*

After his return from Australia Martindale's life continued much as before. Poplar took an increasing part in it, and there were further series of conferences at Farm Street. A new interest was added: the home for Catholic mentally deficient boys at Besford Court, Worcester, which he had visited during the Aloysian year. It was the almost total lack of Catholic interest in the problem of defectives that directed him there.

In Australia he had found it customary to group all sub-normal children together, to disdain any psychiatric approach and to say, 'What does it matter? If they are not fully sane, they can't commit a mortal sin.' This abuse of moral principles appalled him; underlying it was the assumption that nature was in no way the concern of Catholics. Exceptional in approach had been Archbishop Clune of Perth who had made plans for the care of Catholic defectives in his diocese, but he was an old and sick man who had not the strength left to realise them.

Martindale was still very weak. From now on he believed he was fighting a losing battle with his battered health, but this only spurred him to make the most of what he imagined would be the few years of life remaining to him.

While at Besford Court, his tonsils flared up. His accident had affected the antrum below his eye and his system was absorbing much poison. It was decided that he should have another operation. In August 1929 he wrote from Rye:

> I was half off my head with pain . . . On Wednesday I am off to be fattened for the slaughter and return to have my tonsils out and the font of evil in the antrum got at, apparently by dynamiting

half the inside of my nose. This, I am told, will be a bad shock and I shall take ten days or so to buck up.

After his tonsils had been removed, the surgeon described them as 'historical'. The aftermath was bad, and he appeared not to recover his strength.

It was decided that he should be given relief from his London engagements. But before this could be arranged he had several bouts of influenza; at least this is what he called it. His heart was weak, his temperature, for some days in December, rollicked between 96 and 105. He was limping.

Instructed from Rome to rest, but not to take a millionaire's holiday, he proposed to visit South Africa to study the missions. His plan was accepted.

'When I started for the Cape in December,' he wrote in his travel diary,[1] 'I knew no more, and probably less, than everyone knows about South Africa. I went there without any formed opinions about its local, national or racial problems; aware of the dangers that beset tourists; desirous indeed of receiving impressions, but temperamentally almost too reluctant to arrive at conclusions.'

The joy of his outward voyage was his encounter with a stoker, B.S., who became his lifelong friend, a man of remarkable physique, about twenty-two at the time of their meeting, sensual and a constant fighter. Martindale was on his way down to the stoke-hold about midnight, when the young man lurched forward and asked, 'What the hell are *you* doing here?' 'Meeting you, apparently,' Martindale answered, and then explained that he was looking out for any Catholics among the crew. The conversation continued:

*B.S.* If religion ain't free in this ship, what is?

*M.* I can't answer that. But are you by any chance a Catholic?

*B.S.* No, but I want to be.

*M.* Why do you say that?

*B.S.* Come into my head, like.

*M.* But if you want to be a Catholic, I should have to instruct you.

[1] *African Angelus* (Sheed and Ward, 1932), ix.

*B.S.* You take and instruct me.

*M.* Yes, but where? We can't sit cooing on deck. You aren't allowed into my cabin.

*B.S.* Settle it as you please.

The captain agreed that Martindale might meet the man at the steel gate and escort him to his cabin, but he was emphatic he would not, in fact, come. He did, for an hour every night of the voyage. 'What do your mates say when they know you come up here?' Martindale asked him. 'I ain't got no argument,' the stoker answered, 'but you see these fists.'

At Capetown the man asked to be received into the Church. 'On our way back from Madagascar you can make me take my first Communion, even though I go without food or drink till evening.' At 5 p.m. B.S. met Martindale at the Bishop's House in Capetown. Before making his confession he turned white and sweated. Martindale assured him there was no cause for anxiety, that he had already told him in conversation much more than he need say now. 'Ah, but then I was saying it to you: now I'm saying it to God,' he answered.

His ship sailed straight from Madagascar to New Zealand. It was two years before they met again. As B.S. entered his room in London, Martindale jumped up to greet him, but the stoker put his hands behind his back, saying, 'Before we shake hands, I require to ease my conscience.' So he went to confession and then hugged Martindale like a gorilla. Every kind of trouble dogged him, but he remained one of Martindale's closest friends. They met once more when Martindale was on his second visit to New Zealand.

In a letter of 1957 he recalled the story. At the end of it he asked: 'Would you be surprised if my heart had tears of humiliation?'

Also on the way out he read and annotated several books on Africa and continued doing this while he was there. *African Angelus* is full of out-of-date statistics but, if these are cut out, the rest is accurate history and description. Both Sir Godfrey Huggins (later Lord Malvern), the Prime Minister, and Lewis Hastings spoke kindly about it. It would seem that he got to the essence of African problems as they then were, and in some measure to the essence of native psychology.

But he was also very disheartened. He did not romanticise the untouched native; he deplored his pseudo-Europeanisation and would have wished for 'reductions', like those of Paraguay, which, of course, he knew were impossible. In his judgement the Jesuit missionaries in Rhodesia did their job better than the Jesuits at home, but were defeated from the outset by a score of forces they were powerless or unequipped to counteract. His impression was that Africa, though uniquely beautiful, was everywhere a little spoilt, both in its spiritual and physical nature. This frightened him, as can be seen in the two sets of verses he wrote about the Continent. The work of the Europeans struck him for the most part as destructive and vulgar. He believed he had witnessed the debauching of an entire Continent by well-meaning fools. On his return he wrote to a friend:

South Africa was very interesting, but its politics and personal rancours and graft disgusted me—Australia might infuriate you, but South Africa would often disgust you. At least Australia has not got a subject and helpless race, treated alternately with revolting cruelty and with academic uplift. The times when I felt happiest were when I was literally alone (it didn't happen often), with no white man for leagues, but bush, crocodiles, baboons, black men with assegais and, on and off, black babies who are the most trustful and grave little creatures in the world. They sit in your arms and stare at you and make small noises in their throats and show no signs of going away and are perfectly prepared to suck bits of raw goat if you offer them any. (You periodically get a goat given to you. You touch the piece you propose to eat yourself; you supervise its execution and dissection, take your own bit and hand out the other warm, moist, flaccid lumps to the deserving.)

The sheer beauty of the place is incredible, though on the odd side rather than lovely, so to say. Colossal rocks, split in perfectly straight lines fifty yards long, like one gigantic axe-cut; bright red dust; red rocks; dark green metallic scrubby trees; dead grass and brilliant blue sky. So there. Perfect peace, and I am homesick for it, but God save me from the towns.

In another place he added mystically:

I felt as though the bad element in Africa was angry with me for being there, but that underneath was something that wanted me to be there. I could only refer the Continent to the Blessed Sacrament. Here alone was the human-divine and perfectly good. And *force*, which everyone else lacked.

His journey took him from Capetown to Northern Rhodesia. At Salisbury he attended the consecration of his former fellow-novice, Aston Chichester, as the first Catholic Bishop in succession to the Prefect Apostolic.

In other letters from Africa he returned to his passion for being alone. At such times he liked to have what he called a ghostly companion. 'You are often it,' he told his sister Nell. At the Victoria Falls he refused to be escorted. 'I assumed that you were there for the first time and frequently said, "Now, Nell, shut your eyes and do not open them till I tell you." You then clutched my arm and in other ways misbehaved and said, "Oh! Cyril—I'm getting soaked— I'm sure we are too near the edge." '

At Musami he walked alone one afternoon through a baboon- and leopard-infested kopje. He did not mind this. 'The whole scene,' he wrote the same afternoon, 'is as if a dozen giants had pelted it with colossal rocks, cubic, spherical, any shape, the size of houses, and then had taken axes and split them in perfectly straight lines.'

Many times in his last years at Petworth he recalled his happiness in the African bush.

One night I was sitting absolutely alone under a thorn tree and suddenly six vast men lined up out of the dark and I thought, 'There's been a very sticky murder here recently. Is this my turn?' But one of them said, 'We go pray', and they filed off into the mud hut used for Mass and remained in it, pitch dark, no book, no service, and after about a quarter of an hour they returned, lined up again and said, 'Please, blessing.' I, in shorts and vest, stood up and blessed them; and they, with unmoving faces, made the sign of the cross and melted off into the night. There was a little fire some yards off, enough just to see them, i.e. their shape, gleaming eyes, their skin black as the night. One felt, here is the real thing, not raw, but pure.

Or another time, when I didn't know how to get home, another vast man got hold of me and after a while said, 'I show you my flowers', and pointed up a hillock. I said I was too tired to climb. In some mysterious way I suddenly found myself on his back, holding his glistening black shoulders, was deposited, and admired three sunflowers, and then was told, 'You come my house.' It was, of course, round, fire in the middle of the earth floor, fragrant, not at all nasty, smoke. A score of tiny children, absolutely trustful, crawled all over me and were duly patted. The father introduced them: 'This is Helena Two: this is Anthony Four: Mary all these!' The choice of names was limited.

What he remembered with excitement were the episodes that introduced him, often accidentally, into what he called 'pure Africa'. As late as 1957 he would tell how he was sitting alone one day under a scrub-tree. While he was absorbing the heat, he heard a 'thud-thud' from very far off. As it came nearer, he wondered whether it was a drum or human feet thumping the sand. After a quarter of an hour a man passed, throwing his knees high, shaking his assegai, his eyes fixed on the blazing sky. The 'thud-thud' was his voice, pitched alternatingly high and low. He could be heard for ten minutes after he had passed.

Again, only a year before his death, he wrote telling a friend that he was glad to have been in Africa and alone with natives playing their own music; he remembered how they 'crowed with glee' when he tried to play their drums. He and they could laugh in a most friendly way with one another.

Northern Rhodesia was the limit of his journey. On 31 July he sailed from Beira, in Portuguese East Africa, on the *Llanstephan*. Writing from Genoa he expressed his happiness now that he and his father had come to know each other:

I confess my letters home are rather neutral . . . I love Daddy sincerely and far more than I did when I was younger and didn't appreciate him so well; but the fact remains that he thinks along one line and lives along his line far better than I do along mine; and mine will never really intersect with his, nor perhaps yours either.

Later, he explained to his father that in boyhood he had been taught to regard him 'almost as a Chinese God', and that, until he was eighteen, his relationships with his family had been so artificial that he disliked them all. At twenty-one he was beginning to understand what sonship meant. Now between father and son there was respect and devotion and 'that sort of equality that belongs to men who have passed fifty'.

If the lines did not intersect, at least they grew closer. There is an increasing intimacy in his letters to his father after his visit to Africa, and a deepening affection.

2

Soon after his return from South Africa, at the end of August 1931, Martindale tore a ligament in his foot and was confined for a long period to London. But the articles, lectures, sermons, books continued. His most notable, even sensational, achievement was the success of a series of talks on saints, which he broadcast weekly on the B.B.C. every Sunday between 24 January and 8 May 1932. It was said at the time that for incisiveness, clarity, and emphasis he had the best speaking voice ever heard on the B.B.C. Since he was limited to fifteen minutes, he was forced to condense; and, not to kill vitality in restricted space, he re-wrote each of the talks three times. This popular exposition of sanctity was a great advance on the first series of lives, *Cadets of Christ*, for it distilled, frequently in a parenthesis, much of his human experience in the intervening years. The correspondence the talks brought him was immense. When printed under the title, *What are Saints?*, the first edition sold out within two days. The B.B.C. was attacked for allowing itself to be-

come the instrument of Roman propaganda, and a controversy en-
sued in *The Times*. A second series on women saints (the first had
been confined to men), which he had contracted to broadcast, was
postponed, then finally cancelled.[1]

In November 1933 he was asked to lead a pilgrimage of four
hundred and sixty Catholic unemployed men to Rome. To the
amusement of the party the rôle assigned to him was largely taken
over by an irrepressible little Scottish priest. As nominal leader he
did little except insist, when arrangements were made for the public
audience, that the men should not sing Wiseman's turgid hymn,
*Full in the Panting Heart of Rome*, but, instead, the *Credo* in plain
chant and in Latin. He sent a message to Pius XI, asking whether
this would be in order. The Pope replied that he would be delighted.
Only the clergy protested that the men could not do it. A seminarian
intoned the *Credo*, and the men took it up boisterously. The Pope,
enchanted, beat time with his fingers.

In Africa Martindale had suffered a mild bout of malaria; now in
Rome it flared up. On the last day of the pilgrimage, returning from
Tivoli with two of the men, he felt extremely ill. He was given
morphia and assigned two orderlies who nursed him on the train to
London. He lost one and a quarter stone. From Victoria he was
taken in an ambulance to SS. John and Elizabeth Hospital. 'I am
much better,' he wrote on 19 December. 'I hope to say Mass on
Christmas day. Do not imagine I am a crock. I am, in fact, repul-
sively obese owing to eating yeast.'

Inevitably, like most priests of real or reputed distinction in the
thirties, Martindale was asked to join as a lecturer one of the Hellenic
cruises organised by Lunn's tours. 'The miscellaneous tourists,'
Evelyn Waugh has explained, 'whom Sir Arnold Lunn used to coax
into the delusion of being enthusiasts for classical culture, were dis-
posed to think that the price of their tickets included the acquaintance of the savants whose lectures they attended and whose holidays
they subsidised.'[2]

[1] Many years later he published these talks in an altered and expanded form in *The Queen's Daughters* (Sheed and Ward, 1951).
[2] *Ronald Knox*, p. 250.

Martindale was to lecture. He misjudged his audience. The cruise was too luxurious for his taste. Intermittently he permitted himself a sense of intoxication at the beauty of the Dalmatian coast (they had sailed from Venice) and the Greek mainland. But he was still unwell, and wanted to be alone, or preferably, with a silent companion. He made friends with a master from St. Paul's, with whom he visited Tiryns and Mycenae; their understanding of these sites brought them together. At Mycenae his friend clambered about while he sat still and gave the ruins a chance to become alive. Athens contained no ghosts. His happiest hour was when he went swimming opposite Salamis: he removed his spectacles and could see nothing but what the ancient Greeks saw. He wrote later: 'I believe that if I had had a year there, and all my Greek books, I could have realised that I *was* there.' But he felt the warmth of the sun which, to the end of his life, remained the chief attraction of foreign travel; he loved particularly the island landscapes and silhouettes. On his way back to Venice he made no effort to seek out his fellow-voyagers. A Miss Fiennes, a cousin of Gwen's by marriage, asked to be introduced to him, but he did not follow this up.

He judged that the cruise 'was not his way of doing things'.


## 3

Lunn's cruise, however, gave him strength to think of other enterprises. In July 1934, when he was preparing to go to the Eucharistic Congress at Buenos Aires, he claimed that he had the constitution of an ox, and he ascribed this jokingly to Glucose D. His 'personal day', as he called it, began usually at 10 p.m. It was then, often after his return from Poplar, that he answered his letters. 'Life certainly goes fast and one feels one has not made much of it,' he wrote on the eve of his departure for the Argentine. 'Still it has been full of friends, which is something. It is also full of letters.'

All he remembered of his visit is recorded in his book.[1] After Cardinal Pacelli, the papal legate, had made a fine rhetorical speech in Spanish, a French Monsignor, standing next to Martindale, re-

[1] *Athens, Argentine and Australia* (Sheed and Ward, 1935).

marked, 'On voit bien là l'homme qui tient le fouet.' Without reflecting Martindale answered, 'I hope something better will be found to say about our next Pope than *that*.' Only then did he find that all assumed that Pacelli would succeed Pius XI. At Buenos Aires Martindale thought him wooden; later, at Budapest, more mollified.

Since he was continuing immediately from Buenos Aires to Melbourne, he had little time to assimilate the new world he had seen in South America. He tired easily. After the Congress he spent three days in bed. He had been less happy there than at Sydney. The Congress seemed to him not to touch the problems of the country. The money that had been poured into it was calculated to exasperate the Communists, and several hundred were in public gaols which had been whitewashed and embellished for the occasion. The difference between the very rich and the poor, especially in Chile, oppressed him.

In Australia and New Zealand he was again welcomed everywhere with affection. At Melbourne he was the guest of Archbishop Mannix, who had invited him to the centenary celebration of his diocese. He returned happy to have seen Australia once more.

In his absence two close friends from his early days as a priest at Campion Hall had died: F. F. Urquhart, Dean of Balliol, and Professor Bullough of Cambridge, whom he had received into the Church. He paid his tribute to their memory in his next book.[1] Then, shortly after his return, Cardinal Bourne died. 'He reminded me,' he wrote, 'of great French ecclesiastics, with a personal dignity linked to an exalted sense of his ecclesiastical position: not asking to be understood by men, and not always understanding them.' Even before Martindale moved to Farm Street, Bourne had frequently agreed to his request to send letters of greetings to various Catholic Congresses abroad, particularly to *Pax Romana*. The Cardinal trusted him and agreed that he should write, not merely drafts, but the actual letters on his official armorial paper.

Always Martindale had felt impeded by the lack of interest shown by English bishops in Catholic affairs abroad. Bourne had been an exception. Shortly before Martindale's visit to the Argentine, he had

[1] Ibid., 240. Cf. inf., p. 149.

consented to attend a centenary celebration in honour of St. Ansgar at Stockholm, but his last illness had prevented him.[1]

Other Eucharistic Congresses followed at set intervals during the 'thirties: Manila, Dublin, Budapest. Manila he disliked, partly because he travelled on a German ship with a maniac Hitlerite captain, who provoked only a grudging response from his crew when he shot out his arm in the Nazi salute. On the voyage Martindale wrote out most of the sermons which formed his book on Our Lady, which he dedicated to the Madonna at Hartley.[2] Before reaching Manila he received a radio message from the University, asking him to give an address there. He had hardly disembarked when he was seized by a wild priest who commanded him to cancel his engagement. The University was deadly hostile to Catholics and had sworn to admit no priest within its walls or any mention of religion. Quickly it became clear that there existed, as he had discovered elsewhere, two parties among Catholics, one suspicious of the Government (along with the University) as freemason, damnable and untouchable; the other, which included the Jesuits, anxious to bridge gulfs. But he did go to the University, wore his cassock and biretta, and before all the officials gave his address directly on the Congress.

The actual Congress was poorly organised. Archbishop Dougherty of Philadelphia, the Cardinal Legate, could be dissuaded only with difficulty from sitting in front of the Blessed Sacrament exposed for veneration at one of the principal assemblies; the local Archbishop and his vicar-general were not on speaking terms, and the friars were bitter foes of the American Jesuits. He returned sad and bewildered.

The Dublin Congress he found hardly less disheartening. Nationalism pervaded even the sanctuary. A large streamer was blazoned, 'To Christ our *only* King.'

On his way to the Budapest Congress in 1938 he attended as elected delegate a specially summoned General Congregation of the Jesuits in Rome. He found the occasion tedious, since the greater

[1] When it appeared unlikely that Bourne would be able to make the journey, Martindale invited Bishop Amigo, who accepted; then, on hearing that there was a possibility of Bourne's presence, declined. In the end Martindale had to content himself with Canon Smith of Hull.
[2] *Our Blessed Lady* (Sheed and Ward, 1938).

part of the debates turned on governmental machinery. From Rome he wrote:

> While you can get facts across in short speeches (in Latin) you cannot get their perspective or human value. However, I have survived without getting my knuckles rapped. In fact, the General said to me, privately, 'All you say is quite true and everything else is pure theory.' He is a curious man, somewhat hampered by being a Pole, having an enormous ancestry, and having being trained only in court circles, etc. He is as weak as a feather, with unbelievable energy; minute and mouse-like, until he turns into a sort of eagly-steely-wristed (not taloned: he never scratches) creature; meticulously logical but suddenly expanding into astonishing freedoms—altogether a very extraordinary person.

> We have elected a very level-headed young Belgian [Fr. Schurman] to be his vicar until he dies (I mean, till the General does).

Although confined to a minimum of men, the Congregation, in his judgement, was too large for the task it set itself.

During this stay in Rome, Hitler's visit occurred. Pius XI left the city for Castelgandolfo, the Vatican museums were closed, none of the Fathers was permitted to go out, and the public applause was faked. On Ascension Day the Jesuit martyr, Andrew Bobola, was canonised. Pius looked extremely ill and was given injections during the ceremony. He could still have his blue rages, as he did when Cardinal Innitzer welcomed the Anschluss with Germany in March 1938. The Austrian Jesuits immediately left Rome, and the Congregation was quickly wound up.

Martindale had found it difficult to discover what moved in the mind of the General, Fr. Ledochowski. It seemed to him that the General must have known that the Congregation was hopelessly ineffectual, that the Society was now too large to be governed in the old manner, even with the help of a vast bureaucracy in Rome. Yet one day he flared up: 'You *must* realise, Fathers, that you will be going back into a totally different world. *Totally*. We need *totally* new men.' Yet there was no suggestion as to how these men were to be produced. Martindale's own interventions in the debates consisted of tugs back to reality.

Frequently during this time Fr. Ledochowski was unwell and had periodic collapses that rendered him incapable of work. He had several short meetings with Martindale, gave him his sleeping powders and showed him many small kindnesses.

Martindale's most pleasant memories of this stay were his visits to Propaganda, where Australians and others passed hours in conversation with him. In the afternoons he sat often under the ilexes in the piazza of Sant' Onofrio, halfway up the Janiculo, listening to the fountains and resting his mind.

For ten days between the close of the Congregation and his departure by air for Budapest, he rested in the hospital of the Blue Sisters. At Budapest everyone present realised that a world was finishing. The great nobles knew they were wearing their fine ancestral uniforms for the last time. His preoccupation with the awful spectre of Germany blotted out most of his memories of the Congress.

In 1938 a general 'mission' was organised through the archdiocese of Westminster in an attempt to recover lapsed Catholics to the Church. At the Cardinal's request Martindale sent Hinsley a long letter laying out the difficulties he saw in the way of the Church's progress. Today, after a Conciliar commission has attempted to answer the same problems, Martindale's views still have value and importance.

He knew Hinsley well from his visits to Rome and could write frankly without fear of misunderstanding:

> It will not be much good doing over again what we have for long been doing. What we have done, does not seem to have worked. 'Missions' have been described as a success, when lots of people have followed the sermons and been to the sacraments on the final Sunday. But even if the church has been packed nightly, how minute a percentage of the local Catholics does that account for! And I feel no deep conviction as to the lasting effects of missions.

It was his experience that frequently in working-class districts priests were too grand. The people believed that they said certain things because they had to say them. They were out of touch.

At the other extreme, educated people do not meet the clergy or listen to sermons that make them think, or help them to think properly if they are already thinking. And again, they often say (I have accumulated memories on this topic): 'We somehow feel we are not getting the gospel: we get ecclesiastical information; we hear about money; we are taught how to behave and we know that already, whether or no we carry it out; but we understand that these excellent precepts were taught also by the pagans.' So they were, by the Stoics, for example, who invented the four cardinal virtues. And anyway, plenty of modern pagans behave as well as we do and even better, as a matter of course. If we are to be Christians, we ought to know more about Christ.

He confessed that, owing to the divorce between faith and morals in the sixteenth century, Jesuits were as much to blame as anyone for implementing the idea that Catholicism was an affair mainly of personal behaviour. Then he continued:

What certainly troubles me is the apparent loss of dynamism, i.e. the driving power, fascination, inspiration of Christianity. The first Christians were so intoxicated with their election, redemption, vocation, ultimate glorification that they called Mass the Eucharist, Thanksgiving, long before it became called the Dismissal, which is after all what *Missa* means. How many of us, had we to invent a new name for Mass, would now think first and foremost of Gratitude?

Hence I ask myself what sort of mission would, I think, be desirable? Not, anyway, a mere repetition of the old sort of mission, with its emphasis on Hell, or its re-telling what everyone knows already or knows in a 'catechism' way. How many boys and girls does one know who can answer the Catechism properly (it has been taught them well); but no one has made them love what they know.

Under three headings he set forth some guiding principles: 'Love, not fear, atheism-communism, the Mass.'

We may regret the weakening of belief in Hell. It remains that men refuse to be swayed by threats; their imagination responds no more to the old symbolism. Fear, at best, only prevents them from doing wrong and does not develop the Christian life. And, anyhow, the centre of the Christian life is not fear; neither is it softness nor flattery; but it is positive and constructive.

He discussed the problem of the vast numbers of children who abandoned Mass immediately on leaving school. He saw that the Catholic, like the Communist, must make his ideas very clear and give everyone a share in propaganda. He did not advocate Mass in English, either now or later. He believed that all Catholics could be made to answer with meaning in Latin, be taught to sing plain chant, understand the construction of the Mass. That, as he saw it, should be one aim of the mission. Then there should be lectures with slides on the life of Our Lord, which should be presented as a continuous Life, not as a series of detached edifying episodes or items to prove something.

Then as to Communism. We spoil, it seems, our denunciation of its iniquities by not owning up, in considerable detail. The Communists and we see the same things, but recommend different methods. We cannot dare to leave the acknowledgement of facts wholly to them. The Holy Father does not. But we are frightened of applying his words. I may say that *The Clergy Review* has asked to print an article of mine on condition that everything I say about the life of stewards on ships be omitted; for they say the Shipping Lines might take out a libel action. But it is terrible if Catholics are to remain always within harmless generalities.

He urged the need for a brave declaration of Catholic social doctrine during the mission. The clergy ought not to fear being too highbrow. 'I find them often in the rear of the laity in the matter of thoughtful talk.'

He summarised his hopes:

May the mission be Christian, not theist and ecclesiastical only; loving and not abusive or threatening; and may it courageously tackle the problem of the Mass and the active participation of the laity therein, and vigorously demand social justice in some detail, bravely going beyond the Anglican who always hedges and cancels out this by that . . .

I hope then that this mission will be, to some extent, a new kind of mission and reach non-Catholics as well as Catholics, and include, if possible, some lay speakers. I feel that too often missions consist of a priest flogging the laity into 'fervour'.

4

Martindale himself was too unwell to take any active part in the general mission. From June 1938 until October 1939 many months were spent in hospital, or in preparing for it, or in convalescence. The crisis of his illness came in October 1938. On the 14th he had a double operation—for the removal of his appendix, which proved greatly scarred, and for a more obscure complaint. 'Ask your doctor.' he told his father, 'what Meckle's-Mekel's-Mekell's diverticulum is. This was my number two operation.' There was also lung trouble.

He had prepared himself for death. In September he wrote to his father: 'If I die before you—and why shouldn't I?—I repeat (and I really mean this) that there must not be one penny of expense over Tablets, Inscriptions or what not. I should hate it. A gravestone, no doubt, with, "Pray for his restive sprite"; but anything else whatsoever goes to (i) the Sea Apostolate and (ii) the debts of the Archdiocese of Westminster. And I have destroyed everything in my possession that could subserve newspapers.'

Whimsically he comforted his father with the reflection that should he die after his operations, then he would be likely to go into eternity 'more or less' with him. They had been together so little in life.

Between October and Christmas there was talk of his going to Australia to regain his strength. 'I should love it, but it won't happen. And if it did, I should like to stop there for always. Preferably in Queensland, where you can be sure of warmth. But all those are dreams.'

By Christmas he was able to joke about his condition: 'A good deal of my inside is no longer there to worry about.' He wished that his head could have been successfully amputated, scooped out, had its contents replaced, and then re-shouldered. The demands on him were incessant. He considered he had only twenty-five per cent of his vitality available to meet them.

In January 1939 he managed to preach his first sermon for many months, but he had had no proper convalescence. In April he was again in hospital; his physical energy was almost wholly sapped. When an announcement of his condition appeared in the press, a stoker, whom he had met returning from Australia in 1932, came up from Tilbury and offered him a blood transfusion. 'He said he had lots [of blood]. But I didn't need it.'

On 4 June he left hospital in the afternoon, recorded a broadcast talk, then went to the Hudlestons, remote Catholic cousins of his stepmother, at Sawston Hall, Cambridge, for a rest; and from there to Campion Hall.

This was the time when the project of a new translation of the Bible was launched, a piece of Catholic history admirably recorded by Evelyn Waugh in his *Ronald Knox*. At the end of May Martindale had written to his father from hospital:

> I expect to emigrate to Oxford and can quietly help Ronald Knox in his translation of the Vulgate. *He* is enchanted. It is too vast a job for one man. He was sure he could not get me as assistant. Now he has got me.
>
> I am supposed to be ready to work by October, i.e. to go back then to 114 [Mount Street].

Knox and Martindale never met over the project. When Martindale arrived at Campion Hall in July, the committee members—the translation was envisaged by Hinsley as a joint enterprise—had already dispersed. 'It makes no odds,' he wrote to his father from Campion Hall on 10 July, 'because all he [Knox] wants me to do is to make a paraphrase of the more obscure passages in St. Paul and

St. John, which really means guessing how their minds really worked and what thoughts occurred to them which they did not write down. Rather fun, as well as necessary.'

Many uncompleted manuscripts went with him from Mount Street to hospital, and from hospital, via Sawston, to Campion Hall. There was a book, *Letters from their Aunts*, which attracted little attention: aunts who wrote to Demas, John Mark, Timothy and others. Then some doggerel verse, *Poplar Leaves*, written at odd times for children. And meditations on the Psalms that were published under the title *Sweet Singer of Israel*. Then a book that was never finished: four hundred short meditations on the Eucharist. In 1937 he had written *Does God Matter For Me?* for a series entitled 'Needs of To-Day'; now he wanted to contribute a companion volume, *Can Christ Help Me?* This he did, but not until after the war.[1]

Martindale was at Campion Hall on the outbreak of the war. From now until April 1940 most of his letters to his father are on exegetical questions. The committee appointed to translate the Vulgate never functioned, and the work devolved entirely on Ronald Knox.

[1] Rich and Cowan, 1950. The other books were: *Letters from their Aunts* (Rich and Cowan, 1939), *Poplar Leaves and Seaweed* (Sheed and Ward, 1940), *The Sweet Singer of Israel* (Sheed and Ward, 1941).

## II
# Denmark

During the early months of the war Martindale visited many military and Air Force establishments. He continued his writing. In February 1940 he was again unwell, suffering from insomnia and unable to walk up slopes or even to sit upright for long. At the end of the month he was consulted by the Ministry of Information on broadcasts to South America: he had already spoken with success to Brazil. While the B.B.C. was inclined to treat all these countries alike, he insisted that each republic differed from all the others. The preparation of the talks demanded careful rehearsal in Spanish; the only comment he received was that he spoke the language with a 'rather French accent'. He broadcast also to Germany in German, 'but the B.B.C.,' he told his father, 'made so irresponsible a mess of it . . . that the War Office and Ministry of Information (usually called Miniff) gave it the worst dressing-down it had had for a long time . . . Anyhow, it seems to have gone all right in the concrete.'

In the same month, at the prompting of the Foreign Office, he initiated talks with the Italian Embassy for the improvement of Anglo-Italian relations. Also plans were made for a column to appear jointly in England and France, written partly by François Mauriac, partly by himself. He noted: 'Mauriac's half-column should be published in England, translated by me, with an added but consecutive half-column by myself; the same should be published simultaneously in France—his own stuff and my stuff, not translated, but left in the baroque kind of French that I write. I know it amuses the French and they like it. It is quite good, but me-ish.'

Earlier in the year he had written Hinsley's broadcast to New Zealand, which the Cardinal spoke with such admirable effect that the Ministry of Information printed and distributed a quarter of a million copies. Now he was expanding some of Hinsley's English broadcasts into a book.

His success at this kind of work made him an obvious selection for similar tasks in Spain: at the time Lord Lloyd was planning to open British Institutes in Madrid, Barcelona, Seville and Santander. It was judged that he could help with this and with other 'English–Spanish mutual understanding jobs'. He felt that at any moment the 'phoney' period of the war would end and that he would once more be able to throw himself into work for the sick and dying soldiers. He asked his father to pray that he should not have to go to Spain.

Denmark, in any case, was to be visited first. Already, at the end of February, he expected to be sent there, perhaps for three weeks, soon after Easter, to address mainly non-Catholic audiences. The request to lecture in Denmark came from the Catholic Bishop of Copenhagen through Mr. Møller, an ex-diplomat who was later ordained priest with great éclat and shortly afterwards apostatised. On the instruction of his Provincial, Fr. Joseph Bolland, Martindale went to various Ministries to inquire whether it would be wise to accept the invitation in view of possible invasion of Denmark by the Germans. From the Foreign Office downwards he was assured that a German attack was unlikely for a year at least. The Danish Minister (as he then was) confirmed their view, but at the same time sent for his wife to come to England. The Ministry of Information had no answer to Martindale's inquiry as to what would be valuable to say or not to say in Copenhagen. 'I have developed the utmost distaste for the idea of going to Denmark,' he wrote to his father on 21 March.

On 6 April he made his way gloomily to Shoreham airport. On his arrival at Copenhagen via Amsterdam he was interviewed by journalists, then proceeded to the Jesuit residence in Stenosgade in the centre of the city. His German brethren, he noted, gave him 'a pleasant welcome, two eggs and a glass of beer and exquisite bread and butter'. That evening Hitler's army began its march towards the Danish frontier.

On 7 April he wrote a review of Walpole's *Roman Fountain* for

*The Tablet*, then visited Bishop Suhr, the Catholic Bishop of Copenhagen, 'a convert, tall, slender, with a sense of humour; in fact, beautifully at his ease and dignified without being in the least prelatical or jowly'. He received his instructions and stayed to eat his first smørrebrød, followed by 'a terrific creamy cake, beer and coffee'. The papers had written friendly articles on him and had contrasted him with the Dean of St. Paul's, the last ecclesiastical visitor from England. The next day he lunched at the British Legation. The Minister, Howard Smith, a Harrovian, gave his opinion that the Germans were unlikely to invade. That night he sat up preparing his lectures and sermons. The cold took him by surprise; when he got up from his chair, his feet were numb. He fell and pulled a muscle in his right instep. As the Brother was bandaging his ankle in the early morning, flight after flight of German aeroplanes flew low over the house. Later the same morning parts of the city were already occupied. In the afternoon there was shooting outside the Palace. The German propaganda machine was at work that evening. Bishop Suhr was accused of plotting with the Vatican. What for, was never explained.

For three days there were uncertain and conflicting rumours. Martindale's name was put on the Legation list for evacuation to England, then scored off in Berlin. There was an attempt to get him out through the American Legation but this came to nothing. He resolved not to speculate but to look round for possibilities of work. He was still unable to walk; his fingers and toes were cramped with frost. 'Simply nothing would un-ice my body,' he wrote. The struggle to keep warm strained his heart. Within a fortnight of his arrival he was suffering from dropsy.

From the day of his arrival until the liberation of Denmark, and after it, he kept a journal. It runs to more than half a million words, in single-spaced crowded typing on foolscap pages. By means of it he relieved himself of his sadness at the loss of English companionship for which he found no complete substitute in Denmark. At times it is sentimental, morose, even self-pitying; at others it reaches heights of heroic self-abdication. There is detailed self-analysis. On occasional pages in the first section, passages are marked with a pencilled line in the margin. When he himself re-read the early part of it after the war, he was not always certain whether he had been writing ironically, savagely or with a smile. It is utterly objective. There are no corrections. Much space is given to physical discomfort and mental torment, which, in fact, formed a large part of his life. In public he behaved impeccably and with a show of cheerfulness; in private, when he came to write, there were no reserves. He recognised that the origins of his suffering were in part psychological. Nevertheless the pain was continuous.

Perhaps only in these pages, and in his early verses before ordination, did he write for no one but himself. Often he failed to state the main point of an incident or experience. For instance, he goes into detail over a dispute he had with a modern Danish artist without explaining that the man was illustrating a small Christmas book he had written. In many places he is unintelligible. Several persons are referred to simply by initials. Later, he forgot to whom they referred. There are long speculations on spiritual subjects, which, generally but not in every instance, represent a final state of mind or definite intellectual conclusion. The need to express himself was always paramount. The diary was his chief outlet.[1]

On 15 April, while still uncertain whether he might get back to England through American intervention, he reconciled himself to the prospect of spending the remainder of the war in Copenhagen. 'Anyhow, I am certain to have an increased amount of prayers. May they bring warmth and work.' Also on the 15th the German Rector of the house gave him an electric pad which kept his feet warm during the day and made it possible for him to sleep at night. That afternoon there was a triumphal parade of German troops through Copenhagen. The men were from Sudetenland, 'small, ruddy, and very non-Prussian . . . another multitude to embrace with all one's heart.' Later the same day he met some priests who remembered him from his visits to Propaganda in Rome. He appreciated the courtesy of his German brethren—'They must be on an awful rack and are very good and gay about it.' In their community he acquired a reputation for stoical or scholarly indifference, if not for mystical

---

[1] Selections from this diary are now being prepared for publication.

detachment. His complaints were against the folly of the British Legation: 'Miss Lund tells me that the Danish troops were issued with ammunition the day before the invasion. Why, then, didn't Howard Smith act on *that* and tell me to get at least into Holland.' A conversation at table led him to reflect on religious perfection. This was on 26 April.

Now I have not the slightest idea of what Perfection means: unless something so technical that I have forgotten the definition and can't invent it, which shows that the thing is unreal. Therefore I said . . . that I would be amazed if anyone attained perfection. I can't think of anyone I would call perfect or anything like. One can always be better. Everyone could, except Our Lady.

At present I think it awful that anyone should *try* for some special sort of prayer, or keep his eye on himself to see if he had got it. I don't know that I even want to have it. I want to serve God and please Him and haven't any wish to be aware, even, whether I am doing so or not. Anyhow, I know in a flash if I'm praying what I call more *purely* than usual—I mean, from an entirely non-self impetus . . . (without) words, save at intervals, and then only isolated words. Then I say, thank you, when it's finished without making the least attempt to remember or analyse or recapture it, let alone to induce it . . . It does not surprise me at all that God should on and off take some sort of initiative, as indeed He is doing all the while by making me *believe* . . . It is even quite appalling to imagine that God exists. Or that my Self does. I am too terrified to permit the imagination to have anything to do with it. And honestly I don't know whether I like any of this intensive soul-culture. What is very valuable is to see that there is a way of being and knowing well below ideas, which are only a kind of algebraic interpretation . . . In fine, I should absolutely hate to go in for mysticism, either in myself or others.

Two days later, after a fortnight in Denmark, he wrote: 'And it may last for years! I ought to have been at Ogle St. today.' And a week later: 'I feel rather like St. Ignatius at Manresa—can I go on with this for *X* years? Not quite three weeks!' Even so, these weeks

were full of writing, interviews and talks to small groups. His friends
still had hopes for his repatriation through the American Legation.
On 5 May the police removed the two young English-born Danish
Jesuits, the brothers Dorn; it was uncertain whether it was for
arrest or for interrogation. The next day he hurriedly typed out a
testament, which he left in the hands of the Rector to send to England in the event of his arrest. It began:

> Since the Dorns were removed late last night and are not back
> this morning, and since Fr. King[1] also is removed, though they
> may be back quite soon, they may not; therefore the future is
> recognised by the Rector, etc. as precarious. I might be taken to
> Germany, and if the cold is what it is here, minus the helps I get
> here, I should probably die. I wish to say now that should I, in
> delirium, pain, cowardice, anger or semi-consciousness or any
> other form of weakness, say what I should not or act wrongly or
> fail to act rightly or make mistakes of prudence or any other sort,
> I wish to deny the value of anything of the sort before it happens.

Then, after a moving profession of faith, which he signed with his
full name, he added a postscript.

> If I am taken elsewhere and if my stay is a long one, my father
> may probably die without my knowing. I can only hope that my
> affection may be communicated to my family and that unofficially
> prayers may be said for him and them. He will have known my
> sentiments in this regard. I should like Hutton John to become a
> novitiate or study house rather than be sold to just anyone or to
> fall into ruins after so many centuries.

The same evening that he wrote this he became excited on dis-
covering confirmatory proof for the true interpretation of *Ite, Missa
Est*; he had been working on the beginnings of a fourth book on the
Mass.

Referring to his testament, he says:

> Probably better confide this to the Minister, and any other

[1] A Scottish priest who, after serving for many years in the Faeroe Islands, worked in
Copenhagen. He died there in November 1965.

manuscripts, though they are purely pious. . . . It is now certain that *missa* means dismissal—I mean, new evidence of apparently non-Christian kind; I cannot find the article I was reading. A soldier stands at his post *usque ad missam*. One sees how the dismissal of the Catechumens came to be called the Christians' *Missa*.

In the second half of May it seemed likely that he would be left at liberty. He was over military age. On 23 May he had to seek permission from the Danish police to stay on in Denmark. He appreciated the irony of his position: 'Suppose they say, no,' he wrote to his father, 'I should have to charter a private balloon . . . and live outside the three-mile upward limit, if there is such a thing.' He had made a number of Danish friends whom he met at tactful intervals.

In the few letters he was able to send out of the country, he was always anxious not to stress his discomfort or disturb his family or friends. When he caught himself complaining in his diary, he would check himself and enumerate his 'luxuries'—his very comfortable pillows, the electric heating-pad, books, sleep between blankets. Instinctively he sought to help those who were worse placed than himself. When peat was running out, he managed to take a 'plucky old lady' an occasional sack of wood to supplement her allowance of two scuttles of coal a month; and also a tin of golden syrup and a hyacinth. Anniversaries of his birthday, reception, ordination, were often occasions of surprising comfort in prayer: 'It was a special sort of anniversary-goodnight from *Il Signore*, abrupt, unlooked-for, with a queer content, sweet and shut off like electric light.' He struggled to convince himself that his discomfort was entirely due to his own character and physique; he was not in a concentration camp, not even a prisoner of war or strictly interned. He was leading now a sedentary student's life, and was anxious to be more active. Nevertheless, his sense of mental oppression was real enough. And physically he was weakening. Already on 31 May he noted: 'Don't understand puffiness of calves and ankles and almost cessation of kidney-work.' Moreover, the futility of British propaganda maddened him as much as the untruths of the German radio. ' "Exercises over the sea north off Zeeland; owing to thick fog a projectile fell in Sweden." But it was a very clear day.'

Bishop Suhr arranged for him to leave Copenhagen and rest for a time at a sanatorium run by nuns at Farum. Spring had come. He enjoyed the flowers, particularly after the dusty aspidistras in the Jesuit residence. He worked spasmodically in the garden pulling up thistles. The feast of St. Boniface came. He prayed for some more years of life, if only 'to reconcile England and Germany in Christ'. Always it was the restriction of the apostolate that irked him:

> I seem to be losing strength and ground so steadily that I thought perhaps I could not surmount it. Queer, that perhaps for the first time in my life I have been praying to live, because I feel as if there were so much sheer Christianity needed to be preached after the war . . . Difficult to realise one will do no more apostolate when 'dead', simply because when people die it does not look as if they *did* continue to influence, etc. Why have we (the Society of Jesus included) not more *apostles?* Least of all, in England; abroad certain Jesuits do seem to exercise wide, deep, influence. The main line of increase seems to be that of erudition (aimed at, anyway) which is different from wide culture and general education, of which we get none.

He found it difficult to believe that the first virtue in priests should be prudence, so often made the excuse for not taking the lead. As the weather became warmer, depression set in, and a Calvinistic sense that he was damned, due perhaps to his enforced inaction and increasing weakness.

> Had 'light' today when sitting in the garden that I am a *bad* man, i.e. essentially: compare a wound in which worms have laid eggs so that you simply breed worms from within. So the devil injects living poison into the essence of the soul and it breeds. Almost a sense of being damned. Very strongly felt. All you can do is to offer yourself to God and His love, as such. I am certainly conscious that 'though I do not sin', the fountain of it is in

me. I can quite easily see myself as responsible for all the calamities of the Church. . . . Fourth Sunday after Pentecost. Very consoling *Introit*. That was about as far as I could attend! Quite drunk with sleeplessness.

Continually he prayed that in public at least he might never utter a complaint or expression of anxiety or show rufflement, but 'in this house it is difficult since the place is packed with lamenting ladies and elderly male prophets of disaster'. The nuns puzzled him. He judged that there were far too many female religious congregations in Denmark, and that there was no adequate work for them. The lay-sisters were more enchanting, gay, modest and seemingly happier than the choir nuns.

Only slowly did he fully accept his exile. 'My sacrifice is *not* to be in England— . . . to be unable to speak or write, unable to minister . . . I suppose I have never really made any sacrifices, or made them well, all my life: therefore I had better fill my last years with them.'

He found more work, but, on a smaller scale than in England. There were regular articles in the Catholic paper. The first appeared in June. He was told it suited exactly the Danish mentality and found it strange that he had hit on it so quickly. Then in July he conducted the first of many retreats. There were talks on secular and religious subjects to societies or groups; lectures to schoolmasters, religious instruction to boys from the school adjoining the presbytery, individual converts—he received his first in October 1940. In June, back in Stenosgade, he became 'quite excited at the approach of the feast of St. Aloysius'. The day was a turning-point for him. He realised now that it was possible for him 'to begin to emerge with tact', although he still required permission to sleep outside Copenhagen. He visited the King and his family, stayed for two weeks as the guest of the Bishop, and at his suggestion planned a number of small books and pamphlets for translation into Danish. In late June there were rumours that heartened him: 'Apparently the Germans are arranging a large camp not far from Farum for British prisoners. If so, and if it is filled, please God I can get myself put into it and be able to minister to all alike besides Catholics. The life will be hard; but how perfect a joy to finish up with. I should feel my internment was justified, i.e. the whole expedition.'

While the German priests at their residence behaved towards him with exemplary understanding, he did not know what attitude he should adopt to the German authorities: 'I am not only very unhappy about England, but constantly tormented by the question of how I should behave to Germans. I mean, what would be the Christian way? Is it compatible with quiet unyielding dignity? With plain-spokenness? Must one try to be positively friendly also in manner, with the certainty of being misunderstood?' On 20 August he received a letter from de Bélinay. On 22nd there is a note: 'Trotsky R.I.P. Who next?'

Throughout the summer he still wondered how to get 'more sheer occupation'. He resigned himself to remaining in Denmark. He started to learn Danish and, as much for the sake of companionship as for the language, he took lessons. But he found he could not get his tongue round the words, discontinued, and, instead, gave some private lessons in English. He reflected that he could endure it all better if he had been in a Catholic country. The Danes were kind to him and cultured, but he could not understand them. Their appetite for food never failed to astonish him, and their 'Protestant' fuss about health. The cold dulled his wits in winter and his pace of work slowed down. He tired more often. 'I perfectly understand why animals hibernate. After dinner yesterday I rolled myself up in rugs and slept like a dormouse.' He wore a woollen hat indoors; then, in the next winter, had a second lining sewn into it. The cold was said to be severer then than at any time in recorded history. Many people collapsed in the street. The Associated Press reported that 'with the temperature 32 degrees below zero, the weather is so severe that, when trains stop, they frequently freeze to the rails'. The Provincial, on visitation at Stenosgade, received anonymously 50 kroner for 'Fr. Martindale's warmth'. Did he want warmer underclothing, a second electric pad, some bottles of French wine? Martindale was convinced that nothing would make any difference, but promised to tell the Provincial if any need occurred to him.

On 9 November 1940, during the prayers after Mass, he fell asleep with his hands on the altar. He wrote a Christmas play for children. When the news of General Wavell's victories in the western desert reached him, he wrote: 'Anyhow, the Australians will be up after recent events.' He abominated the special beer brewed for the Christmas festivities; also the cold marble-coloured sausage, and sauerkraut, grey or the colour of decayed claret, and 'as sharp as a bayonet charge'.

He noted every book he read and the lines of thought it set him on. St. Angela of Foligno he found alternately dull and enthralling. For days he was puzzled why he could not like St. Catherine of Siena. Probably it was because she described every person and thing as *dolce*; her letters were dreary, diffuse and unsuitable to the recipients; and she had a total disregard for nature: once only did she comment on poppies, simply because the colour reminded her of Christ's blood. How much more subtle a reformation the Church would need after the war than in St. Catherine's time! St. Ignatius, he argued, was not vulgar, nor were any of the Jesuit saints, but what they wrote, save when they unconsciously let themselves go, was instantly vulgarised. Then: 'How one wants our Lord, Shepherd, to play his pipe a little louder, with a more definite tune. But not in this world will He. . . .'

For pages he reflected on things ecclesiastical—the preoccupation of priests, even in Denmark, with administration instead of pastoral work, the jealousies between order and order, old and young, secular and regular, all the dead legislation that needed cutting out from the Church's machine. Surely now there was no discernible difference between 'servile' work and any other kind of work. He could speak about these matters to the Bishop and thought of asking him whether they might lunch together once a week.

Never could he accept the sheer mismanagement and misinformation that had placed him in Denmark. Once in a suburban train he discovered a German soldier with a Norwegian-Danish-German phrasebook. It had been printed in 1938 for use of the invading troops. Then shortly afterwards, he got back to an old personal puzzle as his thoughts turned inward: 'I can see strong clashes of co-existent qualities in me as in Constantine, Helena, etc. but so smudged out compared with them: an itch rather than a scorching fire . . . I suddenly saw myself as *always* here, like the man at the end of *A Handful of Dust*.'

Often he ruminated on his vocation. Although he had first wanted, he did not know how sincerely, to be a Brother of St. John of God, or 'something like that', and nurse the sick, preferably in Spain and without a surname, even now he did not doubt that he had entered the Society under a spiritual compulsion. He reflected moodily on his family. As he had done at St. Beuno's, he wrote much about his mother. He did not see how he could have helped the disharmony in himself. It had always been so, a thing he was incapable of correcting —'I should think, due to my Mother, herself ill, and ill-crossed with my very nervy family, I mean, my Father's. I can never think of hers as mine.'

On 29 January 1942 he was particularly ill. In the afternoon a lady came to him for confession. He was almost unable to talk. Then suddenly, about 4 o'clock, within a quarter of an hour, his strength returned 'like a blind slowly drawing up or lights rising', Then the Rector came to his room to say that he had *des nouvelles douleureuses*. At first Martindale thought he was to be sent to Germany, then when the Rector added 'from Rome', he feared he was involved in some kind of Jesuit row. Cardinal Maglione, the Pope's secretary, had cabled the Bishop news of Sir Arthur Martindale's death on 25 January at the age of eighty-seven.

At great length he went through the changing history of his relationship with his father, a childhood myth who became a real person. He was to blame for his failure to explain himself to his father in his early days as a Catholic and Jesuit. Later, after ordination, they began to understand one another better: '*he* recognising what in me he could not and never would understand—the gaps, gulfs, enigmas, formulas; and humbly taking them all for granted and adhering so devotedly to what he could have of me; and *I*, recognising his Martindale-ish and English and class-ish limitations and intolerances and eagerness to question me about my life, knowing that he would hear so much that meant nothing to him, or that sounded so small or priggish or affected or alien or almost enviable;

and in a way thinking me "brilliant", if not "above" him, poor
man. Well, I was much cleverer than he, but how much more
meretricious! He had no thread of the mystic in him: so just,
honourable, industrious, loving, tolerant, un-climbing.'

Arthur had retired at the age of fifty in the year that his son took
his Final Schools at Oxford. He had been one of Lord Curzon's
most trustworthy servants during his Viceroyalty. In 1904 he had
been created K.C.S.I., then a Knight of Grace of the Order of
St. John of Jerusalem. He had been one of the best known of Indian
political officers of his day. When his obituary notice in *The Times*
reached Cyril, he pinned it into his diary.

The Roman telegram stated that Cyril's father had died *impro-
visamente*. He wondered how sudden had been his death—in the
street, in his chair, in pain or peacefully? Never had he been able to
use his imagination to make the 'dead' living, though he had no
difficulty in believing that they lived more truly than they had done
or he did. A melancholy came over him. A part of his personal history was over. Now he was the oldest generation of his family. 'I did
not feel unhappy,' he wrote in a letter at the end of March, 'but
rather as if the roof, or one side, had been taken off the house, and as
though I was stripped to the winds, so to say.' Yet, as his diary
shows, he was morose. In his dealings with his father, he wrote, 'I
was aloof, unkind, selfish, untruthful, at one time acidly agnostic—
but then, so have I been to everyone. It is awful to see how much
more one has been loved than one has loved. Or is that true? I have
loved you, X, Y and Z, in my fashion. I really have. But very much
in my fashion, for which I am *not* responsible. But what a loathsome
boy and pitiable youth. It remains that I am sorry, sad, bruised, but
cannot make a real effort to help him in Purgatory . . . Well, if he
does begin to "understand" and "see God", he will be so very
different that it will not be he. Cela étant, R.I.P., and wait till you
are more in shape yourself, and, above all, till the insanity of this
cold is over.'

Particularly he remembered his behaviour on the only occasion he
had stayed at Guildford with his father. He had gone out early to say
his Sunday Mass, so as not to interfere with domestic arrangements.

At breakfast his father inquired whether he had a good congregation. Cyril answered that he had not looked, but presumed no one was there, that he had gone early in order to be alone. Naturally this was more than his father could understand. Cyril then explained himself, but in terms he knew would puzzle his father still more: Mass was a sacrifice, something between him and God; there was no need of a congregation.

This had happened shortly after his ordination, but as his relations with his father drew closer, he answered all his father's questions in long and frequent letters; and, towards the end, confided in him information about his own work that he gave to no one else. In July 1937, with a strict injunction that the news was not to go beyond his home, he told him: 'I had a long talk with the ex-Emperor of Abyssinia and have said what I thought. He is now chewing it. I felt like a man putting the last iron-shod heel on a broken, agonising animal. Also with the Queen of Spain: of no real direct importance, but indirectly, please God.' When the Catholic writer Alfred Noyes fell foul of the Holy Office, Cyril gave his father the whole history of the case, into which he himself had been called as a friend both of Cardinal Hinsley, who was under instructions from the Holy Office, and of Frank Sheed, his own and Noyes's publisher. One of his last letters to his father before leaving for Copenhagen explained the technical vocabulary of St. Paul: the three words he used for spirit and the three for man. 'Supernatural,' he concluded, was not a word at St. Paul's disposal, and he showed how in the later Epistles Paul struggled towards this expression. On his side, his father annotated his letters in the margin and between the paragraphs. It was a relationship that sought understanding on both sides and found it only in small measure. In its later period it was full of courtesy and deep mutual respect.

He had disappointed his father in every way. An only son, he had become a papist, then a priest, with 'no chance of being a cardinal and shedding a reflected rose-colour on my dingy family'. On Arthur's side there was never a word of reproach. Cyril appreciated this: 'I hope to hitch on to his belt hereafter.' Henceforth, in his diary, he recalled not his father's anniversary, but the day he received news of his death. His imagination, on this day, was frozen, as he noted in his diary. This makes all the more convincing the experience he had the same evening. In a letter to Miss Beatrice Davis-Cooke, dated 3 March 1942, he recounts it more fully than in his diary:

I wonder if you asked St. Francis de Sales, on his feast, to cheer me up, if I needed it, when I should hear of my father's death. Naturally I thought of St. Francis and of you that morning at Mass, but I fear that I had given him no more thought that day, though I had been studying him—about a year ago, or rather, Sainte Jeanne François de Chantal—more carefully than before. [Then he recounts how he heard of his father's death about 4 o'clock.] We went down to dinner at 6, and perhaps I *was* feeling a little bewildered, . . . Well, you know that I of all people am not given to pious impressionism . . . but thereupon I was (and am) *quite sure* of St. Francis de Sales's presence (much more definitely than of my neighbours at table) just behind me and a little to the right, and, as it were, patting my side (sounds odd, but if I were inventing it, I should say, shoulder), and being *most* kind and encouraging, and yet episcopal and Savoyard-no-sentimentalism-please; in fact, both affectionate and genial *and* grand-seigneur— quite the last mixture I should have administered to *myself*. At first there wasn't any imagination mixed up with this, i.e. no words or sight, but in a moment or two I noticed that my imagination *was* trying, on its own, to add something and was rather fidgeted by the suggestion of a *brown* skirt of a habit (n.b. I couldn't look up over my shoulder, twisting round in my chair, but could have, as it were, squinted a little downwards!) and felt that this was not what I was expecting. Afterwards, thinking it over, I concluded that the mere name, Francis, set going a *Franciscan* train of imagination, whereas I was uneasily conscious that I ought to have imagined episcopal violet and perhaps ermine! This seemed to show that my examining, almost rationalising, spirit was quite active and was rejecting all that imaginative element as *my* contribution; while the 'gift' of his presence and influence was so unmistakably *not* my affair that I thought and think that it was real and a good gift from God and quite likely due to your having told him to take me in hand. Anyway, I just sort of nodded a *Deo Gratias* and hoped to take anything that God meant to give, and went on eating.

He was ill at this time. In the next few days he was sent off first to the Catholic Nursing Home, then, for closer examination, to the Communal Hospital. Within a fortnight he was back at Stenosgade, but unable to say Mass. He had two attacks of angina and before Easter was anointed.

As he came to know Denmark better, his depression increased. The Danes struck him as incorrigible materialists: 'So long as they have enough to eat and drink, they could rock themselves in cradles of illusion.' Even the 'nicest Danes' slammed doors or left them open, dropped tins and crockery in corridors without noticing the crash. But gradually he conquered his suspicion that Danes were 'overwhelmingly kind' only when their kindness was pleasurable to them; yet still at the back of his mind he wondered whether they were capable of 'giving up in order to give at all or to go on giving, even affection'. Certainly he never appreciated the real and great sacrifices they made for his comfort. When whisky was selling at fifteen pounds a bottle on the black market, they saw that he was seldom without it. Regularly he received from them cigarettes purchased at exorbitant prices. They did as much, if not more, than his English friends could have done. On his birthdays he was given presents of flowers, marmalade and cigarettes: 'Sorry,' he wrote on one birthday, 'if God saw fit to make this the last birthday in so wasted a life.'

His condition became worse. In June 1942 he spent a fortnight in hospital. The two flights of stairs up to his room in the Jesuit house were more than he could now manage. It was arranged that he should move to Rygaard convent-school, now emptied of its pupils, at Hellerup in the suburbs of the city. It had a fine garden, and he was kindly cared for by Mother Madeleine Eugenie and the community. From here, when he was well enough, he could visit his friends, and he was accessible to them. Occasionally he met the Queen, more rarely the King. Once, on Corpus Christi, the Queen visited him: 'She has real charm, modesty and dignity. She began in Danish but went on in English. Two such *superb* black horses and lovely scarlet livery.' Another time, repeating his description of the Queen, he added 'almost holiness'. Other visitors, engaged in underground activities, would suddenly ask him: 'Can I lawfully shoot so and so?' They expected an instant answer.

He refused to allow himself to think of England except as a kind of symbol, even to hate the war or get angry about any event: 'If I let myself slip a hair's breadth I should be passionately homesick and exhaust my soul by wanting to get home.' His acutest homesickness came over him when he thought of Abingdon, where Mrs. Spencer-Bull had evacuated the Club after it had been bombed in Poplar.

Before going to Rygaard he had learnt that the Germans had suppressed the Danish police; no longer was Denmark to be the model protectorate. Hitherto he had reported to the police weekly and had to be at home when he received notice of their visits. Also he had made promises, dictated by the Germans, that he would not attempt to escape, or engage in subversive activity. Now he considered these promises no longer binding and moved about within Denmark as he chose. He was not harassed.

Many of his short excursions were errands of mercy. When eggs were rare and expensive, he bought two and 'got sandwiches made for M.B. who had nothing save bread and proposed to travel to a rest-home on it'.

His work continued, as much of it as he could get or could do. In England his writing had always been done in intervals of travel, retreats and ceaseless external activity. Now he found it difficult to adjust himself. The articles, pamphlets, playlets, prayer-books continued, but there was only one work of any substance, published first in Copenhagen, then, after the war, in London. Significantly it was a biography of Camillus de Lellis, a saint whose birthday he shared and whose life had always a special appeal to him. St. Camillus had nursed the sick, organised hospitals, had failed frequently and made new beginnings: a character as full of contradictions as his own. Although war conditions made it impossible for him to do the kind of research that had gone into *The Vocation of St. Aloysius*, it was a careful book. The Camillan Fathers at Aalborg sent him books in French, Spanish, English, German and Italian; he wrote to Oxford for a copy of an original and unpublished letter of St. Camillus there. His motive was to explain Catholic attitudes to Danes, 'for there is a Catholic way of looking at life, and still more, at death; and if it is happier to live in a Catholic atmosphere, it is almost necessary to die in one, if that tremendous act of Death is to be accomplished with full spiritual satisfaction.'[1]

However, the book did not receive the notice he had hoped.

He felt a sense of acute personal loss when he heard of Cardinal Hinsley's death in 1943. On 19 March he wrote: 'I feel Cardinal Hinsley's death more and more. Have written by request about him and seize every opportunity of speaking about him'; then, on 24 March, 'Last night I listened to parts of Cardinal Hinsley's Requiem: knelt all through it and had eyes aching with unsheddable tears.'

Always the future of the Church occupied him, in England, Denmark and universally. Lutheranism, as he observed it now, was very different from what it had been; relics of its old form could not survive into the present generation. As for the Catholic faith, he saw the need for presenting it in an utterly different way if it were to make progress in a changed world: 'The clergy will never do this unless awful disasters and all but extermination come upon us or unless we have a quite miraculous and heroically audacious Pope.' Criticism of seminary and Jesuit training and, most of all, what he saw as the waste of his own life, fill many pages. The lessons for Matins, hymns, phrases from the psalms set him off on new and old trails. 'A lovely example of the absolute in human affairs: *omnis consummationis vidi finem*: a most Greek idea if that is what the Psalmist means. *Per passionem ejus et crucem ad resurrectionis gloriam perducamur.* Felt, oh, yes, am delighted that God should drag me along; so to say, put me through it. I quite trust Him.'

In the last year, and particularly in the last months, of the occupation, the streets of Copenhagen became dangerous. The German

[1] *St. Camillus* (Sheed and Ward, 1946), vii.

authorities had opened the prisons, letting out the dregs of the population as well as the adult defectives. At times there was chaos. Previously, sniping and arrests had been spasmodic. Now there was looting and assassination. The Germans did little to check it, since it gave them the opportunity of proclaiming that it was not their work. At times also the Germans themselves became hysterical and indulged in wild shooting on any pretext. No place or time was more safe than any other, so Martindale paid little attention. Fatalistically, he continued to visit his friends or to take books to and from the library of the Jesuit residence. The only emotion that the shots stirred in him was anger at being made to jump suddenly.

As the activities of the Danish underground increased towards the close of the war, he had to be more careful in his conversation with friends who might repeat his remarks and get themselves, if not him also, into trouble. Allowance had to be made for a certain number of traitors in any country, though it seemed to him that Denmark had too high a percentage, not least among young girls. He taught himself not to speculate in company, or to think aloud, or even to believe what he heard; and this produced in him a stunned effect, which lasted for some time after his return to England.

In the spring of 1945, when the Allied advance was resumed, there was panic in Copenhagen. The Germans prepared to evacuate the city. On 29 April all the bakeries, lorries and bicycles were commandeered. Schools were closed. The next day it snowed. Martindale was still wearing his three winter waistcoats. As the British troops drew nearer, the confusion was worse. On 2 May there were rumours that the city was actively besieged. Many German officers were out of uniform; some surrendered to local postmen. The shootings continued all day. 'It is an exasperation,' he noted, 'not to know who gets killed, and why.'

As in his first weeks in Denmark, the B.B.C. broadcasts infuriated him. On 4 May he corrected the nonsense that came over the radio from London: 'The Danish police have *not* taken over, the Germans have *not* evacuated the island, the King has *not* "returned" to Copenhagen, for he has been there for ages.'

The evening of the same day he was dining with friends when

news came that Copenhagen was liberated at last. The next morning, while he was still in bed, there was shooting around the convent at Rygaard. A shot was fired into the room of another priest, Fr. Wever, and would have killed him had he not been sitting on the floor. 'Many said they were aiming at me, but why? or why, for that matter, at Fr. Wever?' When he turned round at Mass to give Holy Communion, he noticed two girls standing at the foot of the altar with a Danneborg and a Union Jack. '*Longus ille et unus annus*', so his five years in exile appeared to him that day.

On 13 May Field-Marshal Montgomery entered Copenhagen. There was a victory parade. 'The town was maniac about Montgomery, whose face I liked very much; very austere *and* kind *and* amusing.' The next day there is an entry in his diary: 'Have determined to write to Churchill. Tactful if he came; and politically stabilising re Russia.' There is no note of a letter.

Slowly news of his English friends trickled through. Almost compulsively he began work among the British and French troops. On board H.M.S. *Birmingham* he met a number of friends. He said Mass on other ships and preached to French sailors. He remained in Copenhagen, and on 10 July he was visited by Fr. Peter Blake, an Air Force chaplain, who brought him 'so much desperately interesting provincial, national and international news that my mind could not retain it'. The visit raised his spirits: 'the Society of Jesus is so much better than what one might have feared. I am quite sure that the English Jesuits are a fine body of men, and would to God I could come up to them.'

However, the immediate aftermath of war depressed him. He wrote:

The destruction of almost everything, the spread of hate, vengefulness, the incredible misery of millions, oppress me too much. But worse than anything is my feeling that I have not enough *Catholic spirit* to do the only thing that is open to me, i.e. to offer myself as a victim *seriously* for these poor nations, armies, families and so on, because I am afraid of what might happen to me—not from man, but from God's end. But I think I must do something of the sort, and if I *do*, I think I am in for a very tough time. What I have been for a long time clear about is, that I must cut the whole of my past life off from my future. By life I obviously don't mean the faith-element in it: this is the only thing that survives or will or can survive. So I resign all friends, relatives, domiciles, jobs and even sanity to God. But ought that to be difficult? Haven't I always said it? Yes. But meant it? Or realised what I thought I meant? I have lived, really, on (apart from the *Pater*, *Ave* and *Gloria*) four prayers: *Anima Christi*, *Suscipe*, *Sub tuum* and C. de la Colombière's 'Sacred Heart of Jesus, to Thee I offer myself without any reserve'.

Once again, as at Oxford, but with a more mature penetration, he examined the pagan and the Christian parts of himself, the first leading logically to suicide, the second to the total self-abdication he had always sought. He hoped, but was not convinced, that now the Christian element pervaded him more widely than the pagan. He argued with himself persistently, setting forth the alternatives to his ideal and demolishing each in turn:

So I foresee either suicide (which certainly would mean being mad) or wild sensuality (which, at my age, would be not only ridiculous but impossible) or a lapse into complete lethargy (which I know I would be temperamentally incapable of, short of a brain-lesion), *or* complete self-abandonment to God, which He has been trying to make me do ever since my noviceship, and I have always cheated Him. All one can say is—*De multitudine misericordiae Tuae* . . . and *Largire digneris. Largitas Dei* is the thing to fasten on. His work continued among his Danish friends and acquaintances.

August was largely taken up with farewells. He received letters of thanks from the Bishop, editors of papers to which he had contributed, Jesuits, heads of Catholic organisations, for all the work he had done for the Church in Denmark. He felt 'apathetic but grateful, and especially very grateful for so much gratitude. It is better not to look back and try and assess credit and debit.' This was almost the last entry in his Danish diary. On 20 August he preached in the crowded Catholic cathedral at a peace service, which all the ambassadors, except the Russian, attended. Early in September he obtained a place on a plane to London.

In a letter written just a year before his death he recalled the 'five empty years' in Denmark, far worse than any illness, during which he could 'see nothing, hear nothing, say, imagine, believe nothing'—and feel nothing save the cold.

# Last Years

On his arrival in London Fr. Martindale was greeted by the new Provincial, Fr. Martin D'Arcy. He learned that his father had greatly fretted over him in Denmark. He was amazed by the number of prayers that had been said for him, and this he saw as a sign that God wished his soul to be saved and that its salvation demanded such help. Although the community at Farm Street was largely changed, the same fatality continued to beset the decoration of the church. The new statue of Térèse of Lisieux represented the saint as a bad-tempered woman of forty-five, with two large warts on her chin produced by bad lighting. He found his friend, Fr. Steuart, much older, in many ways like himself without his own weakness of character and head, but unable to 'stick to things'. There was work he considered he could still do, and he prayed for strength to do it. The amount of wickedness and sorrow he met on all sides appalled him.

Before 24 September he had completed drafts of B.B.C. talks to Poland and Hungary and begun his contribution on the Apocalypse for the *Catholic Scripture Commentary*. At once he interested himself in Czech and Polish refugees. 'If I can help in their chapel of Our Lady of Czestochowa in Liverpool Cathedral, I kill or animate two birds with one cheque.' In September also he received an invitation to the United States, which he did not take up. From what he heard of the behaviour of certain priests and laymen, he believed that the wartime bombing must have physically shaken people's brains. A friend, just back from Addis Ababa, conveyed to him Haile Selassie's best regards, 'despite our last interview; L. says he is the most democratic autocrat'. An Italian priest from the Rota, whom he met

in London, quoted to him amazing rules based on obsolete sixteenth-
century science, that the Congregation still followed.

It did not take him long to get up to date in his reading. *The Song
of Bernadette*, about which his Catholic friends raved, struck him as
an inferior romance. *The Power and the Glory*, published some months
after his leaving for Copenhagen, set his mind working on the subject
of grace. He thought he could say that Graham Greene was determined to detect the action of grace, or of the Spirit, like a kind of
germ working its way up through a morass of wrong: 'He does not
see the Holy Spirit chiefly as plunging onto men from outside, but
as there already. Without knowing it, he has a lot of Romans VIII
in him.' The book struck him as ghastly and grand; it was also a
grave criticism of Mexican Catholicism. It fitted his mood. 'I am
increasingly overwhelmed by the consciousness of the incredible
mystery of each individual.'

There was much that made him melancholic, mainly his inability
to work as he had done before the war. He could scarcely believe he
had been the recipient of so much affectionate interest among his
brethren: 'Well, more and more, I am astounded by the affection I
get even inside the Society.' Nevertheless, the unmistakable proofs
of this were insufficient to rid him of the feeling that he was only
tolerated and kept on at Farm Street because there was no way of
getting rid of him. His sermons were not, of course, as clearly
audible as they had been; and he was too weak to take his turn at the
routine tasks in the church and parlour. But there was a melancholy
also at a deeper level, when he viewed the condition of the world. As
always he argued with himself:

> There is too much in the world that needs prayer that one would
> be only distracted by trying to know it in detail, let alone imagine
> it, or to pray explicitly about it: so the more one can empty out
> self, wishing God to occupy oneself totally and then overflow and
> energise where He sees one would want Him to, and above all,
> where He wants to.

Constantly he had to reassure himself that he still could serve the
Church. In the November following his return the Provincial,

Fr. D'Arcy, assured him that he had his part to play in London, that he had his complete confidence and wished only that he should say frankly to his Superior what he thought he could do.

When he looked at the Society of Jesus in England, he saw some hope for its usefulness. He found Fr. D'Arcy's direction of the Province imaginative and inspired. Tied for longer periods at Farm Street and more accessible to his brethren, he made discoveries of talent among men to whom before the war he was merely a name. He ranked highly Fr. Frederick Copleston's works. 'Copleston on Nietzsche very, very good.' He came to know Fr. Christopher Devlin, for a brief period stationed at Farm Street after his demobilisation from the Royal Air Force. 'He turns out to be a mystic and modern poet. He showed me the first canto of an epic on Seven Cities, of which the first is the Sphinx. I wrote a long criticism of it which apparently touched him.'

This heartened him but his sense of his own uselessness persisted. After a dinner party at the Savoy before the end of the year, to which both Fr. D'Arcy and Fr. Steuart were also invited, he noted that Fr. D'Arcy was really brilliant and extremely gay, that Fr. Steuart was tragic, quite deaf, haggard, looking miserable and old beyond words; and that Randolph Churchill was paradoxical and noisy. He judged there was no place for him.

After the retirement of Mrs. Spencer-Bull, Poplar was bedevilled by quarrels. The clergy there and elsewhere appeared resolved to keep everything in their hands and yet they produced no ideas. Cardinal Griffin had not the 'tête de l'emploi', the Pope did not really write the kind of encyclical that would reach men in general, 'and if he trusts, as he says he does, bishops and ordinary priests to put them across, what an illusion that is!'

His engagement books are fairly full: sermons, an occasional broadcast, instructions, luncheons, marriage cases, the resumption of old contacts; but he felt himself carried on far beyond his own physical or mental strength by forces outside himself. His life was now, as he described it, 'all slogging'. He believed the saints were his best company. On Francis Xavier's feast, 3 December 1945, he had a 'sense' of the saint, his simplicity and of the transfer of his own self to God's care. 'How delighted I feel and at home when in contact with the saints,' he wrote early in January 1946. Then on the 29th of the same month: 'This is the anniversary of the day St. Francis de Sales was so kind to me. I think that was really a gift. Not only unexpected but unlike what might have been expected. Moreover, such a lot in it. And in the middle of dinner.' He reflected how saints, little enough known, like St. Lawrence, seemed to get hold of him. He tried to tease out the problem presented by Fr. William Doyle:

Willie Doyle was jumping about with glee in the corridor [at St. Mary's Hall] when we had some English disaster in the Boer War. Fr. McCoy overheard him and gave him a refectory penance for 'gross uncharity'. Once he [Doyle] twice fouled R[obert] M[onteith] also very grossly at football. M. said, 'I've stood it twice. There are rules . . . Next time I will make you remember it.' He did it again, and M. had some trick which laid Willie Doyle low for weeks. A religious house! I cannot overcome my dislike for the ejaculatory and 'penitential' part of Doyle's life. Perhaps he began by doing a *generous wrong* thing and earned a late conversion.

He took up once more his book on women saints, *The Queen's Daughters*,[1] which he had started and set aside during the last years before the war. There are passages in it that belong to different periods: some, like his sketch of Mother (now Saint) Cabrini, are brilliant, but it is essentially a patchwork.

There was one final spiritual experience, more in the nature of the two he had during the noviceship than of his third at St. Beuno's. It occurred on 22 September 1946 and in a curious and unexpected manner, as he was coming down from his top-floor room in the lift.

I cannot deny that I felt or rather *was* in close touch with the Trinity as such. I say 'touch', because it was not feeling, imagination or ideas. Yet I suppose any spiritual state cannot but have an effect on the imagination. Certainty that each Person was there and having hold of me. That already is an idea; then absent. No

---

[1] *The Queen's Daughters* (Sheed and Ward, 1951).

result that I know of, save more recollection during the day: presence by faith of the Holy Trinity.

He had long been exercised about the individual relationship of God with the soul. On the preceding August Bank holiday, he had attempted to convince himself, when looking at photographs of the vast crowds on south-coast beaches, that each was a person, the centre of his world: 'it becomes quite overwhelming and seems impossible; yet [if not true] everything else would be more impossible, starting with myself'.

After demobilised troops who had fought in Italy had made Padre Pio, the Capuchin friar and stigmatic, familiar in England, he studied the subject. There were moments when he hoped to be able to accept an invitation to see him, but he was too weak for the journey. The Marchese Patrizi, who was closely connected with the work Padre Pio inspired, provided him with much information. Eric Strauss, an old friend and former convert, now director of the psychiatric department at St. Bartholomew's, discussed with him the psychological elements in the phenomena. He gathered first-hand reports, then wrote in *The Month* what is still the best appraisal of Padre Pio. He was interested in Strauss' theory that there was no physical substratum for the Ascension; that the historic event was an hallucinatory appearance of an ascension permitted by God.

He was also studying the question of possession by evil spirits. 'If we admit that, then why not by good spirits—equivalent to confirming in grace? Perhaps it is that good spirits don't want to possess.' The occasional article by Père Teilhard de Chardin in the Jesuit review, *Études*, stimulated him. He saw nothing in his friend's writings to embarrass the dogma of the resurrection of the body. What Père Teilhard wrote seemed to him in harmony with the Church's teaching on mysticism and on the supernatural life.

But principally it was the life of the priest in the post-war world that agitated him. He was no extreme advocate of lay control but only of cooperation and understanding between laymen and clergy. He insisted that no priest was an oracle, and proposed that in each parish church a triple list should be posted for all to see, giving, first the income from endowments, offertories and gifts, then expenditure, which was to include also 'priestly whisky', and, finally, the parish needs. Where this had been done at his instigation, activity was harmonised. A parish, he pointed out, did not consist of a priest plus a large number of people, who (it was hoped) would go to Mass and the sacraments regularly and give generously, but 'one living body in which (if one must distinguish) the priest is essentially and always the servant of the laity'. Half the priests he met did not see that eventually their responsibilities were far greater than a married man's, yet they were apt to become, not celibates for the love of God, but old bachelors doing a job dutifully, but no more than they need. 'I don't want a priest to be cossetted in material ways and I don't want spiritual respect to be artificial. That a priest should never know he is criticised is bad, for he can't ever correct himself. And it is false that a priest can't ever need correction.' He thanked God he had never been comfortable in his own priestly life, but 'I've often been extremely happy.'

In the pulpit the priest was so often mechanical. On looking back at his own life he could state that he had never preached on a subject about which he was not convinced: the Holy Shroud, for instance, was always an 'inexplicable puzzle'. In the confessional the priest might have to be a theologian, but should not behave as one, for he was dealing there with persons whom he loves and is privileged to help. He preferred to hear men's confessions outside the 'box'; and seamen's confessions as priest and penitent leant over the bulwarks in a state of awe at the sea. Priests who occupied themselves with mortification and were utterly inconsiderate continued to puzzle him.

As his powers of endurance diminished he sought to identify himself more closely in spirit with world events. Even more intensely than in Denmark he reacted to all he heard or read, whether it was news of a flood in India or an air crash in the Atlas or Andes. 'I don't want merely to know about things, I want to *be* them. And, after all, if we are in Christ and Christ is in all those people killed by an earthquake, or wants to be; so can we be, through faith, no doubt, not feeling.' Therefore he prayed for more faith, 'helped out by a spot of feeling now and again'. Reduced activity made him turn in more on himself. He could not get away from the conviction that he had inside him a 'suppressed volcano' and that there were certain things to which he should make a volcanic response. 'I believe this with every fibre of my being: but then God muffles it (the volcano) until there is nothing but faith left.' And he went on: 'I am prepared to wait for heaven for the proper response. I think it would kill me if I realised anything now, that is, in a way corresponding to what I know is realisable.'

An article in *The Times Literary Supplement* on 'changing man' set him thinking how far man had changed or even could change, and what a priest's preparation for this phenomenon should be. He saw the progression of man simply as a zig-zag or at best a spiral. Pain was once considered redemptive; but now no longer. Pagans, save when morbid, hated pain and found no use for it; Christians, more healthy minded, saw how to use it: 'now men are relapsing into the old helplessness. The collective mind changes, if you like, but not the pain nor the man.'

A letter from de Bélinay in December 1948 gave him news of friends from his days at Aix. 'Teilhard n'est pas encore brûlé. Une lettre de Rome, où il est allé récement, nous a dit que son livre (examiné par une douzaine de réviseurs) avait des chances d'être apprové.' De Bêlinay's hopes were premature. In the same month Martindale received a letter from Teilhard:

Moi, je demeure beaucoup trop logistique et intellectuel. Je tâche de cristifier les idées et les courants d'idées. C'est beaucoup trop impersonnel; mais c'est tout ce que je sais faire.

He explained the grounds of his optimism, his radical hostility to existentialists, and ended:

Cette 'froideur humaine', cet agnosticisme ou plutôt scepticisme des 'officiels' catholiques lorsque qu'il s'agit d'un ultra-développement des puissances spirituelles humaines, me paraît être la cause directe de la déchristianisation des masses (et des élites!). Et je trouve cela d'autant plus vexant que nous avons tout, dans un Christ pleinement compris, pour animer exactement le monde comme le monde demande à l'être.

Still, at recurring intervals, he was overcome by the conviction of his uselessness at Farm Street. 'Fr. Provincial was afraid I was asking to resign: he wishes me to stay, though I find myself more and more preoccupied with the Holy Trinity and Death.' His heart was weak and he had developed the 'revolting practice' of walking slowly. Also he was suffering from neuritis.

In the summer of 1947 he accepted an invitation from the Duke and Duchess of Palmella to visit Portugal. He gave some retreats, studied Fatima, was received by Salazar and discovered a new country where, as in France and Italy, he felt at home. Salazar, he wrote afterwards, 'is *the* man for *that* country at *this* time'. Before and during his visit he read much about Portugal, saw 'royalties and peasants, ambassadors and cooks' and, as after his visits to Africa and Australia, wrote his travel recollections.[1] He returned in time to celebrate in London the fiftieth anniversary of his entrance into the Society. In a speech he made at the dinner given in his honour he recalled that he had always been frightened before the opening of every new chapter in his Jesuit life and that, on the whole, his fears had proved ungrounded. He had found the affectionate letters sent to him from literally every continent most treasurable and disconcerting. He considered that he had been 'pitchforked' by Our Lady into the Church, and by St. Aloysius into the Society, independently of his own choice and in contradiction to his character. 'An S.J. life,' he reflected later the same day, 'is not exactly thrilling, but I confess there might be a few cheerful episodes connected with stokers, murderers, Australian dockers, and the submerged tenth generally, who have been kind enough to make friends and remain very loyal ones.' The walls of his room once again were a tapestry of photographs reflecting the patchwork his life had been, 'dukes and dockers, all good friends, really very like one another when one meets the innermost person'. Never had he sought them out or tried to keep hold of them. He had always believed that the time would pass when he could be of use to them, and he had never foreseen a lifelong correspondence.

Alternately he believed that he had many years ahead—his

[1] *Portuguese Pilgrimage* (Sheed and Ward, 1948).

father and grandfather had lived to a great age—and that he might die soon. Ready to accept his unpreparedness, he reflected a great deal on his spiritual condition and his practice of prayer: it is either 'non-existent or continuous,' he wrote; and he confessed to a friend that if thinking always on God and relating all to him was prayer, then he never ceased to pray.

Nearly all my prayer which goes on most of the time and into which I relapse in any break in activity resolves itself into a sort of knowledge of the reality, presence and activity of God, of Christ in me, of the Holy Spirit; and I reject ideas, let alone pictures, and think, at most, of only one or two words in a formula.

As Mass exacted greater physical effort every year, he concentrated less on the actual words he was saying than on the flow of meaning. With little effort of thought he was able, with unformed expression, to know, 'I mean this with the meaning of Christ within me.' Later he noted the same experience again: 'Mass goes in a flash —a satisfactory time of faith with the inner mind much helped by God and held steady underneath its vague floating surface.' Abandonment still eluded him. 'If I could only learn once and for all absolutely to abandon myself to God, no momentary instant in any day but would have its divine everlasting meaning.'

The lines of his spiritual thought had remained little altered since his noviceship. In his old age he looked more at the work God might do on him than through him. In March 1948 he wrote:

When I kiss the floor on rising I mean, and want always to mean one hundred per cent, that I am nothing and know it and look for nothing from myself. This is easy. But then I wish God to do great things *through* me, not that I shall ever know them or that anyone else will, but that is all to the good. I *expect* all sorts of souls to be saved simply owing to God's action through me. This also is fairly easy, and all the easier because I see how shoddy my own work *is*. But then I want God to do great things *to* me, and that is very difficult. Because (1) I see how poor my stuff is, and it is hard to believe that great and good things co-exist in me too; and I see how poor I *am*, and to *be* great at the same time is hard to grasp. And (2) I am frightened of what a 'great thing' done in me might carry with it or exact. But God acts wholly through love and, whatever happens, I *will* believe that love and nothing else accounts for it.

This might have been written at any time in his priestly life. There had been such a mystery in his conversion that he was anxious never to analyse overmuch his own condition. He was convinced that he knew almost from infancy that the Catholic faith was what he must possess and that Our Lady had really left him with no choice.

In 1949 he again visited Portugal. His first visit to Fatima had made him anxious to get at the essential message of the apparitions which so many Catholics found hard, if not impossible, to accept. He believed that there had been a supernatural occurrence there which ignorant children with no words at their disposal had tried but failed to express. The eldest of them, who alone survived, had entered a cloister and had given her account with all the embellishments of the convent dialect she had developed. 'I am trying (quite humbly, I assure you),' he wrote from Sintra in September 1949, 'to disentangle the thing meant from the way in which it was said.' He felt it his duty to write a book for all who found the apparitions a difficulty and deterrent rather than an inspiration. *The Message of Fatima*[1] showed no decline in his powers; he glossed over no difficulties, rigorously reconstructed the time-sequence and produced a convincing story.

This was his last journey abroad. 'You can guess what it is like,' he told a friend in November 1949, 'to return from an ill-behaved essentially Catholic country to an allegedly correctly behaved non-Catholic one.'

In the following spring he had double-pneumonia and received the Last Sacraments. For nearly six months he was convalescent, mostly at Mayfield, writing but in other ways inactive. *The Castle and the Ring*,[2] which he was working on now, traced the story of the Magis' gold down to the present day. For the background he drew a great deal on his boyhood recollections as well as on his reading of

---

[1] Burns, Oates, 1950.     [2] Kenedy (New York), 1955.

history. It had little success, but the reader familiar with his early life can detect in it many reminiscences of interest. On his return to London he had little energy. He complained that he felt ninety-two. He could walk only two hundred yards without danger of an attack of false angina, as the doctors described his condition, yet he was able still to deal with callers at Farm Street. 'There's a man to see you. I've shoved him into parlour one,' a defective boy on the door announced to him. 'I found he was a Royal Highness whom I knew,' Martindale discovered in desperation. 'Luckily an authentic one, so he was very nice and amused.'

In January 1952 his portrait was painted for the first time, a work of competence without distinction. It showed him scowling and heavily muffled 'like the Grand Lama of Tibet about to be mummified or Torquemada regretting his lost opportunities for torturing the innocent'. In February he was again in hospital. A large part of this and the following years were spent in convalescence with friends. Finally in September 1953 it was decided that he should move to a small Jesuit rest home, Burton Hill, a mile from Petworth, Sussex.

2

In the shabby mock-Gothic Jesuit house, with a small community of six ailing Brothers and two, sometimes three, very old or sick priests, he was more happy than he had expected to be in his old age. The strain of London life was lifted, and he was accessible to his friends; there were many books he had still unfinished, and his correspondence increased. Regularly all his friends were remembered at Christmas. Those who had been killed in the two wars were as real still to him as ever; many still living were in remote places. As he grew old, the need to see them passed. Yet he lived a 'populated life, and not merely among memories'.

What he found most difficult to endure was the typically religious hideousness of the house, which was particularly noticeable when an attempt was made at decoration: 'Better plain walls than shoddy oleographs and meaningless pictures of "A Monk with Two Cows" or prints of old Masters crookedly mounted.'

To the end of his life he retained all his noviceship scruples. He could never persuade himself that he was doing otherwise than wrong if he was not working. Scripture again became his principal study. In the next three years he produced for schools a series of commentaries on the four Gospels and the Acts of the Apostles. Augustine's description of the working of St. John's mind seemed to provide the best definition of scriptural inspiration he had met. 'For speak the thing as it is, who can do that. He spoke of God being but a man. Being inspired, he spoke somewhat; uninspired he had spoken nothing; but being a man inspired he spoke, not all that is; but what a man *can* speak, that he spoke.'

He saw the application of this to himself. All that he could say, he had said. The human mystery of his own person puzzled him more as he watched death come nearer. He welcomed the thought of Purgatory and spoke much about it as a process revealing the real man. 'Purgatory means getting us all down to the "real" stuff which God likes, minus all the cocoon we accumulate round ourselves. We may not enjoy the process, but will be terribly happy and always more so.' And it would be over in a flash. As each birthday came round he hoped it would be his last. Friends noticed that he seemed impatient to die. 'I can't hope, though I would like to, that this will be my last birthday. If I am to go this year, it would be very much like a beggar asking to be cleaned up.'

In the summer of 1955 he moved for several months to the Convent of the Daughters of the Cross at Haslemere, in order to write the life of the foundress of the Congregation, Mother Mary Haze. This was the last of his biographies. The autumn of the same year he underwent an operation for hernia at the County Hospital, Chichester. As he regained consciousness, he recognised a priest visitor and inquired how he came to be in Copenhagen. For the next fortnight he had to remind himself that he was not there. His heart was too weak to stand up to much morphia and he suffered greatly. Later he wrote: 'I knew I existed, but I could not think who I was, let alone where. My very I-hood was eclipsed. I *hope* I knew that God anyhow loved this unknown thing... A taste, in fact, of hell.'

He was unfit to travel abroad for convalescence but he let his imagination rove: 'All I ask is to sit still, though I would *like* to see again some distant mountains, to be on a ship; to see some fountains in a lovely garden, and to be warm, in fact, hot.' But the thought of any journey dispelled his fancies. He tired now after fifteen minutes' continuous work. But at the end of the year he was able to travel to London to record his last broadcast.

During 1957 he continued content at Petworth, praying that he might never be sent to live in a large community. He wrote a shorter form of *Jock, Jack and the Corporal*, revised his *Seaman's Prayerbook* and made notes for a background book on the gospels and St. Paul. The work of the Society of Perpetual Adoration and the debts on Liverpool and Southwark cathedrals still concerned him. He collected or directed sums from his friends for these ends. While he complained that he was tired to the inside of his bones, he did not reduce the number of his letters. At night he slept only in short intervals, and for fear of disturbing his sleeping brethren would write his letters long-hand at all hours of the early morning. His gentleness impressed visitors. When a journalist described him as dynamic he was amused, for he could recall no time in his life when he had not felt tired. He had never thought of his own work as anything but third or fifth rate, with occasional flashes of the first rate. All he asked for now was to spend a little time occasionally with people he liked and in surroundings that he liked, particularly with Catholics who did not have to talk about it. There were visits to Newbuildings Place, Southwater, the house of Lady Winifred Tryon, the great-granddaughter of the Lord Lytton who had written his childhood favourite, *The Last Days of Pompeii*. He still seized occasions for apostolic work. In May 1958 he lunched with a friend at an hotel in Midhurst. The barman introduced him to two waiters who were Catholics. Back at Midhurst a week later to have a tooth extracted, he sought them out and heard their confessions.

There was an incident at Oxford, after the first war, that he recalled now with regret: a piece of sharp behaviour, as it seemed to him, unbecoming in a priest. It had stuck fast in his memory. A group in an hotel was 'psychoanalysing' for his sake the Crucifixion;

they were at the next table and talking in loud voices so that he should overhear. One of them leaned over and said: 'We hope we are not shocking you.' 'No,' he had replied, 'By "shock" I mean to "surprise unpleasantly". You are unpleasant, but you don't surprise me.' He commented now: 'I think that was wrong, because cheap.'

The Apocalypse still set him thinking on fresh lines. He believed he saw three or four layers of meaning in what St. John wrote about the 'woman'—the synagogue, the Church, the New Eve or Our Lady.

At the end of August 1959 at Newbuildings he trod on a crumbling garden step, hit his head against a steel scaffolding pole and suffered slight concussion. He wondered whether he would ever say Mass again, he was so frequently in bed. 'One's life is like a sentence in a bracket that must soon close.'

In January 1960 he had a slight stroke and was anointed for the sixth time. 'I always expected seven,' he told a friend when he recovered. He was tempted to wish that the delay would not be long. His thoughts returned regularly to the training of priests. In April 1961 he proposed that every seminarian should be examined in theology by a board of laymen to whom he would have to make himself understood. That precisely had been the aim of his own writing. He had seen something that ought to be written and that he could write, and he had done it. Until the first war he had believed that his life would be one of books, written, read or taught. At Oxford he had found himself thrown among real men: never had he not been shy, yet had always been increasingly happy among them. To the end he had driven himself to the utmost. His belief in Providence was deeply actual, but he had no patience, even now, for those who glibly declared 'The Lord will provide', as though God would make up for the laziness of Catholics, when there were millions starving in India as they had done in the days of his father's administration of Bengal. Sloth and laziness remained the principal sins of his priestly experience.

In September 1961 he was anointed again, 'which makes the seventh time'. He could do little. Too sick to be nursed at Petworth, he was taken to St. Anthony's Hospital, Cheam. He was out in

November. After each succeeding physical crisis he was not quite up to his previous condition.

He continued to reply to letters. 'Nothing but letters,' he told a friend, 'I hope it counts as charity and prayer.' Now he had to be washed and dressed. In May 1962 he wrote: 'Living, not "life", is queer. I'm horribly strong . . . so I may have to hang on quite a bit yet. There are one or two things I'd still like to do, but they require energy.' He regarded the business of going into the next world with total objectivity. He was apprehensive only of sudden changes and shocks, as he had always been. On 5 September he hoped to say Mass, three days later, sitting down now. It was the anniversary of his becoming a Jesuit. It was his last Mass. 'I feel I've let the side down badly,' he wrote that day.

Reflecting on his life his chief cause of gratitude was that God had never permitted any part of His human race to become intolerable to him, as he had once feared it might. Even the very complacent or liars were not over his limit.

There were more falls and an eighth anointing. In his last letter, dictated in early February, he cleared his correspondence. 'I'm pretty ill and, in fact, one night they said the prayers for the Dying by me. I find it hard to be brought back, but the Lord's will is the most lovable of all.'

He died on 18 March 1963.

## 3

In an earlier chapter it was noted that Fr. Martindale, when expecting arrest in Denmark, had written a statement which he left in the hands of the Rector of the house in the event of his death. The introduction and the postscript were given there. The substance of it forms a fitting epilogue to this biography:

'I renew my faith in the Catholic revelation and in all that the Church believes and teaches in the sense in which she does. I am grateful for the gift of Faith, and repose my entire hope in the free goodness of God. I wished I loved Him much better and truly with all my heart, and I wish to offer the whole of my life for the salvation of my fellow-men through and because of Christ. I am very sorry for my sins which do not in the least astonish me, because I have the poorest opinion of my character; nonetheless they have been sins against light and grace and were due not only to weakness but to self-worship, which I renounce.

'I wish to live, yet not I, but Christ in me and I in Him, I in His body and in the Vine and as altogether below, for His sake and in myself, the "lowest" of my fellow-men, whom I have loved and do love and for whom I wish to offer my entire self.

'I am grateful to the Society for its patience with me, and am sorry for having played my part so badly, which is again due to my self-isolation due to self-idolatry. In so far as I can, I wish totally to renounce self for the sake of each and every one of my fellow-men, in Christ, apart from whom neither they nor I have any meaning; but in whom every atom of their body and soul, experience, fears, hopes, sufferings, pleasure, is honourable and by me, please God, is honoured and loved.

'It is quite impossible for me to send my love and trust and thanks to all my friends who have been innumerable and each of whom I wish not to possess, but to give to Christ and to find in Him. Therefore all this matter of friends I hand over to Him and leave no special messages, because the matter would be quite beyond me.

'I wish not a penny to be spent on any "memorial" of me as such. As for Masses, apart from the three S.J. ones, I would like one to be offered in a hospital, one in a prison, one in a ship, if possible at sea (but that does not matter), one in a barracks, and one in a mining village. Also one at Poplar, one at Horseferry Road, and one through the care of Lady Margaret Kerr and Lady Lovat in a poorer church in Scotland. Also one at Lujan (Argentine) and at Antipolo (Manila), and at Czestochowa and at Esztergom. If allowable, one at St. Paul's Tre Fontane and one in the crypt of St. Peter's. Also one in our most purely native mission in S. Rhodesia, to which I attach special value—I mean to Mass there; I wish thus to identify myself with the whole of the Black race. I would also like one in some very poor church of Canada and another in the U.S.A. and, if possible, in China and Japan. But I would also, in particular, ask for one in New

Zealand at Waihi; and in Australia, which perhaps might give me three, at the Toowong Carmel, Perth Cathedral, and one of the Mercy hospitals in Melbourne. In this way my visits will have been responsible for the perfect worship of God in all those places, and will carry up to Him my love of those people and their prayers for me. Certainly I should like one in Notre Dame des Victoires in Paris and one in Germany and one in Spain; but this leads me too far, for I could think of almost anywhere.

'But, speaking reverently of Mass, I would rather have one said seriously for me than an indefinite number of Masses. I confide the consequences of not having many Masses said for me to our Lord Himself, and I shall anyhow be grateful for Purgatory. I would wish those who want to make offerings, to ensure the rapid, strong, simple and *complete* building of the Horseferry Road centre, since this will serve destitute churches all over the world and so ensure many Masses anyhow, and a more dignified Sacrifice, though always, I pray, a simple one. I would rather, I repeat, have one Mass only anywhere than that this work should not be carried through at once. I would also like the completion of Liverpool Cathedral and the paying off of debts in Westminster, Brentwood, Nottingham, Northampton and Menevia and Cardiff dioceses, that constructive work may go forward the more rapidly and that priests may have to talk less about money. I wish this very earnestly. As for the Society, I entrust its future in England and the missions, and, of course, everywhere, to the S.J. saints whom I have tried to study; but the above intentions are those on which I put my stress, being ready to abdicate those too if God wills. All I do ask, in my heart, is that I should *be*, whatever is thought, beneath the feet of the poorest and of sinners, so miserably have I fallen short of the grace of God in all imaginable ways and so wholly do I trust to Him in Xto.

'C. C. Martindale, S.J.'

# APPENDIX 1

## *The Gisborne Connection*

Francis Gisborne, of Holme Hall, Bakewell, was the father of Gwendolen (now Mrs. Gerard Twisleton-Wykeham-Fiennes), Cyril's childhood companion. One of Francis's sisters, Mary, was married to Sir William Evans, of Allestree Hall, Derby, where Cyril's mother had been brought up; another of Francis's sisters, Susan, was married to Sir William's brother, Walter Evans, of Darley Abbey, Derby. Sophy Gisborne, Cyril's Catholic aunt, was the third wife of Francis Gisborne's brother, Henry.

Since there were no children of Sir William Evans's marriage, he left Allestree Hall to the Gisborne family.

# APPENDIX 2

## *C. C. Martindale's Oxford Achievement*

1903 Hertford Scholarship (Latin)
First Craven Scholarship
First Class Classical Moderations
1904 Chancellor's Prize: Latin Verse, *Sertorius* Gaisford Prize: Greek Verse, *Virgil, Georgics IV*, 450–547
1905 First Class in Final Classical School
1906 The Derby Scholarship
1907 The Ellerton Theological Essay Prize

# APPENDIX 3

## *The Writings of C. C. Martindale*

The *Bibliography of the English Province of the Society of Jesus*, published in 1957, gives 487 items below the name of Fr. Martindale. I have had occasion to mention only a few of the seventy-nine books listed there. There were several books written after the compilation of the bibliography. It includes fifty-nine pamphlets, but omits many articles in American and Australian reviews and all his contributions to newspapers and several ephemeral journals.

# Index